Iran's Soft Power in Afghanistan and Pakistan

Iran's Soft Power in Afghanistan and Pakistan

Zahid Shahab Ahmed and Ali Akbar

EDINBURGH
University Press

Edinburgh University Press is one of the leading university presses in the UK. We publish academic books and journals in our selected subject areas across the humanities and social sciences, combining cutting-edge scholarship with high editorial and production values to produce academic works of lasting importance. For more information visit our website: edinburghuniversitypress.com

© Zahid Shahab Ahmed and Ali Akbar, 2023, 2025

Edinburgh University Press Ltd
13 Infirmary Street,
Edinburgh, EH1 1LT

First published in hardback by Edinburgh University Press 2023

Typeset in 10.5/12.5 Times New Roman by
IDSUK (DataConnection) Ltd

A CIP record for this book is available from the British Library

ISBN 978 1 3995 1745 4 (hardback)
ISBN 978 1 3995 1746 1 (paperback)
ISBN 978 1 3995 1747 8 (webready PDF)
ISBN 978 1 3995 1748 5 (epub)

The right of Zahid Shahab Ahmed and Ali Akbar to be identified as authors of this work has been asserted in accordance with the Copyright, Designs and Patents Act 1988 and the Copyright and Related Rights Regulations 2003 (SI No. 2498).

Contents

List of Abbreviations	vi
Acknowledgements	viii
1. Introduction	1
2. Historical Legacy	21
3. Iranian Fears and National Interest	33
4. Geostrategic Interests	54
5. Cultural and Ideological Influences	72
6. Iran's Political Influence	96
7. Economic Relations and Influence	116
8. Recruitment: Shi'a Brigades in Syria	135
9. Conclusion	153
Annexure 1. Afghan Participants	158
Annexure 2. Pakistani Participants	159
Bibliography	161
Index	177

Abbreviations

AAH	Asaib Ahl al-Haqq
ACCI	Afghanistan Chamber of Commerce and Industry
BRI	Belt and Road Initiative
CAREC	Central Asia Regional Economic Cooperation
CIA	Central Intelligence Agency
CNPC	China National Petroleum Corporation
CPEC	China–Pakistan Economic Corridor
ECO	Economic Cooperation Organisation
FTA	Free Trade Agreement
FTZ	Free Trade-Industrial Zone
FUM	Ferdowsi University of Mashhad
HRW	Human Rights Watch
IAC	Institute for Art and Culture
ICRO	Islamic Culture and Relations Organisation
IKRC	Imam Khomeini Relief Committee
IMAFT	Islamic Military Alliance to Fight Terrorism
IRGC	Islamic Revolutionary Guard Corps
IRIB	Islamic Republic of Iran Broadcasting
ISI	Inter-Services Intelligence
ISIS	Islamic State of Iraq and Syria
ISKP	Islamic State of Khorasan Province
ISO	Imamia Students Organisation
ISSI	Institute of Strategic Studies Islamabad
JCPOA	Joint Comprehensive Plan of Action
LNG	Liquefied Natural Gas
MIU	al-Mustafa International University
MoU	Memorandum of Understanding
MWM	Majlis Wahdat-e-Muslimeen
NEPRA	National Electricity and Power Regulatory Authority

NTDC	National Transmission and Dispatch Company
NUML	National University of Modern Languages
OPEC	Organisation of the Petroleum Exporting Countries
PIPS	Pak Institute for Peace Studies
PPP	Pakistan Peoples Party
PTA	Preferential Trade Agreement
PTRO	Peace Training and Research Organisation
RCD	Regional Cooperation for Development
SATP	South Asia Terrorism Portal
SMP	Sipah-e-Muhammad Pakistan
SPA	Strategic Partnership Agreement
TJP	Tehrik-e-Jafria Pakistan
TNFJ	Tehrik-i-Nifaz-i-Fiqah-i-Jafria
TRACECA	Transport Corridor Europe–Caucasus–Asia
TUMS	Tehran University of Medical Sciences
UNODC	United Nations Office on Drugs and Crime
WASSA	Women Activities and Social Services Association
WTO	World Trade Organization

Acknowledgements

Deepest thanks to our research participants from Afghanistan and Pakistan for taking time out from their busy schedules to contribute to our research project. We are also indebted to the support provided by some local institutions, including the Pak Institute for Peace Studies, Quaid-i-Azam University and the Afghanistan Institute for Strategic Studies, with data collection. Without their support, we could not have interviewed many high-profile research participants.

This project would not have been possible without Deakin University's internal funding and for that we are particularly thankful to the University's Alfred Deakin Institute for Citizenship and Globalisation.

We are also thankful to Professor Shahram Akbarzadeh (Deakin University) and Dr Stuti Bhatnagar (Australian National University) for their critical feedback that certainly improved the quality of this research and its outcome in the shape of this book.

1

Introduction

This book explores Iran's soft power in two of its eastern neighbours, namely, Afghanistan and Pakistan. It explores Tehran's soft power in key areas such as the cultural, religious, social, media, ideological and educational spheres, seeking to understand what resources and instruments Iran has used to project its soft power after the establishment of the Islamic Republic in 1979. The book offers the most up-to-date account of Iranian soft power strategies in both countries, and their reception among local Afghan and Pakistani participants interviewed for this research project.

Due to cultural, geoeconomic and geopolitical factors, South and Central Asia are important for Iran. In terms of the cultural and ideological dynamics, this region is significant to Iran because of its sizeable Shi'a population. It is estimated that there are about 36–64 million Shi'as in South Asia.[1] Shi'as comprise 15 per cent of Afghanistan's population and 20 per cent of Pakistan's population.[2] While the number of Shi'as in Afghanistan is not large, owing to its relatively small total population of roughly 35 million,[3] the Shi'a component of Pakistan's 207.8 million population is significant. According to data from the Pakistan Bureau of Statistics, 96.28 per cent of the population are Muslim, 20 per cent of whom are Shi'as, totalling around 40 million Pakistanis.[4] This means Pakistan has the second biggest Shi'a population after Iran.[5] It is partly due to these demographics that Iran has extended its political, cultural and ideological influence into Afghanistan and Pakistan.

Iran's relationship with Pakistan has faced many ups and downs. It started on a high point when Iran became the first country to recognise Pakistan's independence from the British Raj in 1947. During the time of Mohammad Reza Pahlavi, the two countries had a very cooperative economic and security relationship. Since the Islamic Revolution of 1979, the bilateral relationship has drastically shifted to

---

[1] Adam Weinstein, 'South Asia's Shiites are Eschewing Sectarianism', *Foreign Policy*, 7 January 2020, https://foreignpolicy.com/2020/01/07/iran-pakistan-shiism.
[2] Colin Freeman, 'Iran Poised to Strike in Wealthy Gulf States', *The Telegraph*, 4 March 2007, https://www.telegraph.co.uk/news/worldnews/1544535/Iran-poised-to-strike-in-wealthy-Gulf-states.html.
[3] 'Afghanistan', World Bank, https://data.worldbank.org/country/afghanistan.
[4] 'Population by Religion', Pakistan Bureau of Statistics, Government of Pakistan, http://www.pbs.gov.pk/content/population-religion.
[5] Zahid Shahab Ahmed and Shahram Akbarzadeh. 'Understanding Pakistan's Relationship with Iran', *Middle East Policy* 25(4) (2018): 97.

one dominated more by a trust deficit and less by cooperation. Although Islamabad was quick to support the outcome of the Islamic Revolution, Iran and Pakistan had divergent policies on Afghanistan during the Afghan–Soviet War (1979–1989). After the departure of the Soviet troops, Tehran backed the Northern Alliance, whereas Pakistan was part of an international alliance supporting the Taliban.[6] Recently, the two sides have been engaged in negotiations over difficult issues, including Pakistan's reservations about India's intelligence agencies using Iran as a base for clandestine operations in Pakistan, and Tehran's concerns about Jundullah's hideouts in Pakistan. Nonetheless, Iran holds a sacred position in the hearts of the millions of Shi'as in Pakistan. According to an estimate, more than 100,000 Pakistani pilgrims visit Iran and Iraq annually.[7] Among these pilgrims, many visit the Imam Riza shrine located in the Iranian city of Mashhad.[8] Tehran has established Iranian cultural centres, commonly known as *Khana-e-Farhang* (house of culture) in several large cities in Pakistan, including Karachi, Rawalpindi, Peshawar, Lahore and Quetta, which organise Persian lessons and lectures on Persian culture. Iran's influence on Shi'as in Pakistan has also been visible through its recruitment of Shi'a fighters for brigades in Syria (i.e., Liwa Zainebiyoun and Liwa Fatemiyoun). This has included a sophisticated campaign, including on social media. For instance, one recruitment advertisement on Facebook targeting 18–35-year-old Pakistani Shi'as offered a forty-five-day military training camp in Syria, deployment, a three-month holiday and a monthly salary of US$1,100.[9]

The relationship between Afghanistan and Iran can be traced back to the 1930s, when there were functional monarchies in both countries under King Zahir Shah in Afghanistan and the Pahlavi dynasty in Iran. Since the Afghan–Soviet War, Iran has viewed developments in Afghanistan with keen interest. Other than Tehran's concerns about international actors, especially the United States, in Afghanistan, there have been other irritants, including the Taliban – viewed in Tehran as an anti-Shi'a group – and the water dispute over the Helmand and other shared rivers.[10] Afghanistan also benefits from the Chabahar Agreement, although it mainly involves India and Iran, with the former being the key financier of the Chabahar Port. Tehran showed a keen interest in facilitating Afghan peace processes, which, it is important to mention, were organised by China, Russia, the United States and Pakistan. As in Pakistan, Iran also has cultural centres in Afghanistan, including in

---

[6] Paul Hastert, 'Al Qaeda and Iran: Friends or Foes, or Somewhere in Between?' *Studies in Conflict & Terrorism* 30(4) (2007): 327–36.

[7] Zahid Gishkori, 'Flights to Iran being Considered for Shia Pilgrims', *Express Tribune*, 26 September 2011, https://tribune.com.pk/story/260458/flights-to-iran-being-considered-for-shia-pilgrims.

[8] *Hawza News*, '30 Million Pilgrims Visit the Holy Shrine of Imam Reza Annually' (in Persian), 12 March 2022, https://www.hawzahnews.com/news/1013400.

[9] Babak Dehghanpisheh, 'Iran Recruits Pakistani Shi'ites for Combat in Syria', *Reuters*, 11 December 2015, https://www.reuters.com/article/us-mideast-crisis-syria-pakistan-iran-idUSKBN0TT22S20151210.

[10] Fatemeh Aman, *Water Dispute Escalating between Iran and Afghanistan*, Atlantic Council, Washington, 2016; Shahram Akbarzadeh, 'Iran's Policy towards Afghanistan: In the Shadow of the United States', *Journal of Asian Security and International Affairs* 1(1) (2014): 63–78.

Kabul.[11] In addition to ideological and geopolitical factors, a few other factors play a role in Iran's attempts to enhance its reach in Afghanistan. For example, Iran is home to nearly 3 million Afghan refugees.[12] Also, Iran has had concerns about the presence of US military bases in Afghanistan, especially between 2001 and 2021.

Considering Iran's multifaceted influence in Afghanistan and Pakistan, this book is an attempt to uncover the various aspects of its impact in order to understand ground realities and Tehran's motivations. It also investigates Iran's economic, ideological and political influence in Afghanistan and Pakistan in the context of sectarian conflict in the region. This study aims to answer the following questions:

1. What are Iran's resources and instruments of soft power in Afghanistan and Pakistan?
2. How is Iran's soft power received in Afghanistan and Pakistan?
3. What outcomes has Iran been able to achieve through its strategies in Afghanistan and Pakistan?

To answer these questions, data was collected during 2018–2019 through in-person interviews of key individuals in both countries from a variety of backgrounds, including civil society, government, military, media, academia, think tanks and policymaking. Interviews were carried out using a semi-structured questionnaire. In Pakistan, interviews were conducted in English and Urdu, and in Afghanistan, in Dari. A total of fifty-seven interviews, twenty-six in Afghanistan and thirty-one in Pakistan were carried out. Due to security concerns, interviews could not be carried out in some Shi'a-majority areas, such as Herat in Afghanistan, and Balochistan and Khyber Pakhtunkhwa in Pakistan. For ethical reasons, we have anonymised all participants and have allocated them participant numbers: A1–A26 for Afghan participants, and P1–P31 for Pakistani participants. In the annexures, we have included two tables indicating the affiliations of our research participants.

Iran's soft power strategies

Iran has used a variety of tools during the past few decades to increase its soft power in the region. One of the key instruments for increasing Iran's soft power is the Islamic Culture and Relations Organisation (ICRO). ICRO was established in 1995 for the purpose of 'homogenising the Islamic Republic's multifarious cultural diplomacy networks' and for 'coordinating Iran's bilateral cultural initiatives

---

[11] In December 2017, there was a suicide attack on the Iranian cultural centre in Kabul that killed forty-one people.
[12] Ali M. Latifi, 'How Iran Recruited Afghan Refugees to Fight Assad's War', *New York Times*, 30 June 2017, https://www.nytimes.com/2017/06/30/opinion/sunday/iran-afghanistan-refugees-assad-syria.html; Bethan McKernan, 'Iran's "Exemplary" Refugee Hosting Efforts Praised by UN', *Independent*, 16 March 2017, http://www.independent.co.uk.

with other states'.[13] The main activities of the ICRO include organising cultural and religious events in different countries, promoting Persian-language learning centres and building links with cultural institutions in host countries. In addition, it produces books about Iranian culture and the Islamic Republic which are available to the public at the cultural centres associated with the ICRO.[14] ICRO has offices in a variety of countries in the region, including Iran's neighbours Afghanistan, Pakistan, Turkey and Tajikistan.[15] Iran regularly draws on some of its cultural norms to enhance its soft power. For example, Iran often emphasises the celebration of the Persian New Year (*Nowruz*) across the region, and at times invites regional heads to the international celebration of *Nowruz* in Iran. Under former president Mahmoud Ahmadinejad, Iran sought to establish a 'Union of Persian Speaking Nations' between the three Persian-speaking countries, that is, Iran, Afghanistan and Tajikistan, as a means of increasing cooperation with them.[16]

Another instrument used by Iran to extend its soft power reach is its international media, which is under the control of the country's state broadcaster, Islamic Republic of Iran Broadcasting (IRIB). These international media outlets seek to showcase Iranian culture and civilisation as well as Shi'a norms to other countries. IRIB's international branches include Al-Alam, Al-Kawthar, Press TV, HispanTV and iFilm TV. Al-Kawthar was launched in 2006 and focuses more on religious programming in the Arabic language. According to its mandate, Al-Kawthar is committed to promoting 'human values in harmony with the Holy Quran and Sunnah' and supporting 'resistance' against 'global arrogance'.[17] These are guiding principles of Iranian support for Hezbollah and its rejectionist declarations against Israel and the United States. For example, in the Lebanese context, Iran spreads messages such as an anti-Israeli agenda, emphasising the importance of the 'Resistance Front' through media channels associated with IRIB.[18] Another religious channel for non-Persian speakers is Sahar TV, which began broadcasting mainly Pashto programmes in 1997 and aims to export norms associated with the Iranian Revolution abroad and to support Islamic education.[19] In addition to religious programmes, some of these media channels broadcast entertainment programmes such as movies through which the Islamic Republic seeks to promote Iranian cultural values. In particular, iFilm TV is an Arabic-language entertainment channel broadcasting Iranian films, TV series and television shows dubbed into Arabic or English.[20]

[13] Edward Wastnidge, 'The Modalities of Iranian Soft Power: From Cultural Diplomacy to Soft War', *Politics* 35(3/4) (2015): 370
[14] Ibid., 370
[15] Ibid.
[16] Ibid.
[17] Seth G. Jones and Danika Newlee, 'The United States' Soft War with Iran', *CSIS Briefing*, 11 June 2019, https://www.csis.org/analysis/united-states-soft-war-iran.
[18] Pierre Pahlavi and Eric Ouellet, 'Iran: Asymmetric Strategy and Mass Diplomacy', *Journal of Strategic Security* 13(2) (2020): 97.
[19] Jones and Newlee 'The United States' Soft War with Iran'.
[20] Ibid.

Another measure used by the Islamic Republic to enhance its influence is the expansion of branches of Iranian universities abroad. One of the educational institutions used by Iran to export its values and norms is al-Mustafa International University (MIU). MIU has branches in many countries across the region and its goal is to train jurists, clergy, researchers and translators. Its teachings reflect Shi'a ideology, Quranic studies and political goals aligned with Iranian state policies. It also offers online educational services for those who are not able to attend classes at its branches.[21] In addition to MIU, Iran uses its charitable foundations (*bonyads*) as a means of enhancing its soft power. *Bonyads* are para-governmental organisations which appeared from the very beginning of the establishment of the Islamic Republic of Iran. As Jenkins notes, *bonyads* are 'a robust foreign policy tool that effectively cultivates influence in service of Iran's revolutionary and cultural identity and are a long-term source of continuity in Iranian foreign policy outside changing administrations' regional policies'.[22] They are not supervised by elected governments but rather more often connected directly to the supreme leader, and thus are able to pursue long-term strategies regardless of government changes. *Bonyads* offer social and public services, providing assistance to people with disabilities across the region. *Bonyads* are active in countries such as Iraq, Lebanon, Afghanistan, Syria and Tajikistan. Their activities focus on culture, religion and the arts. For instance, in the realm of art, we can point to the Farabi Cinema Foundation, which promotes cinema and acts as a powerful vehicle for spreading Islamic ideology.[23]

The fact that Iran uses soft power strategies to enhance its influence in the region is confirmed by Iranian leaders and policymakers. Hassan Rouhani, who was Iran's president from 2013 to 2021, stated in his 2013 presidential campaign that 'Iran needs soft power'. Mohammad Javad Zarif, Rouhani's foreign minister, once stated that soft power is a key aspect of Iranian foreign policy: 'The Islamic Republic is well suited to draw on the rich millennial heritage of Iranian society and the significant heritage of the Islamic Revolution.'[24] Iran's *sanad-e cheshm-andaz-e bist saleh*, or 'Twenty-year Vision Document', reflects Iranian strategy for combining its soft and hard power to achieve 'regional leadership'. This document describes Iran as a regional leader in economics and science with an 'Islamic revolutionary identity, inspirational [*elham-bakhsh*] in international relations . . . and emphasis on soft-measure action [in achieving this].'[25]

---

[21] Ibid.
[22] William Bullock Jenkins, 'Bonyads as Agents and Vehicles of the Islamic Republic's Soft Power', in Shahram Akbarzadeh and Dara Conduit (eds), *Iran in the World: President Rouhani's Foreign Policy* (New York: Palgrave Macmillan, 2016), 157.
[23] Ibid.
[24] Amin Saikal, *Iran Rising: The Survival and Future of the Islamic Republic* (Princeton: Princeton University Press, 2019), 158.
[25] Jenkins, 'Bonyads as Agents and Vehicles of the Islamic Republic's Soft Power', 161.

While some scholars have investigated Iran's multifaceted relations with Afghanistan and Pakistan,[26] especially its links with Shi'a groups and the Taliban,[27] little attention has been paid to Iran's soft power in these countries. In a postgraduate thesis focusing on Iran's soft power in Afghanistan, Feizi explored the Iranian use of narratives around a 'sense of brotherhood' in terms of its outreach involving Afghan audiences.[28] Feizi argued that 'the strength of this narrative is in Iran's ability to create an emotional connection that is embedded in commonalities between the two countries'.[29] Iran focuses on culturally defined foreign policy objectives to appeal to the Muslim world. Wastnidge argued that key aspects of Tehran's foreign policy, such as the discourse on the dialogue among civilisations presented by former president Mohammad Khatami, represented a key component of Tehran's approach to soft power by drawing on Islamic principles of justice and respect.[30] This is clearly an area that needs further exploration. Iran's soft power projection is noted by many scholars and deserves a careful and empirically grounded study to explore its dynamics and impact. Afghanistan and Pakistan present two very relevant cases for the investigation of Iran's soft power project and will pave the way for other studies to take the scholarship beyond the level of generalities.

Context: Iran's multidimensional influence in Afghanistan and Pakistan

Iran enjoys significant points of connection with the neighbouring countries of Afghanistan and Pakistan which could be instrumental for extending its influence. These points of connection rest on shared history, culture and geographical imperatives, and have a bearing on how Iran fashions its influence in the key areas of economy, anti-Americanism and Iran's regional ambitions. These fields of connections are explored in detail in this book. The following sets the scene for some of the key episodes and points of Iran's soft power projection and interests in Afghanistan and Pakistan.

Trade

The nature of Iran's economic relationship with Afghanistan and Pakistan is very different. Afghanistan, as a landlocked state, has been economically dependent on

---

[26] Ahmed and Akbarzadeh, 'Understanding Pakistan's Relationship with Iran'; Akbarzadeh, 'Iran's Policy Towards Afghanistan'.
[27] Shahram Akbarzadeh and Niamatullah Ibrahimi, 'The Taliban: A New Proxy for Iran in Afghanistan?' *Third World Quarterly* 41(5) (2020): 764–82; Mukhtar Ahmad Ali, *Sectarian Conflict in Pakistan: A Case Study of Jhang* (Colombo: Regional Centre for Strategic Studies, 2000).
[28] Hiva Feizi, 'Discourse, Affinity and Attraction: A Case Study of Iran's Soft Power Strategy in Afghanistan', Graduate thesis, University of South Florida, 2018, https://core.ac.uk/download/pdf/213968957.pdf.
[29] Ibid., vi.
[30] Wastnidge, 'The Modalities of Iranian Soft Power'.

its coastal neighbours, Iran and Pakistan. The fall of the Taliban regime in 2001 following the US invasion of the country provided Iran with numerous opportunities to enhance its economic relations with Afghanistan. After the fall of the Taliban regime in 2001, India – Afghanistan's key development partner – invested in Iran to build the Chabahar Port on the Arabian Sea. Afghanistan is a key beneficiary of trade through this project. In the context of Afghanistan's frequently conflictual relationship with Pakistan, which often leads Islamabad to close its borders with Afghanistan, Kabul has found in Iran a more reliable economic partner. In 2017, Iran overtook Pakistan to become Afghanistan's number one trading partner.[31] Tehran also provided an aid package of up to US$500 million to support the Karzai administration in Afghanistan.[32]

Pakistan has not been able to fully utilise the potential of economic cooperation with Iran – mainly because of international sanctions on Iran. Pakistan's strategic alliance with the United States and Saudi Arabia is also a key factor that explains the lack of economic cooperation between Iran and Pakistan. There have been numerous opportunities to enhance trade between Iran and Pakistan, but those projects have not materialised. Notable among these is the Iran–Pakistan–India pipeline project, which Pakistan has essentially put on the backburner. Iran has built its part of the pipeline and has been demanding that Pakistan should fulfil its commitment to do so. Despite Pakistan's growing energy needs, it is highly unlikely that the gas pipeline project will be completed. In 2009, Pakistan was Iran's fifth largest trade partner, with two-way trade worth US$1 billion per year, yet still far below an estimated potential of US$5 billion.[33] Although, the overall trade between Iran and Pakistan increased in the late 2000s, it significantly decreased from the early 2010s because of US pressure and Western sanctions on Iran. In 2014, the two-way trade between Iran and Pakistan stood at US$217 million, much lower than the volume of trade between the two countries in the early 2000s.[34] After Iran signed the P5+1 nuclear deal or the Joint Comprehensive Plan of Action (JCPOA) in 2015, Iran and Pakistan sought to increase their economic relations. Accordingly, both countries increased their engagement in key areas including trade, investment, banking, finance and energy.[35]

---

[31] 'Iran Biggest Trade Partner of Afghanistan in 2017–18', *Financial Tribune*, 8 April 2018, https://financialtribune.com/articles/economy-domestic-economy/84309/iran-biggest-trade-partner-of-afghanistan-in-2017-18.

[32] Alireza Nader, Ali G. Scotten, Ahmad Idrees Rahmani, Robert Stewart and Leila Mahnad, 'Iran and Afghanistan: A Complicated Relationship', in Alireza Nader (ed.), *Iran's Influence in Afghanistan: Implications for the US Drawdown* (Washington: RAND Corporation, 2014), 5–22.

[33] *Pakistan–Iran Relations: Challenges and Prospects* (Islamabad: Centre for Pakistan and Gulf Studies, 2014).

[34] Najam Rafique, 'Prospects of Pakistan–Iran Relations: Post Nuclear Deal', *Strategic Studies* 36(3) (2016): 1–20, 10.

[35] Baqir Sajjad Syed, 'Iran Wanted Expanded Relations with Pakistan', *Dawn*, 14 August 2015, https://www.dawn.com/news/1200373.

Culture and ideology

The promotion of the Persian language and key cultural norms, such as the celebration of *Nowruz* are instruments that Tehran employs to enhance its soft power in South and Central Asia. Persian was the lingua franca of the Indian subcontinent before British colonisation, and many elites in Pakistan are still fluent in Persian. The language is taught in numerous public sector universities across the country. Moreover, in addition to the history of the Persian Empire covering the territory that now constitutes Afghanistan, there are cultural connections based on linguistic ties. Dari, an official language of Afghanistan, is a dialect of Persian. Another factor pertaining to Iran's soft power strategies is the promotion of Shiism and support for Shi'a communities beyond its borders. Pakistan is home to the world's second largest Shi'a population after Iran; in Afghanistan, almost 20 per cent of the Muslim population follow Shi'a Islam. As a Shi'a majority state, Iran is a significant source of inspiration for Shi'as in the region.

Since the 1980s, Iran has been supporting Shi'a groups in Afghanistan and Pakistan and several Iranian proxies are engaged in promoting Iranian interests in those countries. In Pakistan, evidence of ideological links surfaced following the killing of Iran's Quds Force Commander Qassem Suleimani by US drone in 2020. Two Shi'a groups, Majlis Wahdat-e-Muslimeen (MWM) and the Imamia Student Organisation, condemned the killing strongly at a public rally in Islamabad.[36] On 9 February 2020, many Shi'a groups across Pakistan, especially in Karachi, observed *Chehlum* (the fortieth day after Soleimani's death).[37] We will explain these later in the book.

The Shi'a–Sunni divide has grown in Pakistan since the 1980s, at times erupting into open conflict at the community level. Two trends were central in this process. Under General Zia-ul-Haq, Pakistan was a frontline partner in the Afghan–Soviet War, with the recruitment and training of mujahideen from Pakistan managed by the US Central Intelligence Agency (CIA).[38] This led to the creation of many Sunni militant groups in Pakistan. At the same time, Pakistan went through a process of Islamisation which involved legal reforms, including the introduction of a religious tax (*zakat*). This new tax was seen by Shi'as to be targeting them unfairly. Shi'a mobilisation against *zakat* led to mass protests in 1980 and enjoyed support from Iran. The Shi'a won a concession to be exempt from *zakat*,[39] but the episode

---

[36] 'Official: Iran Biggest Trade Partner for Afghanistan', *Islamic Republic News Agency*, 26 February 2020, https://en.irna.ir/news/83692144/Official-Iran-biggest-trade-partner-for-Afghanistan.

[37] 'Shia Parties Will Observe Chehlum of Qassem Suleimani in Pakistan', *Shiite News*, 21 January 2020, https://shiitenews.org/shiitenews/pakistan-news/item/108498-shia-parties-will-observe-chehlum-of-qassem-soleimani-in-pakistan.

[38] Zahid Shahab Ahmed, 'Political Islam, the Jamaat-e-Islami, and Pakistan's Role in the Afghan–Soviet War, 1979–1988', in Philip E. Muehlenbeck (ed.), *Religion and the Cold War: A Global Perspective* (Nashville, TN: Vanderbilt University Press, 2012), 275–96.

[39] Weinstein, 'South Asia's Shiites are Eschewing Sectarianism'.

put the sectarian divide on public display and served to fuel community distrust and tension.

Sunni and Shi'a militant groups in Pakistan clashed repeatedly in the 1980s. In 1988, Arif Hussain al-Hussaini, a prominent Shi'a leader of Tehrik-i-Nifaz-i-Fiqah-i-Jafria was killed. In a subsequent attack by Sunni militias on a Shi'a village in Gilgit approximately 400 people were killed.[40] Cases of sectarian violence increased significantly in the following decades. There were 3,072 incidents of sectarian violence that led to the deaths of 5,602 people in Pakistan between 1989 and 2018.[41] Sectarian violence in Pakistan has declined in recent years, and according to a report by the Pak Institute of Peace Studies, the number of violent sectarian incidents decreased from 220 in 2013 to 12 in 2018.[42]

Following the removal of the Taliban from power in Afghanistan in 2001 and escalating tensions between Iran and the United States, particularly after President George W. Bush named Iran as a member of an 'axis of evil', Iran reviewed its position towards the Taliban. The subsequent regime change in Iraq in 2003 brought more US troops to Iran's doorstep and accelerated a strategic review in Tehran. Iran continued to promote an anti-American discourse in Afghanistan and beyond, which resulted in growing ties with the Taliban. Indeed, Iran appeared to be running two contradictory agendas in Afghanistan. Iran benefited from the fall of the Taliban, gaining an unexpected opportunity to expand its influence in Afghanistan, including through its relationships with government officials. Former president Hamid Karzai confessed that Iran made payments to Afghan officials.[43] Iran established cultural centres in different Afghan cities such as Kabul, Mazar-e-Sharif, and Herat. Iran's humanitarian/charity organisations, such as the Imam Khomeini Relief Committee (IKRC), also operate in Afghanistan, providing generous scholarships to Afghan nationals to study in Iran. Tehran also hosts fee-paying Afghan students in different Iranian universities. According to one estimate, there were 38,000 Afghan students in Iran as of January 2019.[44] To expand its outreach in Afghanistan, several Iranian universities also offer on-campus and online education in Pashto, including at Allameh Tabataba'i University. A few Iranian universities have also opened campuses in Afghanistan; these include Islamic Azad University, MIU and Payame Noor University. This cultural influence is further expanded through the media. To counter the influence of Western media, IRIB operates TV channels

---

[40] 'Pakistan's Sectarian Mire and the Way Forward', *Pak Institute of Peace Studies*, 22 March 2019, https://www.pakpips.com/article/book/pakistans-sectarian-mire-the-way-forward.

[41] 'Sectarian Violence in Pakistan', *South Asia Terrorism Portal*, http://www.satp.org/satporgtp/countries/pakistan/database/sect-killing.htm.

[42] 'Pakistan's Sectarian Mire and the Way Forward', 8.

[43] Dexter Filkins, 'Iran is Said to Give Top Karzai Aide Cash by the Bagful', *New York Times*, 23 October 2010, https://www.nytimes.com/2010/10/24/world/asia/24afghan.html.

[44] 1- تحصیل مشکلات و ایران مقیم افغان دانشجویان ؛شد مطرح ایرنا میزگرد در (Afghan University Students in Iran and Their Problems: Discussed at IRNA), *IRNA*, 2 January 2019, https://www.irna.ir/news/83155937.

in Dari and Pashto in Afghanistan. It is reported that as part of its soft power strategy in Afghanistan, Tehran invests US$100 million per annum in media, civil society and religious programmes.[45]

Geopolitics

During the Afghan–Soviet War, both Iran and Pakistan played a key role in recruiting and training mujahideen. By the 1990s, Iran had become a key player in Afghanistan, backing the government of Burhanuddin Rabbani. When the Taliban captured Kabul, Iran began supporting some opposition groups against them, including the prominent group Hezb-e Islami, a Pashtun dominated organisation led by Gulbuddin Hekmatyar. After the formation of the Taliban government in 1996, Hekmatyar fled to Iran and remained there until the fall of the Taliban in 2001. It has been reported that Iran had supported Hezb-e Islami in attacking US bases and other targets in Afghanistan.[46] In addition to forging relations with political groups in Afghanistan, Iran has also used the refugee card to maintain some influence in Kabul. Over the past decades, millions of Afghans have taken refuge in Iran. This has given Iran important leverage over Afghanistan, allowing Tehran to threaten the deportation of Afghan refugees or disrupt remittance payments to Afghanistan.

Since the beginning of the twenty-first century, Tehran's political influence has grown in the Middle East as well as across Iran's eastern borders. To underline this phenomenon, King Abdullah of Jordan coined the term 'Shiite crescent' in 2004.[47] It should be noted that Iran's relationship with Pakistan is complex. While sharing cultural ties and some geopolitical ambitions, there is also mutual mistrust. Iran is particularly concerned about the Sunni extremist group Jaish ul-Adl, based in Pakistan. This group has carried out several attacks in Iran, including an attack on the Iranian military on 13 February 2019, which killed twenty-seven soldiers.[48]

After the deployment of US troops in Afghanistan in 2001, Iran actively sought to guard against the prospect of Afghan territory being used by Washington to launch attacks on Iranian territory. This is possibly because tensions between Iran and the United States significantly increased in the context of concerns over Tehran's nuclear programme. Due to this concern, Iran reviewed its position on the Taliban and developed ties with them, providing it with support – mainly material and intelligence – to fight the United States and its NATO allies in Afghanistan. At the same time, however, Iran did not want the Taliban – an anti-Shi'a group – to be

---

[45] Amie Ferris-Rotman, 'Insight: Iran's "Great Game" in Afghanistan', *Reuters*, 24 May 2012, https://www.reuters.com/article/us-afghanistan-iran-media-idUSBRE84N0CB20120524.
[46] Nader et al., 'Iran and Afghanistan: A Complicated Relationship'.
[47] Kayhan Barzegar, 'Iran and the Shiite Crescent: Myths and Realities', *Brown Journal of World Affairs* 15(1) (2008): 87–99.
[48] Saurav Sarkar, 'Understanding Iran's Moves in the Afghan Endgame', *South Asian Voices*, 26 March 2019, https://southasianvoices.org/understanding-irans-moves-in-the-afghan-endgame.

the only dominant group in Afghanistan after the withdrawal of the US-led NATO mission. An analyst explained that Tehran 'desires neither a pro-US government in Kabul nor political system rule by the Taliban or Sunni extremists under the influence of Saudi Arabia and Pakistan'.[49] Therefore, Tehran at times provided simultaneous support to the Taliban and the US-backed Afghan government. Iran also had concerns over the Afghan peace processes facilitated by other actors, because it feared that its Persian Gulf rivals, such as the UAE and Saudi Arabia, could exploit such negotiations.

Pakistan, on the other hand, has historically had friendly relations with Iran from its formation in 1947.[50] However, since the 1978 coup by General Zia-ul-Haq in Pakistan and Iran's Islamic Revolution in 1979, competing forms of Islamisation in the two countries have significantly changed the domestic politics and foreign policies of both states. This, alongside swiftly changing geopolitical dynamics, put them in opposing camps, for example, Pakistan cooperated in the US-led 'War on Terror'. Besides geopolitical divergences, the bilateral relationship has also suffered because of sectarian violence in Pakistan, about which Tehran has always expressed serious concerns. Sectarian conflicts within Pakistan have also been reinforced by the geopolitical rivalry between Tehran and Riyadh, as elsewhere in the Middle East and South Asia regions. Despite having clear ideological and political links with Iran, Pakistani Shi'a groups claim that they do not receive any funding from Tehran. Tehrik-e-Jafaria Pakistan (TJP), which is the largest Shi'a political organisation in Pakistan, has direct links with Tehran. In 2011, Sajid Naqvi of TJP travelled to Iran to participate in the first International Islamic Awakening Conference. Similarly, a prominent Shi'a student-led organisation, the Imamia Students Organisation (ISO), claims that it receives no funding from Iran.[51] It could be true that these groups have local sources of funding and support Iran's ideological and political agenda solely due to their shared religious affiliation. There is no evidence to suggest that Iran provides any direct funding.

Recruitment of Shi'a militants from Afghanistan and Pakistan

Tehran declared its support for the besieged regime of Bashar al-Assad in Syria, and has provided military assistance to the country after the outbreak of a popular revolt in 2011. An important aspect of Iran's involvement in Syria is its active recruitment and deployment of Shi'a combatants from South and Central Asia, mainly from Afghanistan and Pakistan. Iran appears to have taken advantage of its cultural links with Shi'as in Afghanistan and its influence over Afghan refugees in Iran for the recruitment of paramilitary fighters, known as the Liwa Fatemiyoun, named after Prophet Muhammad's daughter and Imam Hussain's mother. Liwa Fatemiyoun was

---

[49] Ibid.
[50] Ahmed and Akbarzadeh, 'Understanding Pakistan's Relationship with Iran'.
[51] See a media release from the ISO Media Cell, https://imamia.wordpress.com/about.

founded in 2013 to support the Assad regime in Syria, and it appears to have been funded, trained and equipped by Iran's Islamic Revolutionary Guard Corps (IRGC). Foreign fighters operate under the command of Iranian officers. As of 2017, there were 10,000–20,000 fighters serving in Fatemiyoun brigades, mostly comprising Afghan Shi'as recruited from inside Iran. A report from the US Institute of Peace pointed out that the marginalisation of Shi'as in Afghanistan, particularly Hazaras, has facilitated Iran's recruitment drive for the war in Syria. According to one estimate, 897 Afghans were killed between January 2012 and July 2018 in Syria, the second highest number of foreign nationals killed in that period after the 1,232 Lebanese.[52] There are already reports of the return to Afghanistan of combatants from the Fatemiyoun division. Those trained Shi'a fighters may serve Iranian interests in Afghanistan in the future. A report from the Middle East Institute suggested that some Shi'a militias are engaged in armed action against anti-Hazara and anti-Iran groups in the Wardak province of Afghanistan.[53]

Iran has also recruited Pakistani Shi'as to fight in Syria, who serve primarily in the Liwa Zainebiyoun militia force. The brigade, named after Prophet Muhammad's granddaughter and Imam Hussain's sister, is a pro-Assad brigade made up of Shi'a Pakistani residents of Iran, Shi'a Hazaras living in Quetta, and Shi'a Pakistanis based on the city of Parachinar and the province of Khyber Pakhtunkhwa. Some reports suggest that these recruits have been trained by the IRGC. According to a newspaper report, the brigade consisted of 1,000 fighters in 2015.[54]

It was in 2015 that frequent reports of Iran's recruitment of Pakistani Shi'a started to appear in the international media, with some coverage in Pakistani newspapers. One report suggested that most of the Pakistani recruits were aged between 18 and 35, who were offered a forty-five-day military training course and a monthly salary of 120,000 Pakistani rupees.[55] There is no precise data available of the number of Pakistani Shi'a recruited to fight in Syria, but reports estimate Zainebiyoun numbers to range between 200 and 1,000 fighters. As will be discussed in detail in Chapter 8, while many of our research participants in Pakistan reported that the government is not doing enough to address the issue of Iran's recruitment of Pakistan Shi'as, security agencies in Pakistan have been closely monitoring this matter. The government of Pakistan has quietly launched a security crackdown against suspected members of Liwa Zainebiyoun, which has been linked to the disappearance of many young

---

[52] Ali Alfoneh, 'Four Decades in the Making: Shia Afghan Fatemiyoun Division of the Revolutionary Guards', Arab Gulf States Institute, Washington, 25 July 2018, https://agsiw.org/four-decades-in-the-making-shia-afghan-fatemiyoun-division-of-the-revolutionary-guards.

[53] Tobias Schneider, 'The Fatemiyoun Division: Afghan Fighters in the Syria Civil War', Middle East Institute, 15 October 2018, https://www.mei.edu/publications/fatemiyoun-division-afghan-fighters-syrian-civil-war.

[54] 'Iran Recruits Pakistani Shias for Combat in Syria', *Express Tribune*, 11 December 2015, https://tribune.com.pk/story/1007694/iran-recruits-pakistani-shias-for-combat-in-syria.

[55] Dehghanpisheh, 'Iran Recruits Pakistani Shi'ites for Combat in Syria'.

Pakistan Shi'as.⁵⁶ According to one report, 140 Pakistani Shi'a disappeared during 2016–2018, and local Shi'a activists believe that they were picked up by the state's intelligence agencies.⁵⁷ The families of Shi'a missing persons have held protests in Pakistan to demand the release of their family members and the Missing Persons' Relatives Committee has been very active, in collaboration with other human rights groups, such as the Human Rights Commission of Pakistan.⁵⁸ Their combined pressure has led to the occasional release of some Shi'as, including four who were released in May 2019.⁵⁹

Soft power

We use soft power theory in this research to explore and analyse Iran's influence in Afghanistan and Pakistan. Soft power as a concept emerged at the end of the Cold War through debates surrounding the decline of the United States' influence on global politics. The American political scientist Joseph Nye, is known as the progenitor of the academic discourse on soft power. Nye defines soft power as co-optive power that works by 'getting others to want what you want' without the use of hard power means such as military intervention.⁶⁰ In other words, soft power represents 'the ability to get what you want through attraction rather than coercion or payments'.⁶¹ This means that attraction is a key concept associated with soft power. Nye notes, 'soft power is the ability to affect others through the co-optive means of framing the agenda, persuading, and eliciting positive attraction in order to obtain preferred outcomes'.⁶² As will be discussed in the next chapter, Iran's ancient civilisation and its historical relationship with Afghanistan and Pakistan offer great potential to Tehran for exercising influence and increasing its attractiveness and prestige in both countries.

Nye further argues that any state can develop its soft power capabilities by drawing on the three key sources of culture, political values and foreign policy.⁶³ Instead of using military force or physical strength and threat, a country that utilises its soft power draws on these capacities to persuade others to modify or change their behaviour. Each of these sources can increase a country's attraction, generating the

---

[56] Secunder Kermani, 'The Story of Pakistan's "Disappeared" Shias', *BBC News*, 31 May 2018, https://www.bbc.com/news/world-asia-44280552.
[57] Ibid.
[58] In May 2019, a demonstration was held in Karachi outside the residence of Dr Arif Alvi, president of Pakistan.
[59] Imtiaz Ali, '4 "Missing Persons" Return after More than Two Years: Committee', *Dawn*, 10 May 2019, https://www.dawn.com/news/1481436.
[60] Joseph S. Nye, Jr, 'Soft Power', *Foreign Policy* 80 (1990): 167
[61] Joseph S. Nye, Jr, *Soft Power: The Means to Success in World Politics* (New York: Public Affairs, 2004), x.
[62] Joseph S. Nye, Jr, *The Future of Power* (New York: Public Affairs, 2011), 20–1.
[63] Joseph S. Nye, Jr, 'Public Diplomacy and Soft Power', *Annals of the American Academy of Political and Social Science* 616(1) (2008): 94–109.

admiration of people in the target country. According to Nye, 'If [a country's] culture and ideology are attractive, others more willingly follow.'[64] The cultural norms of a country that exercise influence in another country can be displayed 'in places where ... [they are] attractive to others'.[65] Such influence can also be achieved by various means, such as student exchange programmes, granting scholarships to foreign students, convening seminars and conferences, and broadcasting programmes through media channels.[66] Nye gives the example of student exchange programmes and American soft power capability in the context of the Cold War, noting that 'from 1958 to 1988, 50,000 Russians visited the United States as part of formal exchange programs', and that these programmes facilitated the dissemination of US values to tens of thousands of Soviet citizens.[67] Indeed, exchange programmes comprise a significant aspect of soft power. Some studies suggest that exchange students often return home with a more positive view of the country in which they studied – confirming that international graduates comprise a resource that can enhance the host country's soft power.[68]

One aspect of cultural soft power that has the potential for a given state to exercise influence on target countries is language. Nye notes that there is a direct link between language and soft power. For example, he argues that Japan's weakness in foreign languages makes it difficult for the country to exercise its soft power. According to Nye, although Japan seeks to alleviate this weakness through the Japan Exchange and Teaching Programme, Japanese is not widely spoken in the world and Japanese foreign language skills rank among the lowest in Asia – factors that prevent Japan from extending its soft power.[69] The promotion of a country's language in another country can be conducted, for example, 'through preparing and selection of teaching materials and providing a comprehensive insight into the culture and values of the country and its people'.[70] Examples of countries that promote their language outside their borders include China through Confucius Institutes, the United Kingdom through the British Council, France through Alliance Française and Germany through the Goethe Institute. As will be discussed, Iran has used a variety of cultural tools including its language to exercise influence in Afghanistan and Pakistan.

Soft power gained currency as states acknowledged its value in advancing their foreign policy and pursuing their interests. Beyond the literature on the United States during the Cold War era, international relations scholars have focused on how

[64] Nye, 'Soft Power', 167.
[65] Nye, *Soft Power: The Means to Success in World Politics*, 11
[66] Ibid., 109
[67] Joseph Nye, 'Soft Power and Higher Education', *Forum*, 2005, http://forum.mit.edu/articles/soft-power-and-higher-education.
[68] Carol Atkinson, 'Does Soft Power Matter? A Comparative of Student Exchange Programs 1980–2006', *Foreign Policy Analysis* 6(1) (2010): 3.
[69] Nye, *Soft Power: The Means to Success in World Politics,* 97, 110.
[70] Natalia Yudina and Oksana Seliverstova, 'External Language Policy and Planning as Part of Soft Power Policy', 4th International Scientific and Practical Conference, 1–4 October, Volgograd, Russia, 2019.

developed states and the emerging economies of the global South seek to enhance their soft power capabilities.[71] States can use a variety of soft power resources and instruments, for example, public diplomacy, at the bilateral and multilateral levels. Such strategies also help states to boost their international agendas,[72] for example, through international organisations.

One needs to also pay attention to the post-Cold War context in which hard power resources have been very costly. As Chong claims, 'military power was becoming increasingly costly to wield in an era of nuclear weapons proliferation, nationally awakened populations in underdeveloped countries, rising economic interdependence, and a growing public aversion in advanced capitalist democracies to protracted and expensive conventional wars'.[73] In the post-Cold War era, as Nye claims, the United States maintained its advantage over other states because of its democratic values, despite a decline in terms of its dominance as an economic and military power.[74] Nye extended his theory in the context of the 'War on Terror', arguing that the United States should not exercise its hard power at the expense of losing its soft power. In the context of the 'War on Terror' and 'the information age', Nye argues, 'success is not merely the result of whose army wins, but also whose story wins. Hard military power is not enough. We also need the soft power attraction.'[75] In this sense, Nye criticised the United States' heavy reliance on hard power means, stating that a significant aspect of soft power is capturing the hearts and minds of the people of the target states, which can be achieved not through hard power measures such as military intervention, but through soft power measures.[76]

When it comes to resources, the key difference between soft and hard power is that 'resources associated with hard power include tangibles such as force and money', whereas the resources that are associated with soft power include 'factors such as institutions, ideas, values, culture, and the perceived legitimacy of policies'.[77] Economic means are attributed to either soft or hard power depending on the context. Providing economic relief programmes with the aim of capturing the hearts and minds of people – or a certain group of people – in a target country

---

[71] Mathilde Chatin and Giulio M. Gallarotti, 'The BRICS and Soft Power: An Introduction', *Journal of Political Power* 9(3) (2016): 335–52; Jean-Marc F. Blanchard and Fujia Lu, 'Thinking Hard About Soft Power: A Review and Critique of the Literature on China and Soft Power', *Asian Perspective* 36(4) (2012): 565–89; Tim Winter, 'Geocultural Power: China's Belt and Road Initiative', *Geopolitics* 26(5) (2021): 1376–99.

[72] Hongying Wang and Yeh-Chung Lu, 'The Conception of Soft Power and Its Policy Implications: A Comparative Study of China and Taiwan', *Journal of Contemporary China* 17(56) (2008): 425–47.

[73] Alan Chong, 'Smart Power and Military Force: An Introduction', *Journal of Strategic Studies* 38(3) (2015): 233–44.

[74] Joseph S. Nye Jr, *Bound to Lead: The Changing Nature of American Power* (New York: Basic Books, 1990).

[75] Joseph S. Nye Jr, Book Review: 'Smart Power', *Democracy Journal*, 2006, https://democracyjournal.org/magazine/2/smart-power.

[76] Nye, *Soft Power: The Means to Success in World Politics*, 1.

[77] Nye, *The Future of Power*, 21.

is an example through which a country can exercise soft power.[78] Other prominent examples in the economic arena which could be considered a source of soft power include the Marshall Plan in 1948 and China's Belt and Road Initiative (BRI). In his most recent work, Nye refers to such a relationship between hard and soft powers, noting that some resources that are commonly associated with hard power can at times produce soft power. For example, in 2004, the provision of tsunami relief to Indonesia by US naval ships became a source of American soft power since it increased the attractiveness of the United States in the eyes of Indonesians.[79]

The literature on soft power notes a link between soft power and identities.[80] Nye notes such a relationship, stating that we naturally 'like those who are similar to us'.[81] In this sense, religion can be used as another source to increase soft power, though Nye does not emphasise it as a significant source of soft power. This is due to the fact that Nye's theory of soft power reflects American liberal values and is mainly secular in nature. Indeed, Nye clarified that his work on soft power 'stemmed from American culture, values, and policies that were broadly inclusive and seen as legitimate in the eyes of others'.[82] Therefore, compared with other cultural means, Nye does not discuss in detail how and the extent to which religious values can contribute to a country's soft power and even, at times, considers religion to be a 'double-edged sword'.[83]

Despite this, a number of scholars have noted the important contribution that religion can make to a given country's soft power, thereby giving rise to the concept of 'religious soft power'. Jödicke notes that in the contemporary international system, especially in societies and contexts in which religion is deeply rooted, religion can be considered a key source of soft power.[84] Mandaville and Hamid identify 'religious soft power' as 'the phenomenon whereby states incorporate the promotion of religion into their broader foreign policy conduct'.[85] One example of 'religious soft power' identified by them is Saudi Arabia's effort to build mosques around the world through which the country seeks to spread its ideology, in turn increasing receptivity to Saudi initiatives among Sunni Muslims worldwide.[86] Indeed, if one considers religion a

---

[78] See economic examples Iran has used to exercise influence in Syria: Ali Akbar, 'Iran's Soft Power in Syria after the Syrian Civil War', *Mediterranean Politics* 28(2) (2023): 227–49.
[79] Joseph S. Nye, Jr, 'Soft Power: The Evolution of a Concept', *Journal of Political Power* 14(1) (2021): 196–208.
[80] See Ty Solomon, 'The Affective Underpinnings of Soft Power', *European Journal of International Relations* 20(3) (2014): 720–41.
[81] Nye, *The Future of Power*, 92.
[82] Nye, Book Review: 'Smart Power'.
[83] Nye, *Soft Power: The Means to Success in World Politics*, 59.
[84] Ansgar Jödicke, 'Religious Soft Power in the South Caucasus: The Influence of Iran and Turkey', Brookings Institution, 2018, https://www.brookings.edu/blog/order-from-chaos/2018/12/13/religious-soft-power-in-the-south-caucasus-the-influence-of-iran-and-turkey.
[85] Peter Mandaville and Shadi Hamid, 'Islam as Statecraft: How Governments Use Religion in Foreign Policy', in *The New Geopolitics Middle East* (Washington, DC: Brookings Institution, 2018), 6.
[86] Ibid., 10.

significant source of identity, one can conclude that it has the potential to be employed by states to influence others with the same religion living outside its borders. As will be discussed, religion is an aspect of Iranian soft power tools employed by Tehran; it gives Iran an opportunity to establish strong connections with Shi'a groups in both Afghanistan and Pakistan.

Ohnesorge has suggested that soft power may be examined on the basis of resources, instruments, reception or outcomes.[87] While resources and instruments can be controlled by a state investing in soft power, reception and outcomes are dependent on the dynamics in targeted states.[88] In his soft power framework, Ohnesorge further focuses on receivers' potential responses, such as attraction, apathy or repulsion, which can result in compliance, neutrality or opposition.[89] Generally speaking, the soft power literature focuses more on the attributes, actions and assets that states possess to exercise influence on other countries, while the reception aspect of soft power is relatively neglected and there are only a few studies that explore it.[90] This aspect has obvious relevance for our examination of the scope of Iran's soft power project.

In recent years, we have witnessed greater scholarly interest in the hard–soft power nexus. As discussed, hard power depends on coercive power achieved through inducement and threat, and is therefore based on military strength, coercive diplomacy and at times economic might.[91] While hard power is easy to measure through data on aid, trade or economic dependency, weapon supply and troops, soft power is much harder to measure because it requires more data focusing on cultural, ideological and institutional indices.[92] Although the soft–hard power dichotomy is visible in Nye's work, some scholars have noted that 'practices commonly labelled and understood as soft power and hard power are closely interconnected'.[93] With regard to the hard–soft power nexus, the literature has also noted that some non-state actors use religion to gain support and to even recruit militias. This means that religion, as a source of soft power, has the potential to be employed in the exercise of hard power.[94] In the context of the Middle East, states such as Iran and Saudi Arabia use

---

[87] Hendrik W. Ohnesorge, *Soft Power: The Forces of Attraction in International Relations* (Cham: Springer, 2020).
[88] Ibid., 204.
[89] Ibid.
[90] See, e.g., Joanna Szostek, 'The Power and Limits of Russia's Strategic Narrative in Ukraine: The Role of Linkage', *Perspectives on Politics* 15(2) (2017): 379–95.
[91] Joseph S. Nye, Jr, *Understanding International Conflicts* (New York: Pearson, 2009); Ernest J. Wilson, 'Hard Power, Soft Power, Smart Power', *Annals of American Academy of Political and Social Science* 616 (2008): 110–24.
[92] Eric Li, 'The Rise and Fall of Soft Power', *Foreign Policy*, 20 August 2018, https://foreignpolicy.com/2018/08/20/the-rise-and-fall-of-soft-power.
[93] Linus Hagström and Chengxin Pan, 'Traversing the Soft/Hard Power Binary: The Case of the Sino-Japanese Territorial Dispute', *Review of International Studies* 46(1) (2020): 37.
[94] John O. Voll, 'Trans-state Muslim Movements and Militant Extremists in an Era of Soft Power', in T. Banchoff (ed.), *Religious Pluralism, Globalization, and World Politics* (New York: Oxford University Press, 2008), 254.

certain religious and cultural resources in regional rivalries as well as in competition against outside powers.[95] As explained above, Iran has certain advantages in South and Central Asia, for example, proximity to Afghanistan and Pakistan, the sizeable Shi'a populations in these countries and the imperial legacy of the Persian Empire. These factors offer Tehran the opportunity to exercise ideological, economic and political influence in its neighbourhood. The extent to which Iran has employed soft power resources and instruments to advance its agenda in Afghanistan and Pakistan is the key theme that this book aims to explore.

Chapter descriptions

The book is divided into nine chapters, including this Introduction and Conclusion (Chapter 9). The Introduction is followed by Chapter 2, which traces Iran's historical influence in Afghanistan and Pakistan from the pre-Islamic era until the early modern period. The chapter shows how the flow of ideas, people, language and trade between Iran and the Indian subcontinent and between Iran and Greater Khorasan occurred over the course of history. It demonstrates that Iran benefits from its imperial legacy (the Persian Empire) to promote goodwill in neighbouring Afghanistan and Pakistan in the contemporary period.

Chapter 3 explores the dynamics of Iran's relations with Afghanistan and Pakistan with a particular focus on Tehran's key concerns. In the case of Afghanistan, there are three main concerns for Tehran: the illicit trade in opium from Afghanistan to Iran; the influx into and the presence of a large numbers of Afghan refugees in Iran; and the water-sharing dispute over the Helmand River. In the case of Pakistan, Iran has been concerned about the rise of sectarianism and jihadist Sunni Baluch militant groups that have taken refuge in Pakistan. As examined in this chapter, our research participants identified several key sources of tension in terms of Iran's relations with Afghanistan and Pakistan. In particular, our Afghan interviewees were very critical of Tehran's attitude towards the Afghan refugees living in Iran and also considered the water dispute to be a key pending dispute between Afghanistan and Iran. Our Pakistani interviewees mentioned the Saudi factor and border security issues between Iran and Pakistan as sources of mistrust and tension between Iran and Pakistan.

Chapter 4 examines how Afghanistan and Pakistan are significant for Iran's geostrategic goals in South and Central Asia. As in Chapter 3, analysis in this chapter relies on primary data collected in Afghanistan and Pakistan. This chapter explains that besides its interest in exporting natural gas to energy-deficient Pakistan and India via a pipeline through Pakistan, Iran was troubled by the presence of Soviet troops in Afghanistan during the 1980s. Similarly, in Afghanistan, Iran was deeply concerned by the presence of the United States and other international

---

[95] For example, see Dilip Hiro, *Cold War in the Islamic World: Saudi Arabia, Iran and the Struggle for Supremacy* (New York: Oxford University Press, 2018).

troops between 2001 and 2021. When it comes to Pakistan, while Tehran views the Chabahar and Gwadar projects as 'sister ports', Pakistan views the Chabahar Port as a threat to its national security because its arch-rival India has been mainly involved in this project.

Chapter 5 focuses on Iran's ideological and cultural influence in Afghanistan and Pakistan. It presents an analysis of the resources and instruments that Iran uses to leverage its ideological and cultural connections to promote goodwill in Afghanistan and Pakistan, and how such measures have been received in both states. As this chapter argues, Iran has certain advantages such as demographics in the form of a sizeable Shi'a population in both countries and the deep imprint of the Persian legacy due to which it can employ a variety of instruments, including Persian heritage and the promotion of Shi'a ideology, to create a positive image of itself in both countries. The impact, however, varies between the two states. Iran enjoys a much deeper influence in Afghanistan than in Pakistan because Tehran has been able to invest in infrastructure, particularly through the creation of educational and media institutions, to achieve its national interests. In contrast, Iran's influence in Pakistan is not as multifaceted and is largely limited to Shi'as, especially in the Shi'a-majority areas of Gilgit-Baltistan and Parachinar. In terms of how its ideological and cultural influence is received in both these states, interviewees largely reflected on Iran's influence on Shi'a populations in both countries for political gain.

Chapter 6 explores Iran's political influence in Afghanistan and Pakistan, with the intent of demonstrating how Tehran has employed a variety of tools to gain influence over certain political groups in the two countries. Since the Iranian Islamic Revolution in 1979, Tehran has initiated activities with the goal of gaining and expanding its political influence in Afghanistan and Pakistan. This, however, has achieved different results because of the differing dynamics of the target countries. While Iran's political influence in Pakistan is largely limited to Shi'a groups, including those with limited political impact and the Pakistan Peoples Party (PPP), Tehran's political influence in Afghanistan has been more visible and multifaceted. Indeed, while Iran managed to exercise influence on government policy in Afghanistan, especially under the Karzai administration, it has not been successful in achieving such a goal in Pakistan. As discussed in this chapter, Iran has tried to gain a greater influence in Afghanistan through direct connections with policymakers and government officials. In Pakistan, Iran's influence has remained limited to Shi'a groups and has not been fully expanded to formal political parties and the parliament, although some Shi'a groups, such as the MWM, have often participated in formal politics.

Chapter 7 focuses on Iran's economic relations and influence to understand whether Tehran has used economic tools, for example, coercive diplomacy and economic sanctions, to achieve its political goals. The chapter also explores how Iran's economic influence is viewed in both countries. The fall of the Taliban regime in 2001 provided Iran with an ideal opportunity to expand its economic relations with Afghanistan and gain economic influence, which is significant in the western parts of the country. Conversely, Iran's economic relationship with Pakistan has had its ups and downs. In the early years of the establishment of the Islamic Republic, the economic relationship between the two countries grew significantly, but during the 1990s there was a decline because of international sanctions on Iran. These sanctions have prevented both countries from exploiting the full potential of their economic cooperation.

Chapter 8 explores the extent to which Iran's soft power strategies in both Afghanistan and Pakistan have enabled Tehran to recruit Shi'as from both countries – leading to the formation of Liwa Fatemiyoun and Liwa Zainebiyoun – to support the Bashar al-Assad regime in Syria. Iran's recruitment of Shi'as from Afghanistan and Pakistan does not meet the standard definition of hard power, which focuses on the use of economic coercion and military power to influence the behaviour of other political bodies or countries. As neither Kabul nor Islamabad played a role in the recruitment managed by Iran's IRCG, we cannot label this as a typical example of hard power. Iran's ability to recruit Shi'as from both countries, however, provides enough evidence to suggest that it can benefit from its soft power in Afghanistan and Pakistan for military and geopolitical gains. While most Afghan combatants, mainly Hazara refugees, were lured into participation through promises of permanent residency and financial benefits, this study found that most of the Pakistani participants embarked on their mission in order to protect sacred Shi'a shrines in Syria. Despite Iran's influence on Shi'a groups in both countries, we found no evidence to suggest that local religious groups were involved in the recruitment process.

In the concluding chapter, we present a synthesis of our key arguments from the preceding chapters to show how Iran's soft power instruments have been employed and received in both countries. We focus particularly on how Iran's soft power resources, instruments and strategies differ in Afghanistan and Pakistan. Considering the recent developments in Afghanistan in the shape of the Taliban's second takeover, we also focus on how Iran's soft power strategies might change. It is important to note that while the majority of the analysis presented in this book concerns events that occurred before the Taliban's return to power in August 2021, we do touch on the Iran–Afghanistan relationship in late 2021 and 2022 in some sections, addressing how the new developments in Afghanistan in the shape of the second Islamic Emirate of Afghanistan influence ties between Iran and Afghanistan.

2
Historical Legacy

Among the variety of resources and instruments that Iran uses to promote its soft power is the 'capitalization on an imperial legacy'.[1] Michael Rubin argues that 'Modern Iranian culture is a mélange of the influences which dominated in various incarnations of the Persian Empire and Iranian State'.[2] As we examine in this study, Iran has been benefiting from its imperial legacy or that of the Persian Empire to promote its goodwill in other countries. This aspect is particularly visible in neighbouring Afghanistan and Pakistan.

The Persian Empire was founded in 550 BC and soon became one of the largest powers with territories under its control extending from Europe's Balkan Peninsula to India's Indus Valley. Persians of the Achaemenid Empire promoted their art and crafts, including metalwork, weaving and architecture, to areas under its control.[3] The remnants of those can still be seen in areas presently known as Afghanistan, India and Pakistan. As Tehran continues to benefit from the legacy of the Persian Empire in terms of its soft power, it is important to look at the roots of the historical connections of Persia with territories presently under the control of Afghanistan and Pakistan.

Persian legacy in Afghanistan

As a political entity independent of both the Safavid and Mughal empires, the history of modern Afghanistan goes back almost two and a half centuries, when Ahmad Shah Durrani established an Afghan kingdom based in Kandahar.[4] Before this, what we know as Afghanistan today, had been part of the province of Khorasan, which in the pre-Islamic era and during the rule of the early caliphs (the Umayyad and Abbasid caliphates) included the whole of Iran east of the city of Ray. From a few medieval sources, we have evidence of the existence of a tribe called 'Afghan'.

---

[1] Michael Rubin, 'Strategies Underlying Iranian Soft Power', American Enterprise Institute, 7 March 2017, https://www.aei.org/research-products/journal-publication/strategies-underlying-iranian-soft-power.
[2] Ibid.
[3] 'Persian Empire', History, 30 September 2019, https://www.history.com/topics/ancient-middle-east/persian-empire.
[4] D. Balland, 'Afghanistan x. Political History', Encyclopaedia Iranica, online edition, 1982, http://www.iranicaonline.org/articles/afghanistan-x-political-history.

The anonymous Persian geographer who wrote *Hudud al-Alim* (*The Limits of the World*) – a manuscript written around 982 – and the historian Muhammad ibn Abd al-Jabbar al-Utb in the early eleventh century acknowledged the existence of a tribe called 'Afghan' living in the Suleiman Mountains (the borderland of today's Afghanistan and Pakistan). Similarly, al-Biruni mentions various Afghan tribes living west of the Indus River.[5]

The relationship between Iran and the country today called Afghanistan dates back to the pre-Islamic era. Today's Afghanistan was part of Iran's Khorasan Province, historically referred to as Greater Khorasan. This province comprised a large part of the Persian Empire in the pre-Islamic era. Before the fall of the Sasanian Empire and the Muslim conquest of Persia in the seventh century, Greater Khorasan was the Sasanian Empire's eastern province (*satrapy*) and home to cities such as Balkh and Herat in today's Afghanistan, as well as Nishapur in Iran and Merv in Turkmenistan. Balkh and Herat together with Sistan was one of four key Sasanian provinces, governed by a Sasanian general, or an *ispahbadh*.[6] The transmission of Sasanian-origin myths, especially the Zoroastrian legends that Zoroaster died in Balkh and that his patron built the city, as well as the presence of Zoroastrian fire temples in and around Balkh demonstrate the Iranian cultural and religious influences on the regions that comprise Afghanistan today.[7]

In Herat, we can find a stronger Sasanian presence. The city itself served as a Sasanian mint, and its name 'Harev' (*hryw*) is listed in the inscription of the Sasanian ruler Shapur I (r. 239–270). The name '*Hariy*' (*hr'y*) is also mentioned in the Pahlavi catalogue of the provincial capitals of the empire.[8] Sasanian seals and engraved gemstones are reported to have been found in and around Herat.[9] The gold coins from the location now called Herat include a fire altar on the reverse and the portrait of the ruler on the obverse. As noted by Vogelsang, 'the name of the ruler is often identical to one of those listed on the Sasanian coins, and this would indicate that the Sasanian governor in the northeast of the Sasanian Empire at times also controlled the Herat district'.[10] It should be noted that beyond Balkh and Herat, in areas such as Tukharistan's rural metropolises of Samangan and Rob, as well as Bamiyan, the southern point of the area of Balkh, we find a weaker Sasanian presence. In Bamiyan, we can observe the stronger influence of Buddhism. The Chinese Buddhist pilgrim Xuanzang travelled to this area in the 630s and described

---

[5] C. E. Bosworth, 'Iran and Afghanistan in Contact and Interaction through the Ages', in Peter J. Chelkowski (ed.), *The Gift of Persian Culture: Its Continuity and Influence in History* (Salt Lake City, UT: University of Utah Press, 2011), 99.
[6] Arezou Azad, 'The Beginning of Islam in Afghanistan', in Nile Green (ed.), *Afghanistan's Islam: From Conversion to the Taliban* (Berkeley: University of California Press, 2017), 44.
[7] Azad, 'The Beginning of Islam in Afghanistan', 45.
[8] Markwart, *Provincial Capitals*, cited in W. J. Vogelsang, 'Herat ii: History, Pre-Islamic Period', *Encyclopaedia Iranica*, 2003, http://www.iranicaonline.org/articles/herat-ii.
[9] Vogelsang, 'Herat ii: History, Pre-Islamic Period'.
[10] Ibid.

the presence of two colossal Buddha statues at Bamiyan, which were built in the sixth or the seventh century.[11]

Another area of present-day Afghanistan which was part of the Sasanian domain was Sistan. It included Afghan cities and regions such as Ghazna, Zarang, Kandahar, Kabulistan and Zabulistan (the lands between Ghazna and Kabul), with Zarang later becoming an Umayyad base in 652 and used by the Arabs to launch their eastward campaigns. The term Sistan itself is derived from the Middle Persian *Sakastan*, which is also mentioned in an inscription of the Sassanid ruler Shapur. Under the Sasanian Empire, Zoroastrianism was a well-established religion in Sistan and a number of historical sources indicate the presence of chief *mobad*s (Zoroastrian priests) and fire temples in the area.[12]

After the conquest of Balkh in 708–709, the Umayyad caliphate began to exercise control over the lands that are Afghanistan today. Following the example of the Sasanians, the Umayyad dynasty ruled over Greater Khorasan from its regional command centre at Merv. Therefore, the influence of Sasanian political and cultural norms continued in Greater Khorasan after the rise of Islam in the region. The ties of Afghanistan with the wider Iranian world, particularly with Greater Khorasan, were gradually strengthened. By the late ninth century, as the Arab component of the Islamic civilisation began to decline, a new form of Islamic culture grounded in the Persian language and Iranian traditions flourished in Khorasan and Sistan, and we can identify many Persian poets and Sufis from these regions who produced poems and writings in the Persian language.[13]

In the later ninth century, two military adventurers, the Saffarids Yaqub and Amr b. Layth from Zarang in Sistan established a vast empire. Their empire not only included the whole of southern Iran, but also extended as far east as Kabul and eastern Afghanistan. Yaqub defeated local rulers in the region of Ghazna, as far as Kabul on the first occasion, and then defeated Kabul on the second occasion as well as Bamiyan and Balkh.[14] The Saffarids eventually gained control of Greater Khorasan, and their empire spanned not only half of modern Iran but also much of modern Afghanistan, including the cities of Herat and Balkh. According to Bosworth, the achievement of the Saffarids was unique because even the Sasanians did not have such effective control over regions in Afghanistan such as those located in east of Merv.[15]

The ties between Afghanistan and the wider Persian world continued under the Ghaznavids, an Islamic dynasty of Turkish origin (366–582/977–1186) which

---

[11] Azad, 'The Beginning of Islam in Afghanistan', 46.
[12] Ibid.
[13] Ehsan Yarshater, 'The Persian Phase of Islamic Civilization', in Peter J. Chelkowski (ed.), *The Gift of Persian Culture: Its Continuity and Influence in History* (Salt Lake City, UT: University of Utah Press, 2011), 60–1.
[14] C. E. Bosworth, *Sistan under the Arabs from the Islamic Conquest to the Rise of the Saffarids (30–250/651–864)* (Rome: Istituto Italiano Per Il Medio Ed Estremo Oriente, 1968), 119–21.
[15] Bosworth, 'Iran and Afghanistan in Contact and Interaction through the Ages', 104.

ruled a large proportion of Iranian lands, spanning from Ray to Kharazm and from Baluchestan to northwestern India. Ghazni became the capital of the empire from which the Ghaznavids ruled directly most areas of present-day Afghanistan, much of northwestern India and nearly all parts of today's eastern and northern Iran.[16] Sultan Mahmud, the founder of the Ghaznavid dynasty, brought other regions as far west as Isfahan and Hamadan under his control, and many Afghans together with Iranians residing in western parts of Iran served in his army.[17] This means both eastern and western parts of what we know today as Iran retained ties to Afghans.

The city of Herat was the capital of the Timurid dynasty between 1405 and 1507. From the time of Timurid ruler Shahrukh ibn Timur (r. 1405–1447) onward, Herat was the capital of an empire that ruled large parts of Iran, Afghanistan and central Asia. During the fifteenth century, Herat became a centre of Persian culture. It should be noted that Greater Khorasan had already been one of the regions in which Sufism flourished, and important works of Persian religious poetry and prose were composed in regions such as Herat and Ghazni by figures like Hakim Sanai, Abdullah Ansari and al-Hujwiri.[18] The Naqshbandi Sufis flourished under the Timurid dynasty in Afghanistan, and stronger connections between Iran and what we know today as Afghanistan were shaped during this period. Interest in the Persian mystic-poetical tradition characterised by the works of Abd al-Rahman Jami (d. 1492) was linked to the important political role played in central Asia at the time by the Naqshbandi Sufi order. In addition, in the second half of the fifteenth century, under the influence of the main schools of Shiraz, Baghdad and Tabriz, Herat witnessed the development of a new style of miniature painting which was characterised by the perfection of the techniques of colour and composition.[19] In this sense, we may point to the painting of miniatures by the artist Kamal al-Din Behzad and his school in Herat.[20] Therefore, during the late fourteenth and fifteenth centuries, Herat became a regional capital and a cultural centre in various fields such as Persian literature, architecture and book production, and was successful in absorbing not only the work of Khorasani figures (such as painters, scientists, Sufis and religious scholars), but also trends from the central and western areas of Iran.

During the sixteenth century, the control of Khorasan was a matter of dispute between the Shaybanids and the Safavids. With the notable exception of the years 1588–1598, the Safavids (r. 1501–1722) controlled Herat until the fall of the

---

[16] C. E. Bosworth, 'Ghaznavids', *Encyclopaedia Iranica*, 2001, http://www.iranicaonline.org/articles/ghaznavids.

[17] Bosworth, 'Iran and Afghanistan in Contact and Interaction through the Ages', 105.

[18] Nishin Arbabzadeh, 'Women and Religious Patronage in the Timurid Empire', in Nile Green (ed.), *Afghanistan's Islam: From Conversion to the Taliban* (Berkeley: University of California Press, 2017), 56–8.

[19] Maria Eva Subtelny, 'Arts and Politics in Early 16th Century Central Asia', *Central Asiatic Journal* 27(1/2) (1983): 125–6.

[20] Bosworth, 'Iran and Afghanistan in Contact and Interaction through the Ages', 105.

dynasty. The influence of the Safavids on Afghanistan is particularly important since the Safavids are often considered to be responsible for the conversion of the Afghan Hazaras to Shiism, given that the Safavids proclaimed Twelver Shiism as the state religion.[21] From Shah Abbas' era (1588–1629) onwards, the Afghan Hazaras retained their strong connection to Iranian cities in Khorasan. For example, after the Hazaras were persecuted under Abd al-Rahman Khan (r. 1880–1901) and some of them were enslaved and then sold by Pashtun and even Hindu slave traders, many thousands of Hazaras escaped to Mashhad and remained there for years before they were granted permission by Abd al-Rahman's successor Habibullah Khan to return home.[22]

In the early eighteenth century, the collapse of the Safavid and Mughal empires led to the rise of Durrani rulers. Although Durrani rulers sought to consider Kandahar an imperial capital of their own, close connections remained between religious centres in Afghanistan and other established religious centres in Iran especially those of Mashhad. During the nineteenth century, religious centres in Iran exercised significant influence on Afghanistan because access to religious learning was possible mainly through languages such as Arabic and Persian rather than Pashto and Uzbek.[23] However, in terms of political influence, although the recovery of some Afghan cities, especially Herat, remained an important element of Qajar political discourse and Qajar kings sought to increase their influence there, attempts made towards this objective were, by and large, unsuccessful.[24]

Iran and Afghanistan not only have deep historical and cultural bounds, but also a shared language, and Iran exercised significant influence in the development of the Persian language in Afghanistan. There are currently two major languages spoken in Afghanistan: Pashto[25] and Persian. Persian, which is also called Dari, is spoken in the central, northern and southern parts of Afghanistan, as well as in Kabul and the historic town of Ghazni. Persian is an official language and is spoken in bazaars and in conversation between individuals of different backgrounds in Afghanistan. The origin of the language and its introduction to Afghanistan dates back to the Sassanid era and the official language of the Sasanian Empire – Pahlavi. The Persian language was then reinforced throughout the centuries due to the close contact between Iranians and Afghans. According to Bivar, the language 'may have been introduced during the Kushano-Sasanian occupation (A.D. 230–350) in the garrison centres,

---

[21] Hasan M. Kakar, *The Pacification of the Hazaras of Afghanistan* (New York: Afghanistan Council of the Asia Society, 1973), 2.
[22] Nile Green, 'Introduction', in Nile Green (ed.), *Afghanistan's Islam: From Conversion to the Taliban* (Berkeley: University of California Press, 2017), 15.
[23] Green, 'Introduction', 15.
[24] Maria Szuppe, 'Herat iii. History: Medieval Period', *Encyclopaedia Iranica*, online edition, 2003, http://www.iranicaonline.org/articles/herat-iii.
[25] This language is spoken by Pashtun ethnicities living in east and southeast Afghanistan. The language itself is one of the eastern Iranian or Arian-originated languages, a group that includes most major current languages of Europe, the Iranian plateau and the Indian subcontinent.

forming a nucleus reinforced much later by detachments of Persian-speaking Qizilbash left from the eighteenth-century armies of Nader Shah'.[26]

Our Afghan research participants spoke about the importance of the historical legacy of the Persian Empire on present-day Iran's influence in Afghanistan. It was argued, for example, that 'Iran wants to be superior in the region', and this is rooted in what is referred to as the 'dreams' of the revival of the ancient Persian Empire.[27] The historical affinity between the two countries and Iran's rich culture developed throughout both the pre- and post-Islamic eras were considered by some Afghan participants to be important elements which enable Tehran to exercise influence in Afghanistan. According to an Afghan political analyst, Iran is the most influential country in Afghanistan, given the deep-rooted cultural and historical relationship between the two countries.[28] On a contrary note, another respondent was cautious and talked about Iran's influence being present only in some regions of Afghanistan because of 'a mutual history with Iran'. Historically, it was argued, there has been always proximity in language, culture and tradition between Afghanistan and Iran.[29] Deep-rooted historical connections between Iran and Afghanistan are therefore considered as an important element that gives Iran an opportunity to continue to increase its soft power in Afghanistan.

Persian roots in Pakistan

Iran's influence in Pakistani society is evident in a few aspects such as language, culture and religion. Persia has indeed been an integral part of South Asian culture and the life of people in the Indian subcontinent for many centuries. The flow of ideas, people and trade between Persia and the Indian subcontinent goes back to the pre-Islamic era. In particular, the Sasanian Empire exerted cultural and political influence on the northwest of the Indian subcontinent. In 270 CE, under the Sassanid king Shapur I, the Sasanian conquest of the entire Indo-Iranian frontier brought direct rule by a Persian dynasty to the northwest of the Indian subcontinent – present-day northwestern Pakistan (Gandhara) and the Peshawar Valley.[30] Shapur I named four administrative entities within the region, two of which were Hind (or the land watered by the Indus River) and Makran as appendages of Sistan.[31] The inscriptions

---

[26] Adrian Bivar, 'Introduction', in Peter J. Chelkowski (ed.), *The Gift of Persian Culture: Its Continuity and Influence in History* (Salt Lake City, UT: University of Utah Press, 2011), 17.

[27] A17, interviewed on 16 June 2019 in Kabul. This participant was an adviser at Afghanistan's State Ministry for Parliamentary Affairs.

[28] A11, an independent political analyst, interviewed on 9 June 2019 in Kabul.

[29] A22, interviewed on 29 May 2019 in Kabul; he is an independent analyst; A14, interviewed on 12 June 2019 in Kabul. At the time of the interview, this participant was serving as a senior adviser at the Office of the President of the Islamic Republic of Afghanistan.

[30] Pierfrancesco Callieri, 'India iv. Relations: Seleucid, Parthian, Sasanian Period', *Encyclopaedia Iranica*, online edition, 2004, http://www.iranicaonline.org/articles/india-iv-relations.

[31] Brian Spooner, 'Baluchistan i. Geography, History and Ethnography', *Encyclopaedia Iranica*, 1988, http://www.iranicaonline.org/articles/baluchistan-i.

of Shapur I at Naqsh-e Rostam mention a region called Balashakan under the rule of the Persian Empire and the Balaschik as subjects of the Sasanian king.[32]

In the fourth century, the Sasanian king Shapur II ruled over the southern region of the Indo-Sasanian region, in present-day Baluchestan. According to Richard Frye, the eastern boundaries of the Sasanian Empire, including areas such as Sindh, Sistan and Turan, came under the domination of the Sasanians.[33] The fourth century therefore witnessed the propagation of Zoroastrian motifs and Sassanid political ideas in the region. Documents from the Sasanian era demonstrate the institutionalisation of Zoroastrianism from Babylonia to Peshawar and the Makran, regions that are part of Pakistan today.[34] The influence of the Sasanians remained in the northwest of the Indian subcontinent for centuries, even after the Arab conquests of Persia in the seventh century. During the early centuries of Islamic history, when the process of Islamisation was taking place in the Indian subcontinent, Sasanian inspiration remained recognisable in the sculptures of the northwestern Indian subcontinent, particularly in the shapes of crown ribbons and hairstyles.[35]

Iranians themselves migrated in large numbers to the Indian subcontinent throughout the centuries, and this played a significant role in the culture of the subcontinent, including in present-day Pakistan. During the late Sasanian period and the early centuries of Islamic history, Makran and Baluchestan (including those areas of Baluchistan which are today part of Pakistan) were important transit points for the movement of people between the Iranian and Indian worlds. Muslim historian Maqdisi (d. 991) states that both western and eastern Makran (the southeast of Iranian Baluchestan and Pakistani Balochistan today) were united, with a capital at Bannajbur, the Panjgur oasis in present-day Pakistani Makran.[36] According to Bosworth, the first migrations towards the east started in the late Sasanian years, initiated by the prevailing unsettled conditions in the Caspian area. These migrations took place in several waves across a few centuries, most probably from the eighth century to the eleventh century.[37]

When Sindh was integrated into the Saffarid kingdom by Yaqub Layth around the third quarter of the ninth century, the region encountered the Persian culture.[38]

---

[32] Naseer Dashti, *The Baloch Conflict with Iran and Pakistan: Aspects of a National Liberation Struggle* (Bloomington, IN: Trafford Publishing, 2017), 15.

[33] Richard. N. Frye, 'The Persepolis Middle Persian Inscriptions from the Time of Shapur II', *Acta Orientalia* 30 (1966): 84–5

[34] Prods Oktor Skjærvø, 'Kartir', *Encyclopaedia Iranica*, 2011, http://www.iranicaonline.org/articles/kartir.

[35] Susan. L. Huntington, *The Art of Ancient India: Buddhist, Hindu, Jain* (New York: Weatherhill, 1985), 357.

[36] J. Elfenbein, 'Baluchistan, iii. Baluchi Language and Literature', *Encyclopaedia Iranica*, 1998, http://www.iranicaonline.org/articles/baluchistan-iii,

[37] C. E. Bosworth, 'The Kūfichīs or Qufṣ in Persian History', *Iran* 14 (1976): 10.

[38] Muzaffar Alam, 'The Culture and Politics of Persian in Precolonial Hindustan', in Sheldon Pollock (ed.), *Literary Cultures in History: Reconstructions from South Asia* (Berkeley: University of California Press, 2003), 132. It should be noted that when the Umayyad general Muhammad Qasim invaded and conquered Sindh, many people from Shiraz (Fars) served in his army.

In the early eleventh century the Muslim army arrived in India's northwest, and by the thirteenth century Indo-Islamic states had been established in the north and northwest of the Indian subcontinent. In this period, the vast territories between the Balkans and the Bay of Bengal came under Persian influence and adopted many aspects of its cultural norms. By the early eleventh century, Persian culture dominated areas such as Multan and Sindh. When Sultan Mahmud of Ghazni chased Qarmatians in Multan and Sindh, he observed that it was in Persian that the Friday sermons were delivered from the pulpits of the mosques.[39] According to Yarshater, many Islamic dynasties that ruled the Indian subcontinent from the Ghaznavids in the eleventh century onwards were originally drawn from Persia or Afghanistan.[40] It was at this time that large numbers of Persian-speaking people settled around Lahore (the capital of today's Punjab in Pakistan).[41] Accordingly, Persian became the administrative language of the western areas of the subcontinent in the eleventh century, and not only rulers but also their viziers supported writers, scholars and poets to produce Persian work.[42]

Under the Ghaznavids, Lahore became 'something like a provincial capital' which witnessed 'a nucleus of Persian secretaries and financial officials, who contributed to Lahore's eventual role as a center for Persian culture'.[43] It was at this time that we hear of figures such as Qadi Abul-Hasan of Shiraz being sent to Lahore to carry out tasks including the regular collection of taxation. In the later Ghaznavid era, especially from the mid-eleventh century onwards, Lahore absorbed Persian culture to a significant extent, and certain Persian poets like Masud-e Sa'd-e Salman and Abul-Faraj Runi appeared there.[44] According to Bosworth, 'Lahore seems to have been a more vibrant center of Persian culture at this time than Ghazni itself.'[45] In this sense, the head of the Divan in Lahore was himself the translator of *Kalila va Demna* – a text which was considered a model of Persian prose style for centuries.[46] Towards the end of the thirteenth century, Multan also became another important centre of Persian literature. It was at this time that Prince Muhammad, the viceroy of Multan who was appointed by his father, assembled many poets who composed Persian poems; prominent among them were Amir Khusrau and Hasan Dihlavi.[47] Persian cultural domination in the subcontinent was not confined to the areas of poetry, language and literature, but also extended to other forms of art, such as calligraphy, especially during the

---

[39] Alam, 'The Culture and Politics of Persian', 132.
[40] Yarshater, 'The Persian Phase of Islamic Civilization', 63.
[41] Alam, 'The Culture and Politics of Persian', 133.
[42] Yarshater, 'The Persian Phase of Islamic Civilization', 63.
[43] C. E. Bosworth, 'India v. Relations: Medieval Period to the 13th Century', *Encyclopaedia Iranica*, 2004, http://www.iranicaonline.org/articles/india-v-relations-medieval-period-to-the-13th-century.
[44] Alam, 'The Culture and Politics of Persian', 135.
[45] Bosworth, 'India v. Relations'.
[46] Ibid.
[47] Alam, 'The Culture and Politics of Persian', 139.

thirteenth and fourteenth centuries. Traces of one form of script called *nastaliq* can be recognised in the *nastalq* of Afghan, Indian and Pakistani calligraphers.[48]

As Islam moved eastward, it encountered the Hindu and Buddhist cultures. Islamic culture had a profound impact on the Indian subcontinent. In particular, the Sufi movement that flourished in Iran, especially in Khorasan, held great attraction for Indians, and today Sufism is prominent in many parts of Pakistan such as in Sindh and Punjab.[49] The Sufi movement itself played an important role in increasing the number of converts from Hinduism and Buddhism to Islam, as there are close links between these religions and a pietistic and mystical form of Islam. We may point to Sufi orders such as the Qadiris, Naqshbandis and Jalali Sohravardis (which had Persian or Transoxanian origin) 'that provided some of the framework for the conversion of what is now Pakistan to Islam, having come to Punjab and Sindh from Bukhara in the thirteenth century'.[50] That is, Iranian/Islamic culture from the eleventh to the thirteenth centuries continued to exercise a great influence on the areas identified today as Pakistan.

From the sixteenth century, after the rise of the Safavid Empire in Iran and Iran's turn to Shiism, some Iranians left Iran and migrated to the Indian subcontinent for various reasons ranging from economic factors to religious repression. The subcontinent was ruled at this time by the Mughals who looked to Iran as the model for imperial style.[51] From this time onward, Iranians significantly contributed to the development of Shiism in the subcontinent, given that some Persian immigrants were Shi'as.[52] Open preaching of Shiism and its key tenets became common in different parts of the Mughal Empire, including those areas of the Indian subcontinent which became West Pakistan after Pakistan's independence in 1947, such as the Jhang District in Punjab and Sindh. Andreas Rieck identifies several Shi'a preachers at the time such as Shah Jiwna (d. 1564), who settled in a village near Jhang, as well as S. Muhammad Raju Shah Bukhari of Rajanpur (d. 1591) in Punjab and Sindh.[53] The Shi'a preachers (some of whom immigrated to the subcontinent from Persia and others who were inspired by Shi'a *ulema* in Iran) played a significant role in encouraging the conversion of nobles and regional rulers to Shiism. Accordingly, from Bengal in the east to Kashmir and Punjab in the west of the subcontinent, many nobles and newly established regional rulers converted to Shiism during the sixteenth

---

[48] Golam Hossein Yousefi, 'Calligraphy', *Encyclopaedia Iranica*, online edition, 1990, http://www.iranicaonline.org/articles/calligraphy.

[49] Stephen P. Cohen, *The Idea of Pakistan* (Washington, DC: Brookings Institution Press, 2004), 16.

[50] Juan R. I. Cole, 'Iranian Culture and South Asia: 1500–1900', in Nikki R. Keddie and Rudi Matthee (eds), *Iran and the Surrounding World: Interactions in Culture and Cultural Politics* (Washington: University of Washington Press, 2002), 27.

[51] For details, see Juan R. I. Cole, *Roots of North Indian Shiism in Iran and Iraq* (Berkeley: University of California Press, 1989).

[52] Alex Vatanka, *Iran and Pakistan: Security, Diplomacy and American Influence* (London: I. B. Tauris, 2019), 9.

[53] Andreas Rieck, *The Shias of Pakistan: An Assertive and Beleaguered Minority* (New York: Oxford University Press, 2015), 7.

century.[54] Later, the peasants who lived on the lands of their overlords became Shi'as through their lords who had converted over the course of eighteenth and nineteenth centuries.[55] In the nineteenth century, the old leading Punjabi Shi'a families, such as the Faqirs of Lahore, Shah Jiwna *sayyids* of Jhang and the Gardezis and Quraishis of Multan, used their wealth and influence to sponsor Shi'a ceremonies such as *ta'ziya* and to construct Shi'a shrines and mosques.[56]

It should be noted that the large number of Shi'a Qizilbash troops brought by Nader Shah from Iran to northern India during his 1738–1740 campaigns also played a significant role in the strengthening of Shiism in Punjab.[57] The Shi'a Qizilbash held high positions in the army of Nader Shah and were gradually settled in areas such as Lahore. During the late nineteenth and the early twentieth centuries, the descendants of the Qizilbash family became the greatest sponsors of Shi'a mosques and madrasas as well as Shi'a ceremonies such as *ta'ziya*.[58] According to Rieck, 'since the late nineteenth century, *ta'ziya* processions in Lahore have been among the most sumptuous in the subcontinent, surpassed only by those in Lucknow (and, after the foundation of Pakistan, in Karachi)'.[59]

The legacy of these conversions, which eventually led to the strong presence of Shiism is evident today since in Pakistan Shi'as are estimated to make up around 20 per cent of the population. The largest number of Pakistan's Shi'as outside the major towns live today in the areas where Shi'a *muballigh* of the sixteenth century preached Shiism, namely, the districts of Attock, Rawalpindi, Jhelum, Mianwali, Sargodha, Dera Ismail Khan, Bhakkar, Jhang, Dera Ghazi Khan, Multan and Muzaffargarh.[60] Among the feudal landed Shi'a families in today's Pakistan, as Alex Vatanka notes, we may mention those of former President Asif Ali Zardari and his deceased wife, former prime minister of Pakistan, Benazir Bhutto.[61]

Language is another area in which Iranian and Persian culture exercises influence in Pakistani society. Pakistan's national anthem is almost entirely written in the Persian language by Hafeez Jalandhari.[62] The Persian language, as already explained, was a well-established language in the subcontinent during the Ghaznavid era and was even spoken by some common people in the streets, as well as at the court and among literary figures and poets. The influence of the Persian language continued during the medieval and early modern periods. According to Juan Cole, in the period 1500–1900, 'The centrality of the Persian language to

---

[54] Cole, 'Iranian Culture and South Asia: 1500–1900', 26.
[55] Ibid., 27–8.
[56] Rieck, *The Shias of Pakistan*, 9.
[57] Nader Shah defeated the Mughal forces ruled by the emperor Muhammad Shah (r. 1719–1748) at the battle of Karnal near Delhi in February 1739.
[58] Rieck, *The Shias of Pakistan*, 10.
[59] Ibid., 11
[60] Ibid., 7
[61] Vatanka, *Iran and Pakistan*, 9.
[62] Ibid., 5.

chancery and bureaucratic practice in South Asia contributed to the creation of a large Persophone population who could transmit Iranian cultural achievements in poetry, philosophy, theology, mysticism, art, travel accounts, technology, ethics, statecraft and many other fields.'[63] The Mughal dynasty, which was established in north India almost simultaneously with the rise of the Safavids in Iran, made Persian the official language of their court. The Persian-speaking areas in pre-partition India included the coastal regions of Sindh to the present-day modern Pakistani city of Multan.[64]

Further, Persian has long had a great linguistic influence on Punjabi which is the language of Punjab with 60 million speakers in Pakistan. Before its replacement by Urdu following the British conquest of Punjab in the 1840s, Persian was the main language of administration in the region of Punjab from the era of the Ghaznavids from the eleventh century onwards.[65] Imran Khan who served as the prime minister of Pakistan from August 2018 until April 2022 stated during a press conference with then Iranian President Hassan Rouhani in April 2019 that Persian was the *language* of the court and the elite in Mughal India for almost six hundred years. Referring to the need for an 'interpreter' in bilateral talks, Imran Khan noted, 'Had the British not come to India, Persian would have been our common official language.'[66] The development of Urdu is also indebted to Persian since Urdu is a mixture of what we would refer to as Hindi grammar with Persian vocabulary, written in the Arabic script.[67] The Indian subcontinent was host to Persian literature in the modern period, and there were some poets writing in Persian during the twentieth century in the subcontinent. One may point to Muhammad Iqbal of Lahore who wrote his major works in Persian.

Similar to the views of Afghan participants, Pakistani interviewees spoke about the historical legacy of the Persian Empire and its continued influence in Pakistan. It was highlighted that 'during the Mughal Era, the Persian Empire had great influence in the subcontinent',[68] and that from 'a traditional and cultural viewpoint, every region of Pakistan has traces of Iranian influence'.[69] A former ambassador and lieutenant general in the Pakistan Army also highlighted the role of Iran in the Indian subcontinent and argued that present-day Iran continues to benefit from this historical connection to promote its goodwill in Pakistan.[70] The significant

---

[63] Cole, 'Iranian Culture and South Asia: 1500–1900', 15.
[64] Vatanka, *Iran and Pakistan*, 8.
[65] Christopher Shackle, 'Punjabi', *Encyclopaedia Iranica*, online edition, 2005, http://www.iranicaonline.org/articles/punjabi-indo-aryan-language.
[66] 'Had British Not Been Involved in the Region, We Would Have Spoken Persian', *Mehrnews*, 22 April 2019, https://www.mehrnews.com/news/4597227.
[67] Cole, 'Iranian Culture and South Asia: 1500–1900', 29.
[68] P5, interviewed on 14 May 2019 in Islamabad; he is a professor at Quaid-i Azam University, Pakistan.
[69] Ibid.
[70] P18, interviewed on 30 May 2019; he is former ambassador and lieutenant general in the Pakistan Army.

influence of Persian in this part of the world was also noted 'as a tool of communication in the Mughal Emperor's court'.[71] It was broadly argued that Iran benefits from its rich imperial legacy, and that this has given Tehran a special position from which to increase its soft power in Pakistan.[72] Iran's influence in Pakistan today, it was noted, is rooted in Iran's idea that it is 'a successor of the Babylonian and Persian civilizations'.[73]

Conclusion

As analysed in this chapter, Iran has certain advantages in Afghanistan and Pakistan owing to the legacy of Persian influence in certain regions of both countries. The ties between Iran and Afghanistan and Pakistan date back to the pre-Islamic era and have continued in post-Islamic times until the modern period. While participants from both countries talked about the deep influence of the legacy of the Persian Empire and how Iran benefits from this legacy in terms of its soft power in Afghanistan and Pakistan, this topic deserves more attention. In subsequent chapters, we examine the degree to which Iran uses its Persian heritage alongside other instruments, including its language and cultural norms and values, to shape its soft power in Afghanistan and Pakistan.

---

[71] P16, interviewed on 27 May 2019 in Islamabad; he is a journalist from *Dawn*.
[72] P1, interviewed on 16 May 2019 in Islamabad; he is executive director of Iqbal International Institute for Research and Dialogue.
[73] P15, interviewed on 29 May 2019 in Islamabad; he is a professor of international relations at Quaid-i-Azam University, Pakistan.

3
Iranian Fears and National Interest

As we discussed in Chapter 1, hard power projection is a costly enterprise. But that is not the only way states promote their interests outside their borders. Soft power projection is a cheaper alternative and has been widely used in the post-Cold War era. Nye considers soft power to be a strategy of pursuing the national interest outside a country's borders through persuasion and role-modelling rather than invoking fear and compulsion.[1] While hard power is about coercion using military means, soft power is about co-opting others: this can be achieved by employing a variety of tools, such as culture and institutions, including international organisations and NGOs.[2] Through investment in soft power, for example, through cultural cooperation, states ultimately aim to increase their goodwill in other countries. Hence, soft power is intrinsically linked to the promotion of national interests, such as achieving a degree of cooperation and influence that helps states to address challenges beyond their own borders. As we will discuss in this chapter, there are a number of contentious matters between Iran and Afghanistan and between Iran and Pakistan. Sources of contention may affect Iran's soft power in both countries. In this chapter, we use our interview data to explain how our Afghan and Pakistani participants reflected on some of the existing tensions between Iran and their countries, and the extent to which they considered these tensions as obstacles to Iranian efforts to exercise its soft power.

Fears concerning Afghanistan

In the case of Afghanistan, three key challenges have been of serious concern for Iranian policymakers: the flow of narcotics from Afghanistan to Iran; the presence of large numbers of Afghan refugees in Iran; and the dispute over water-sharing from the Helmand River. We will deal with regional geopolitical dynamics in the next chapter.

---

[1] Damien Spry, 'What is Soft Power? Hint? It's Not Footing Sam Dastyari's Bills', *The Conversation*, 7 September 2016, https://theconversation.com/what-is-soft-power-hint-its-not-footing-sam-dastyaris-bills-65026.

[2] Nye, *Bound to Lead*.

Narcotics

Opium production in Afghanistan and its increasing use in Iran is seen in Iran as a serious threat. As the largest producer of poppies and opium, Afghanistan accounts for two-thirds of the total global opium poppy cultivation.[3] According to *The Economist*, Afghanistan has at times produced 90 per cent of the world's opium.[4] The illicit opiate industry in Afghanistan was worth US$2.8 billion in 2014, which was equivalent to 13 per cent of its gross domestic product (GDP) in the same year. The illicit opiate industry's worth has grown significantly since 2014, reaching up to US$6.6 billion in 2017, equivalent to 32 per cent of Afghanistan's national GDP.[5]

During the period of the US-led NATO troops in Afghanistan (2001–2021), the export of drugs from Afghanistan to other countries increased significantly. The Taliban has benefited from opium production and exports, allegedly earning a profit of US$400 annually from 2011 onwards.[6] Opium exports have also assisted in financing insurgencies and terrorism in the Middle East and beyond.[7] The opium industry in Afghanistan is a threat to the country's security and reconstruction, and also to the security and stability of other countries. Opium trafficking from Afghanistan not only affects its neighbours, but also impacts Europe, Russia and India, contributing to increasing drug addictions in these countries.[8] For instance, rising drug addiction has alarmed Russian leaders, with Moscow blaming the issue on the inability of NATO forces to control the drug trade in Afghanistan before 2021. The years 2005 to 2009 witnessed a sudden increase in opium output in Afghanistan, with 4,000–7,000 tons produced annually in this period: there was a significant increase in drug addiction in Russia at this time.[9] At that point, drug addiction, for example, heroin addiction, was blamed for killing 30,000 Russians every year.[10] Tehran has been particularly worried about drug trafficking from Afghanistan, especially since 2001; Iran has suffered more than other countries in the region and beyond from the illicit drug trade from Afghanistan. According to an estimate, 60 per cent of Afghanistan's opium is trafficked across Iran's

---

[3] Andrew Houk, 'Iran's Response to Drugs from Afghanistan', Stimson Center, 29 January 2011, https://www.stimson.org/2011/irans-response-to-drugs-from-afghanistan.
[4] 'What Does Taliban Control Mean for Afghanistan's Opium Economy?' *The Economist*, 1 September 2021, https://www.economist.com/the-economist-explains/2021/09/01/what-does-taliban-control-mean-for-afghanistans-opium-economy.
[5] See, 'Opium Poppy Production in Afghanistan: From 9/11 to the Long War', ArcGIS StoryMaps, https://www.arcgis.com/apps/Cascade/index.html?appid=9e6420db54f043e487ba2831a74cb38f.
[6] Dawood Azami, 'Afghanistan: How Does the Taliban Make Money?' *BBC News*, 22 December 2018, https://www.bbc.com/news/world-46554097.
[7] Nasser Saghafi-Ameri, 'The Afghan Drug Problems: A Challenge to Iran and International Security', *Iranian Review of Foreign Affairs* 1(2) (2010): 217.
[8] Ibid.
[9] Simon Shuster, 'Is NATO to Blame for Russia's Afghan Heroin Problem?' *Time*, 12 June 2010, http://content.time.com/time/world/article/0,8599,1996120,00.html.
[10] Ibid.

borders.[11] This means that Iran has emerged as the most important transit country for the illicit trade of Afghan opium around the world; with approximately 30 per cent of Afghan-produced drugs remaining in Iran.[12]

The use of drugs is a long-standing problem in Iran. Afkhami labels it Iran's most disturbing problem.[13] In particular, Iran witnessed an increase in the trade of heroin across its eastern border with Afghanistan in the 1980s after the Soviet invasion of Afghanistan and the subsequent rise of the Afghan mujahideen.[14] In 1998, it was estimated that 2 million Iranians were drug users.[15] The trafficking and use of opium and heroin in Iran dramatically increased after the US invasion of Afghanistan in 2001.[16] Owing to the fall in the price of opium and its easy accessibility in Iran, the number of addicts in Iran increased. In 2015, it was estimated that the number of Iranian opium users had risen to 6 million, making Iran's drug-using population one of the largest in the region.[17]

Since 2001, Iran's deteriorating economy and increasing joblessness have further worsened its drug problem. Easily accessible drugs offer temporary relief from the economic struggles and rampant unemployment facing Iranian youth, who form the majority of Iran's population, that is, roughly 60 per cent.[18] Indeed, young unemployed Iranians are easy targets for drug dealers.[19] A UN report in 2012 claimed that Iran was the world's fourth highest importer of pseudoephedrine.[20] According to the 2014 *World Drug Report*, Iran accounted for 74 per cent of the world's opium seizures and a quarter of the world's heroin and morphine seizures in 2014.[21] In 2016, Iran accounted for 75 per cent of global opium, 61 per cent of global morphine and 17 per cent of global heroin seized.[22] Opium has also been found to be the drug 'most associated with overdoses'.[23]

---

[11] Saghafi-Ameri, 'The Afghan Drug Problems', 217.

[12] Ibid.

[13] Amir Arsalan Afkhami, 'From Punishment to Harm Reduction: Resecularization of Addiction in Contemporary Iran', in Ali Gheissari (ed.), *Contemporary Iran: Economy, Society, Politics* (New York: Oxford University Press, 2009), 194–210.

[14] Ibid., 194.

[15] Ibid., 203.

[16] Golnar Nikpour, 'Drugs and Drug Policy in the Islamic Republic of Iran', *Middle East Brief*, 2018, https://www.brandeis.edu/crown/publications/middle-east-briefs/pdfs/101-200/meb119.pdf'

[17] 'Inside Iran: Millions Continue to Battle Drug Addiction', *Al-Arabiyya*, 21 May 2015, https://english.alarabiya.net/perspective/features/2015/05/21/Inside-Iran-Millions-continue-battle-drug-addiction; Saikal, *Iran Rising*, 182.

[18] Faranak Bakhtiari, 'World Youth Day: Can Iran Meet Growing Youth Population's Needs?' *Tehran Times*, 12 August 2020, https://www.tehrantimes.com/news/451175/World-Youth-Day-can-Iran-meet-growing-youth-population-s-needs.

[19] Nader et al., 'Iran and Afghanistan: A Complicated Relationship', 19.

[20] Maziyar Ghiabi, 'The Paradox of Iran's War on Drugs and its Progressive Treatment of Addiction', *The Conversation*, 3 July 2014, https://theconversation.com/the-paradox-of-irans-war-on-drugs-and-its-progressive-treatment-of-addiction-28701.

[21] *World Drug Report 2014* (Vienna: United Nations Office on Drugs and Crime, 2014).

[22] *World Drug Report 2016* (Vienna: United Nations Office on Drugs and Crime, 2016).

[23] *World Drug Report 2017* (Vienna: United Nations Office on Drugs and Crime, 2017).

Owing to the magnitude of its drug problem, particularly the trafficking of drugs from Afghanistan, Iran employs several methods to curtail the flow of opium from Afghanistan and Pakistan. These include, for instance, the construction of '260 kilometers of static defenses such as concrete dams blocking mountain passes, antivehicle berms, trenches, minefields, forts, and mountain towers – measures that cost the Iranian government upwards of US$800 million.[24] Iran has also deployed 100,000 personnel from its police force, army and the IRGC to its eastern frontiers, especially the Iran–Afghanistan border, to stop the trafficking of drugs into Iran.[25] This has also led to losses of life of members of the Iranian security forces during clashes with drug smugglers. By the end of the 1990s, it was estimated that 2,800 Iranian security force members had lost their lives in such clashes.[26] In addition to the clashes between Iranian security forces and drug traffickers, the opium trade could also potentially destabilise the border between Iran and Afghanistan. The UN Office on Drugs and Crime (UNDOC) reported that more than 3,700 Iranian officers were killed and over 12,000 law enforcement officials were injured in counter-narcotics operations over the past three decades, and that Iran allocated millions of dollars to its border security in order to prevent the flow of narcotics over its eastern borders.[27] Another strategy used by Iran to control drug smuggling is through passing strict drug trafficking laws and raising the threshold that triggers the death penalty in the case of drug possession.[28] Sentences for trafficking and possession of drugs in Iran are claimed to have been among the toughest in the world.[29]

Despite all these efforts, the flow of drugs from Afghanistan into Iran continues unabated. Iran has called on the government in Afghanistan to strengthen its border defence to prevent the flow of opium into Iran, but the Afghan government has little capacity to do so, due to political instability in Afghanistan during the past two decades. As noted by Saikal, 'Afghanistan does not have sufficient security, border, and customs forces to control the crossing [of drugs] from its side'.[30] Tehran's own resources do not seem to be strong enough to stop the flow of drugs through its territory. The drug issue has therefore been a considerable source of tension between Iran and Afghanistan, with Tehran regularly complaining about Kabul's inattention or unwillingness to address the issue.[31]

After the return of the Taliban to power in August 2021, it seems that some changes are taking place concerning the production of poppies in Afghanistan and

---

[24] Afkhami, 'From Punishment to Harm Reduction', 202.
[25] Ibid.
[26] Ibid.
[27] 'Islamic Republic of Iran: Drug Trafficking and Border Control', United Nations Office on Drugs and Crime (UNDOC), https://www.unodc.org/documents/islamicrepublicofiran/UNODC_Iran_Country_Partnership_Programme_2016-2019_-_en.pdf.
[28] Nikpour, 'Drugs and Drug Policy in the Islamic Republic of Iran', 1.
[29] Ghiabi, 'The Paradox of Iran's War on Drugs and its Progressive Treatment of Addiction'.
[30] Saikal, *Iran Rising*.
[31] Nader et al., 'Iran and Afghanistan: A Complicated Relationship', 21.

its supply to other countries. After the Taliban's takeover of Kabul, Zabihullah Mujahid, the spokesman for the Taliban, declared the Taliban's full opposition to drug production and trafficking, stating that the country would seek assistance from the international community to replace poppy cultivation with alternative agricultural crops: 'From now on, Afghanistan will be a narcotics-free country but it needs international assistance. The international community should help us so that we can have alternative crops.'[32] In April 2022, the Taliban insisted again that they are committed to halting poppy production in Afghanistan, declaring that its production, use and transit are strongly forbidden, and that violators would be punished under Sharia law.[33]

These public declarations may have a significant impact on illicit drug trafficking from Afghanistan to other countries, including Iran, in the long run. Iran initially welcomed the Taliban's decision, expressing Tehran's readiness to assist Afghanistan in producing alternative crops.[34] However, despite the declaration of the prohibition of poppy production and transportation, there are several reasons why Tehran may continue to harbour concerns. First, even if the Taliban is genuine in its opposition to poppy production and trade, given the unstable security situation in Afghanistan, the administration may not be able to put new rules about narcotics into practice effectively. Secondly, given the poor economic conditions in Afghanistan and the variety of social and political problems the Taliban is encountering, it seems unlikely that the Taliban considers the new rules concerning poppy production and trade its top priority. On top of these reasons, we should consider that the overall economic condition of Afghanistan is currently extremely poor, and this may not allow the Taliban to oppose what is a lucrative source of income for it as well. History also favours this point of view because the first Taliban regime greatly benefited from the production and trafficking of illicit drugs and implemented strict measures against poppy cultivation only once it was no longer lucrative due to a massive reduction in the price of drugs.[35]

Afghan refugees

Another problematic issue between Iran and Afghanistan is that of Afghan refugees. After Pakistan, Iran hosts the second largest number of Afghan refugees in the

---

[32] 'Transcript of Taliban's First News Conference in Kabul', *Al-Jazeera*, 17 August 2021, https://www.aljazeera.com/news/2021/8/17/transcript-of-talibans-first-press-conference-in-kabul.

[33] 'Is the Taliban's halt of Poppy Production too Good to be True?' *The Diplomat*, 12 April 2022, https://thediplomat.com/2022/04/is-the-talibans-halt-of-poppy-production-too-good-to-be-true.

[34] 'Iran Offers Afghanistan Help to Replace Cultivation With Others', *Iran Daily*, 5 April 2022, https://irandaily.ir/News/320799.html?catid=3&title=Iran-offers-Afghanistan-help-to-replace-poppy-cultivation-with-others.

[35] 'Opium: Afghanistan's Drug Trade that Helped Fuel the Taliban', *Al Jazeera*, 16 August 2021, https://www.aljazeera.com/economy/2021/8/16/opium-afghanistans-illicit-drug-trade-that-helped-fuel-taliban.

world, particularly Hazaras and Tajiks.[36] Afghan refugees began to flood into Iran following the Soviet invasion of Afghanistan.[37] The number of Afghans who fled from Afghanistan to Iran in the early years of the Soviet occupation of Afghanistan is estimated to be between 1 and 1.5 million.[38] During the 1980s, in line with the principles of Islamic solidarity, Iran felt obliged to offer refuge to Afghans escaping a communist regime. Iran adopted an 'open door' refugee policy and considered the refugees to be 'religious migrants' because many of them, such as the Hazaras, were Shi'as.[39] This shaped the foundation of what later became Iran's refugee policy. According to Nader, the first waves of Afghan refugees were treated well; they were allowed to settle anywhere they found work and were able to access health care for themselves and basic education for their children.[40] After the withdrawal of Soviet troops from Afghanistan, the rise of the civil war in Afghanistan between 1989 and 1993 led to a new wave of Afghan refugees migrating to Iran.[41] By 1993, Iran was hosting more than 3 million Afghan refugees.[42] Eventually, Iran's economy became dependent on the labour of Afghan refugees, since Afghans living in Iran engage in construction, agriculture and municipality services.[43]

After the rise of the Taliban and the establishment of the Islamic Emirate of Afghanistan in 1996, the number of Afghan refugees increased in Iran again, this time including many undocumented immigrants.[44] In the second half of the 1990s, many Hazara Shi'as fled Afghanistan to avoid religious persecution.[45] Despite the presence of a large number of Afghans in Iran, during what is known as the third wave of migration from Afghanistan to Iran, the government in Tehran gradually put strategies in place to limit the number of Afghan refugees, even encouraging and at times compelling Afghans to repatriate. These reactions were initially guided by Iran's deteriorating economic situation following the Iran–Iraq War (1980–1988) and its inability to deal with the cost of supporting nearly 2 million Afghans.[46] Considering its own economic condition and the lack of external support for

[36] Ibid., 20.
[37] Ibid.
[38] Akbarzadeh, 'Iran's Policy towards Afghanistan', 66.
[39] Graeme Hugo, Mohammad Jalal Abbasi-Shavazi and Rasoul Sadeghi, 'Refugee Movement and Development: Afghan Refugees in Iran', *Migration and Development* 1(2) (2012): 267.
[40] Nader et al., 'Iran and Afghanistan: A Complicated Relationship', 21.
[41] Hugo et al., 'Refugee Movement and Development', 264.
[42] See Bruce Koepke, 'The Situation of Afghans in the Islamic Republic of Iran Nine Years after the Overthrow of the Taliban Regime in Afghanistan', in J. Calabrese and J-L. Marret (eds), *Transatlantic Cooperation on Protracted Displacement: Urgent Need and Unique Opportunity* (Washington, DC: Middle East Institute Press, 2012), 57–69.
[43] Bruce Koepke, *Iran's Policy on Afghanistan: The Evolution of Strategic Pragmatism* (Stockholm: Stockholm International Peace Research Institute, 2013), 4.
[44] Ibid.
[45] Diane Tober, 'My Body is Broken Like My Country: Identity, Nation and Repatriation among Afghan Refugees in Iran', *Iranian Studies* 40(2) (2007): 267.
[46] Mitra Naseh, Miriam Potocky, Paul H. Stuart and Sara Pezeshk, 'Repatriation of Afghan Refugees from Iran: A Shelter Profile Study', *Journal of International Humanitarian Action* 3(13) (2018): 1.

managing the costs of Afghan refugees, Tehran has often articulated the significant expense involved in providing health and other services to Afghan refugees.[47] As the refugee issue became a key problem for Iran, Tehran used other strategies to reduce the number of Afghan refugees. For example, the Iranian government began to grant temporary registration cards to Afghan refugees rather than giving them indefinite permission to stay or permanent residency.[48] Further, in 1995, Iran closed its border with Afghanistan and refused to accept more Afghan refugees. In the following years, Iran controlled refugees' access to education and health services, and consequently many Afghan children were unable to continue their education in Iranian schools.[49]

Despite these efforts, the number of Afghan refugees in Iran significantly increased after the US invasion of Afghanistan in 2001, with many living in Iran without legal residency documents. In 2011, Iran reported that there were 300,000 Afghan primary school students and 5,000 Afghan university students in Iran, of which more than 600 had been granted scholarships by the country.[50] According to Ali Akbar Salehi, then foreign minister of the Islamic Republic of Iran, more than 160,000 Afghans had received permanent residency in Iran.[51] However, Iran pursued its efforts to encourage and sometimes force Afghans to return home during these years. According to a UNHCR report, 920,161 Afghans returned home from Iran between 2002 and 2014.[52] Yet the number of Afghan refugees living in Iran remained high. By 2016, Iran was reportedly hosting nearly 3 million Afghan refugees, including about 950,000 registered with the United Nations since the Iranian government has not provided all Afghan refugees with the opportunity to legally claim asylum.[53]

As the Iranian economy deteriorated due to international sanctions, especially in the late 2000s, the status of Afghan refugees deteriorated and resentment grew among Iranians who accused Afghans of stealing their jobs. The Afghan deputy minister of trade and commerce, Muzammil Shinwari, spoke about the impact of Iran's deteriorating economic conditions on the status of Afghan refugees: 'We are hugely concerned over the Rial's drop . . . many Afghans are living and working there and will likely be the first to lose their jobs'.[54] After 2001, some refugees returned to their homeland, but a significant number of them returned to Iran because of instability in Afghanistan, further exacerbating the tensions between locals and the Afghan

---

[47] Tober, 'My Body is Broken Like My Country', 269.
[48] Naseh et al., 'Repatriation of Afghan Refugees from Iran', 2.
[49] Ibid.
[50] Kayhan Barzegar, 'Iran's Foreign Policy in post-Taliban Afghanistan', *Washington Quarterly* 37(2) (2014): 121.
[51] Cited in Barzegar, 'Iran's Foreign Policy in post-Taliban Afghanistan', 121.
[52] Naseh et al., 'Repatriation of Afghan Refugees from Iran', 3.
[53] Patrick Strickland, "Why are Afghan Refugees leaving Iran?" *Al-Jazeera*, May 17, 2016, https://www.aljazeera.com/indepth/features/2016/05/afghan-refugees-leaving-iran-160511103759873.html
[54] Cited in Akbarzadeh, 'Iran's Policy towards Afghanistan', 68.

refugees.[55] In 2006, about 150,000 Afghan refugees were deported from Iran. This number significantly increased in 2007 and from April to mid-June 2007, Iran deported more than 100,000 undocumented Afghan immigrants.[56] In 2012, the Iranian government declared that it would deport 900,000 Afghan refugees from Iran by 2015. While no such action was taken and these words remained at the level of a threat, they demonstrated Iran's use of the refugee card to pressurise Kabul.[57] However, on some occasions, Iran deported Afghan refugees who held Iranian permanent residency. For example, in early 2009, as the governor of Nimruz claimed, Iran forced around 800 Afghan refugees back into the Nimruz province of Afghanistan, even though many of them had a legal permit to live in Iran.[58] This expulsion occurred despite an agreement between Iran and Afghanistan in December 2008 which stipulated that Iran would stop expelling refugees until March 2009.[59] The forcible repatriation of Afghan refugees has also led to growing friction between the two countries.

Another issue concerning Afghan refugees is that since 2001 Afghan refugees inside Iran have been treated very poorly. Violations against Afghan refugees in Iran include physical abuse, forced labour, the forced separation of families and detention in inhumane conditions.[60] Iran's supreme leader Ayatollah Seyyed Ali Khamenei issued a decree in 2015 stressing that all Afghan children should be allowed access to education, but Afghans were still denied basic services, including access to health care, jobs and even housing.[61] The expelling of Afghans continued during these years.[62] The poor treatment of Afghan refugees in Iran became a contentious issue, and protests took place in Afghanistan against it. On one occasion, Afghanistan's Ministry of Refugees and Repatriations urged its Foreign Ministry and the Afghan embassy in Tehran to put pressure on Iranian authorities to punish those who harmed Afghan refugees.[63] Afghans living in Iran highlighted their poor living conditions and the lack of education available to their children.[64]

Iran frequently uses the refugee card to gain political leverage in Afghanistan. In 2012, Iran's ambassador to Afghanistan warned an Afghan official that Iran would deport Afghan refugees en masse to Afghanistan if the Karzai government signed a security pact with the United States.[65] Also, an Afghan parliamentarian told Human

---

[55] Mohsen M. Milani, 'Iran's Policy Towards Afghanistan', *Middle East Journal* 60(2) (2006): 249.
[56] Nader et al., 'Iran and Afghanistan: A Complicated Relationship', 21.
[57] Ibid.
[58] Alireza Nader and Joya Laha, *Iran's Balancing Act in Afghanistan* (Washington: RAND Corporation, 2011), https://www.rand.org/content/dam/rand/pubs/occasional_papers/2011/RAND_OP322.pdf.
[59] Ibid.
[60] Nader and Laha, *Iran's Balancing Act in Afghanistan*.
[61] Frud Bezhan, 'Afghan Migrant Boy's Rough Treatment in Iran Sparks Outrage', *Radio Liberty*, 26 July 2019, https://www.rferl.org/a/afghan-migrant-boy-s-rough-treatment-in-iran-sparks-anger/30077657.html.
[62] Ibid.
[63] Ibid.
[64] Nader et al., 'Iran and Afghanistan: A Complicated Relationship', 21.
[65] Ibid.

Rights Watch that 'every time there is a big problem between the US and Iran, Iran deports a bunch of Afghans, to show that they can put pressure on Afghanistan whenever they want'.[66] According to Saikal, it is unlikely that Iran would expel large numbers of Afghan refugees at once since this would greatly harm its relationship with Afghanistan. Despite this, as Saikal explains, Tehran expelled almost 195,000 refugees in 2016.[67]

Some of our Afghan participants agreed that Iran at times raises the issue of refugees for political advantage in its dealings with Afghanistan. According to one, who is an economic and political expert, Iran has often used 'Afghan refugees as tool to pressurize the Afghan government'.[68] He notes that the issue is often raised in the context of other problems between Afghanistan and Iran, such as the water dispute. Iran threatens the Afghan government that if Afghans do not 'let [the requested] water go into Iran, they will deport our refugees'. He referred to the statements of Iranian officials who from time to time announce that Tehran will deport a significant number of Afghan refugees.[69] Another interviewee explained that Iran often threatens the Afghan government that it will deport refugees. Such threats are made whenever 'any problem or disagreement' arises between the two states, or when Kabul chooses to enter into agreements with the United States.[70]

Another issue about Afghan refugees, which we came across in our data, is that many of our interviewees were very critical of Tehran's behaviour towards the Afghan refugees. According to a research participant, 'Iran pressurizes our refugees there shamelessly and cruelly . . . They are not allowed to go to school or colleges, not allowed to work and always being threatened with deportation.'[71] Similarly, another participant who was a member of the Afghan parliament stated that 'Our refugees are annoyed so much by [the] Iranian government; they do not have opportunities to study, do not have opportunities to work; they do not have ownership rights, to own a car, or a shop.'[72] Another participant noted that at times Afghan refugees are arrested by Iranian police on drug charges.[73] An academic from Kabul shared that 'Iran has no [just] law regarding refugees and refugees have no rights in Iran. Refugees have the worst situation in Iran.'[74] Similarly, another participant was very critical of the mistreatment of Afghan refugees in Iran: 'Our refugees must be treated in accordance with international refugee laws; there is no doubt that our refugees in Iran are being harassed', and are at times used as pawns in Iran's foreign

---

[66] 'Unwelcome Guests: Iran's Violation of Afghan Refugees and Migrant Rights', *Human Rights Watch*, 20 November 2013, https://www.hrw.org/report/2013/11/20/unwelcome-guests/irans-violation-afghan-refugee-and-migrant-rights.
[67] Saikal, *Iran Rising*, 182.
[68] A22, interviewed 29 May 2019, in Kabul; an independent political analyst.
[69] Ibid.
[70] A10, interviewed on 2 June 2019, in Kabul; a political analyst.
[71] A6, interviewed 22 May 2019, in Kabul; an independent political analyst.
[72] A15, interviewed 12 June 2019.
[73] A6, interviewed 22 May 2019.
[74] A26, interviewed 22 May 2019.

policy posturing.⁷⁵ Another research participant used the term 'structural violence', stating that many Afghan refugees in Iran are being mistreated.⁷⁶

Given the security, economic and human rights problems that Afghans have been experiencing since the Taliban's return to power in August 2021, Iran has faced an intensifying influx of Afghan refugees. Various reports from Iranian official media outlets demonstrate that a large number of Afghans are seeking to enter Iran. It is reported that within only few months of the Taliban's takeover of Afghanistan, 300,000 Afghans took shelter in Iran.⁷⁷ Between August 2021 and May 2022, according to one estimate, almost 1 million Afghans sought refuge in Iran.⁷⁸ Iranian Foreign Ministry spokesman Saeed Khatibzadeh lamented in May 2022 that 'waves of displaced Afghans cannot continue [coming] to Iran' because Iran's 'capacities are limited'.⁷⁹ On several occasions, Iranian officials have stated that Afghans should stay in refugee camps set up along the border until they can return to Afghanistan.⁸⁰ The International Organisation of Migration confirmed that in the first three months of 2022, Iran's deportation of Afghan refugees 'jumped 60% each month'.⁸¹

Iran continues to have significant concerns about the influx of Afghan refugees after the Taliban's return to power. On several occasions, Taliban authorities have raised concerns about Iran's mistreatment of Afghan refugees and their forced deportations. As Taliban spokesman Zabihullah Mujahid stated in April 2022, 'We have received reports that Afghans in Iran are being mistreated . . . We call on the Islamic Republic of Iran not to mistreat Afghan refugees.'⁸² Also, Afghan foreign minister Amir Khan Muttaqi raised concerns with the Iranian ambassador, stating that 'The ill-treatment of Afghan refugees in Iran adversely affects relations between the two countries . . . allowing antagonists to conspire.'⁸³ Taliban authorities also raised concerns about forced deportations of Afghan refugees, with the

---

⁷⁵ A13, interviewed 11 June 2019.
⁷⁶ A18, interviewed 16 June 2019; Afghanistan Analyst Network.
⁷⁷ 'Humanitarian Needs in Iran Rise as 300,000 Afghans Arrive since Taliban Takeover', *Norwegian Refugee Council*, 10 November 2021, https://www.nrc.no/news/2021/november/humanitarian-needs-in-iran-rise-as-300000-afghans-arrive-since-taliban-takeover/#:~:text=Humanitarian%20needs%20in%20Iran%20rise%20as%20300%2C000%20Afghans%20arrive%20since%20Taliban%20takeover,-Published%2010.&text=The%20Norwegian%20Refugee%20Council%20calls,the%20border%20to%20Iran%20daily.
⁷⁸ Mehdi Fattahi and Isabel DeBre, 'As Iran–Taliban Tensions Rise, Afghan Migrants in tinderbox', *The Diplomat*, 2 May 2022, https://thediplomat.com/2022/05/as-iran-taliban-tensions-rise-afghan-migrants-in-tinderbox.
⁷⁹ Ibid.
⁸⁰ See Mohsen Solhdoost and Mahmoud Pargoo, 'Iran's Nontraditional Security Challenges Under the Taliban Rule', *Global Policy* 13(1) (2022): 148.
⁸¹ Emma Wallis and Reza Shirmohammadi, 'Iran: Tensions Intensify for Afghan Migrants, as Red Cross Chief Visits', *Info Migrants*, 10 May 2022, https://www.infomigrants.net/en/post/40414/iran-tensions-intensify-for-afghan-migrants-as-red-cross-chief-visits.
⁸² 'The Spokesman for Taliban: We Ask Iranian Government to Not Harm Afghan Refugees', *BBC Persian*, 5 April 2022, https://www.bbc.com/persian/afghanistan-60981581.
⁸³ Fattahi and DeBre, 'As Iran–Taliban Tensions Rise'.

Taliban's deputy minister of refugees stating in May 2022 that he had asked Iranian authorities to stop expelling Afghan refugees from Iran.[84]

Water dispute: Hirmand (Helmand) River

Another dispute between Iran and Afghanistan is over the water resources of the Helmand River, which is one of the longest rivers in Afghanistan that also enters Iran. It crosses southwest through the desert of Dashti Margo to the Sistan marshes and the Hamun Lake region near Zabol on the border between Iran and Afghanistan. This river is an important source of water for both states that suffer from increasing water insecurity. According to a report released by the US National Intelligence Council, Iran is 'heavily dependent on fossil and imported water' and could become embroiled in conflicts with neighbours over dwindling water from shared river basins by 2030.[85] According to another report released by Iran's deputy minister of energy for water and wastewater Rahim Meidani, 87 per cent of Iran's water resources are under threat: 'This cannot be justified by climate change and drought alone ... Even before the impact of climate change in Iran became visible, ground water tables were dropping in Iran's plains.'[86] The Helmand River is an important water source for millions in both Iran and Afghanistan. It flows into the Iranian province of Sistan and Baluchestan from Afghanistan. Sistan and Baluchestan itself is the driest region in the country, and over 1 million Iranians live near Hamun Lake, which is fed by the river.[87] The river is also a crucial resource for Iran's agriculture industry.[88]

The tension between the two countries over water allocation began in the early twentieth century.[89] Before the Iranian Revolution of 1979, in 1973, the then Iranian prime minister Amir Abbas Hoveida and Afghan prime minister Mohammad Musa Shafiq signed a treaty that 'accepted the flow of water into Iran at twenty-two cubic meters per second with an option for Iran to purchase an additional four cubic meters per second in "normal" water years'.[90] This accord, however, was never fully implemented owing to subsequent events, including the 1973 coup in Afghanistan, the 1979 Iranian Revolution and the Taliban's rise to power in Afghanistan in 1996.

Under the Taliban, Iran and Afghanistan did not reach a water-sharing agreement in connection with the Helmand River. The Taliban decreased the amount of water

---

[84] 'Taliban: 700,000 Afghans Returned Home from Iran', *Shafaqna*, 30 May 2022, https://af.shafaqna.com/FA/521624.
[85] National Intelligence Council, 'Global Trends 2030: Alternative Worlds', December 2012.
[86] Aman, 'Water Dispute Escalating between Iran and Afghanistan'.
[87] Saikal, *Iran Rising*, 181.
[88] Bill Samii, 'Iran/Afghanistan: Still No Resolution for Century-Old Water Dispute', *Radio Free Europe*, 7 September 2005, https://www.rferl.org/a/1061209.html.
[89] Amir M. Haji-Yousefi, 'Iran's Foreign Policy in Afghanistan: The Current Situation and Future Prospects', *South Asian Studies* 27(1) (2011): 64.
[90] Aman, 'Water Dispute Escalating between Iran and Afghanistan'.

flowing from the Helmand River to Iran, forcing Iran to take the issue to the United Nations.[91] In turn, Tehran accused Afghanistan of politicising the issue. The Taliban government blocked the Kajaki Dam and thus blocked water to Iran during 1998 and 2001 – years when the province of Sistan and Baluchestan suffered a drought.[92] The blockade had a catastrophic impact on the ecosystem of the region and led to a significant migration from the affected areas. For example, in 2001, drought forced the residents of the province to abandon 124 villages that depended on the Helmand River for their water supply.[93]

After the fall of Taliban regime in Afghanistan in 2001, the intensity of the water dispute between Iran and Afghanistan decreased but was not solved. As Aman noted, even though Iran and Afghanistan have no major territorial disputes, 'disagreement over allocation of water from the Helmand River is threatening their relationship as each side suffers from droughts, climate change, and the lack of proper water management'.[94] Iranian officials have regularly criticised Kabul's failure to implement the 1973 accord. For example, Iranian parliamentarian Alaedin Borujerdi said on 1 September 2002 that 'the least we expect [of Afghanistan] is implementation of the accord signed between Iran and Afghanistan before the Islamic revolution in Iran'.[95] Although water reached Iran on 25 October 2002 from the Helmand River, Iranian officials complained that it was not enough.[96] The then Iranian foreign minister Kamal Kharazi said during a conversation with President Karzai that Afghanistan should respect existing agreements concerning water-sharing by allowing Iran to have more water.[97] Afghan officials on their part have said that Iran receives more water than its share.[98]

Some infrastructure projects in Afghanistan have also led to tensions between the two states. In 2006, Afghanistan recommenced construction of the Bandi Salma hydroelectric dam along the major Harirod River, which flows from Herat province through Iran. This construction heightened tensions between the two countries because the dam affected the amount of water available to Iran.[99] Tehran expressed its concern about the likelihood of a water shortage because of the Bandi Salma Dam.[100] The Kamal Khan Dam project also became another contentious issue. This project began in 1996, but was delayed until 2011 due to the war in Afghanistan. The dam was constructed across the Helmand River about 95 km from the city of Zaranj in Nimruz Province, Afghanistan. Iran was concerned that the dam would

[91] Milani, 'Iran's Policy towards Afghanistan', 245.
[92] Aman, 'Water Dispute Escalating between Iran and Afghanistan', 4.
[93] Nader et al., 'Iran and Afghanistan: A Complicated Relationship', 18.
[94] Aman, 'Water Dispute Escalating between Iran and Afghanistan'.
[95] Samii, 'Iran/Afghanistan'.
[96] Ibid.
[97] Ibid.
[98] Nader et al., 'Iran and Afghanistan: A Complicated Relationship', 17.
[99] Paula Hanasz, 'The Politics of Water Security between Afghanistan and Iran', Strategic Analysis Paper, 1 March 2012, https://www.futuredirections.org.au/publication/the-politics-of-water-security-between-afghanistan-and-iran.
[100] Ibid.

limit water flow into Sistan and Baluchestan. In 2011, a captured Taliban commander claimed that he had been offered US$50,000 to sabotage the Kamal Khan Dam.[101] Afghans called on their government to build the dam in 2011, and Afghan president Ashraf Ghani vowed to complete not only the Kamal Khan Dam, but also two others.[102] As tensions escalated, Iranian media reacted by calling Afghans 'ungrateful [people] ... who do not appreciate what Iran has done to help them', and also accused the Afghan government of violating the 1973 agreement. In response, official Afghan media outlets stated that Iranian concerns were baseless and that 'it is the right of Afghanistan to construct dams on its soil'.[103] Iranians also accused Afghanistan of depriving Iran of water from the Helmand River.[104] In 2012, a member of Afghanistan's Nimruz provincial council accused Iran of conducting an insurgency in Afghanistan to prevent Afghans from completing the Kamal Khan Dam project.[105] It is important to note that the water dispute between Iran and Afghanistan also has a great impact on the status of Afghan refugees who often get blamed for water shortages. For example, in 2016, a parliamentary representative from the city of Torbat-e Heydarieh in Khorasan Province, Iran, said that 'We have close to 4 million Afghans in Iran. If each person uses daily 100 liters [of water], the Afghans living in Iran use 400 million liters.'[106]

The water dispute continued to be a key pending issue between the two states under Hassan Rouhani's administration. In October 2015, Iranian foreign minister Mohammad Javad Zarif said the Kamal Khan Dam project had severely affected Iran's share of water from the Helmand River and would severely affect the flow of water coming into Sistan and Baluchestan Province in Iran. Zarif was asked in a parliamentary session to exert pressure on the Afghan government to obtain more water. Zarif in turn promised that his ministry would do everything to make that happen. He went on to say that 'the issue is not all political ... restoring the Hamouns can benefit everybody'.[107] In the same year, Basir Azimi, a spokesman for Iran's Ministry of Energy and Water, stated that it is important for Iran to measure the water share it receives.[108] In February 2016, Afghanistan announced plans to build twenty-one dams to boost the country's agricultural sector and produce electricity. This plan, as President Ashraf Ghani stated, was expected to produce 42 MW of electricity and irrigate around 75,000 hectares of agricultural land, contributing to the stability of

---

[101] Nader et al., 'Iran and Afghanistan: A Complicated Relationship', 18.
[102] Fatemeh Aman, 'Iran–Afghanistan Differences over Helmand River Threaten Both Countries', *Atlantic Council*, Washington, 17 March 2016, https://www.atlanticcouncil.org/blogs/iransource/iran-afghan-differences-over-helmand-river-threaten-both-countries.
[103] Fatemeh Aman, 'Afghan Water Infrastructure Threatens Iran, Regional Stability', *Al-Monitor*, 5 January 2013, https://www.al-monitor.com/pulse/originals/2013/01/afghanwatershortageiranpakistan.html.
[104] Ibid.
[105] Ibid.
[106] Aman, 'Water Dispute Escalating between Iran and Afghanistan'.
[107] Cited in Aman, 'Water Dispute Escalating between Iran and Afghanistan', 4–5.
[108] Ibid., 6.

the country.¹⁰⁹ These plans added to Iran's worries in terms of its water dispute with Afghanistan, and in May 2016 the matter was discussed between Iran's supreme leader Ayatollah Khamenei and Afghan president Ashraf Ghani at their meeting in Tehran. In this meeting, Ayatollah Khamenei called for an expedited solution, and Ghani, in turn, promised to hold urgent meetings about the issue.¹¹⁰ The chairman of a Hamun revitalisation committee and member of the Iranian parliament's national security commission claimed in the same year that that the lack of attention given to the Hamun situation has caused the emigration of 130,000 people.¹¹¹ Further, the governor of Iran's Zabol Province, Hooshang Nazeri, stated that the Helmand River dispute has created many problems for Afghanistan and Iran, calling for the help of experts to resolve the issue: 'Universities and scientific centres of both countries can resolve all issues with the help of agreements and memorandums of understanding ... using collective wisdoms.'¹¹² Iranian officials stated in the same year that the water Iran receives is less than its entitlement, asking Afghanistan again to implement the 1973 agreement, with Hossein Ali Shahriari, head of a parliamentary health committee, stating that Afghanistan has intentionally caused 'the water not to reach Sistan'.¹¹³ In response, the Afghan ambassador to Iran insisted that 'Iran is receiving more water than its share defined by the agreement'.¹¹⁴

Tensions continued over the next few years. In 2018, Zarif stated that the Helmand dispute was a national matter, and added that Iran had communicated its objection on the overuse of water by Afghanistan to the government in Kabul.¹¹⁵ Another dimension of the tension over water was reflected in the remarks of Afghan president Ashraf Ghani in March 2021. After inaugurating the newly built Kamal Khan Dam in Nimruz, Ghani stated that his country is committed to giving Iran its share of the water under previous agreements, but stressed that Afghanistan would not give additional water to Iran. Ghani insisted that Afghanistan 'will not give free water to anyone'. He even went on to say that 'If you [Iran] give us oil you can then ask for [more] water, or give us something [else] in return.'¹¹⁶

Some of our Afghan participants identified the water dispute as a source of contention between Iran and Afghanistan. A senior adviser from the Office of the President of the Islamic Republic of Afghanistan indicated that there are a few contentious issues between Iran and Afghanistan, the most important of which comprise security-related matters, the refugee problem and the water dispute. According

---

[109] 'Work of Construction of 21 Water dams to start in near future', *Khaama*, 20 February 2016, https://www.khaama.com/ghani-work-on-construction-of-21-water-dams-to-start-in-near-future-0120.
[110] Aman, 'Water Dispute Escalating between Iran and Afghanistan', 5.
[111] Aman, 'Iran–Afghanistan Differences over Helmand River Threaten Both Countries'.
[112] Ibid.
[113] Ibid.
[114] Ibid.
[115] In Persian: DW, 6 May 2018, https://p.dw.com/p/2xFsI.
[116] Ayaz Gul, 'Afghan Leader Demands Iranian Oil in Exchange for River Water', *Voice of America*, 24 March 2021, https://www.voanews.com/south-central-asia/afghan-leader-demands-iranian-oil-exchange-river-water.

to him, compared with other contentious matters, 'fewer agreements are made on the water issue'. This means that the water dispute is the most important tension that exists in the Iran–Afghanistan relationship.[117] According to another interviewee, Iran and Afghanistan have often had tensions over the water-sharing issue. He believed that a 'large amount of Afghanistan's water goes to Iran, since Afghanistan was not able to make use of its water or make dams to stop waters from going to Iran'.[118] He referred to Iranian foreign minister Zarif's statement that Tehran is worried about the construction of water dams in Afghanistan.[119] Another participant, an adviser to the State Ministry for Parliamentary Affairs, stated that there is no other significant source of contention between Iran and Afghanistan except the water dispute: 'We need 6 million tons of wheat yearly and we can only produce 4 million ourselves. And we need water for this . . . If we solve our water problem, we would not have any problem with Iran.'[120] A few of our participants were very critical of Iran's actions with regard to the water dispute. For example, a professor from Herat University stated that 'in some areas like Farah and Nimruz, Iran seeks to stop projects related to Afghan Water Dikes from functioning'.

After the return of the Taliban to power in 2021, the tension between Iran and Afghanistan over the water issue has lessened, with the Taliban demonstrating signs of cooperation with Tehran and willingness to offer some concessions. In January 2022, the Taliban released water from the Kamal Khan Dam into Hamun Lake in Iran. This decision was welcomed by Iranian authorities, and the Iranian special envoy for Afghanistan, Hassan Kazemi Qomi, thanked the Islamic Emirate of Afghanistan for 'fulfilling their promise' by releasing water from the Helmand River.[121] Later, the Taliban spokesman for the Ministry of Water and Power denied the claim that the release of water was conducted for the purpose of the Helmand's water reaching Iran, suggesting that this action was designed to irrigate agricultural land in the areas surrounding the dam.[122] However, local Afghans rejected this claim, with some even stating that 'the water was intentionally released to flow into Iran'.[123] Some reports confirm that a delegation from the Ministry of Water and Power travelled to Iran to assure the Iranian authorities that the Taliban is committed to the water agreement between Iran and Afghanistan.[124]

---

[117] A14, interviewed on 12 June 2019, Kabul.
[118] A22, interviewed on 29 May 2019, Kabul; an independent political analyst.
[119] Ibid.
[120] A17, interviewed on 16 June 2019, Kabul.
[121] 'In Sign of Deepening Ties, Taliban Increases Afghanistan's Water Flow to Iran", *Gandhara*, 26 January 2022, https://gandhara.rferl.org/a/taliban-increases-ties-water-iran/31672858.html.
[122] In a video published on Twitter: https://twitter.com/Zabehulah_M33/status/1483737858913587200?s=20.
[123] 'In Sign of Deepening Ties'.
[124] 'Conversation of Taliban with Iran about Problems in Implementing the Right of Helmand Water', *ISNA*, 20 June 2022, https://www.isna.ir/news/1401033021183.

Fears concerning Pakistan

There are a few factors which have complicated the Iran–Pakistan relationship. One key issue is the rise of Sunni Baluch militant groups since 2000, including Jundallah (Soldiers of God) and its offshoots Jaysh al-Adl (Army of Justice) and Harekat-e Ansar-e Iran (Movement of the Partisans of Iran). Jundallah considers itself to be fighting for the rights of Iranian Baluch Sunnis, possibly with the 'long-term objective of gaining autonomy or independence'.[125] Jundallah claims to fight discrimination against the Sunni minority and the Baluch by the Shi'a majority-led government in Tehran.

The Iranian province of Sistan and Baluchestan is poor but enjoys many natural and strategic resources such as the Chabahar Port. This Indian-funded port is of strategic importance for both Iran and India because it is on the Gulf of Oman, at the entrance to the Strait of Hormuz. Sistan and Baluchestan Province suffers sectarian issues, with one scholar noting, 'With regards to Sistan-Baluchestan area, there is an ethnic and sectarian nature to the issue – there is the Baluchi versus Persian, and there is Sunni versus Shiite.'[126] Baluch grievances against Tehran have led to the rise of militant groups in the province, which have launched a series of suicide attacks in Iran since 2003. According to Basit, in the years 2003–2016, these militant groups conducted fifteen attacks in Iran targeting both civilians and soldiers.[127] During these years, as will be discussed later, Tehran strongly believed that the militants took refuge in Pakistan and that there is a connection between Pakistan's intelligence services and Jundallah, although Pakistan has consistently denied such allegations. Also, Iran fortified its border a few years after the establishment of Jundallah in 2002 and has developed various strategies to counter externally launched militant actions, but has been unable to stop Jundallah from undertaking terrorist attacks inside Iran. In a statement posted on the Internet in September 2009, the group declared that it would help the Baluch to gain freedom: 'This regime [the Iranian government] killed hundreds of youths of this province by firing squad, execution or torture. The Baloch people . . . are determined to stand against injustice and to obtain their freedom till the last drop of their blood.'[128] Tehran is deeply concerned that some Jundallah leaders live in Pakistan and these allegations have often caused frictions in the Iran–Pakistan relationship. According to Raja Muhammad Khan:

> The organization [Jundallah] indeed comprises of locals of the Sistan-o-Balochistan who considered that Iranian Government has ignored them in every sphere of life. Guised

---

[125] Saikal, *Iran Rising*, 183.
[126] Raja Muhammad Khan, 'Towards Harmonization of Pak–Iran Relationship', *Margalla Papers* (2010): 99.
[127] Saira Basit, 'Explaining the Impact of Militancy on Iran–Pakistan relations', *Small Wars & Insurgencies* 29(5/6) (2018): 1041.
[128] 'Iran Blames US and Pakistan for Attack', *Dawn*, 20 October 2009, https://www.dawn.com/news/497566/iran-blames-us-and-pakistan-for-attack.

in the Sunni sectarian group, the organization indeed has elements that are professional criminals and are part of drug barons having strong linkages with foreign intelligence agencies.[129]

To quell the Baluch insurgency, in 2007, the Iranian government began to fence its 700-km border with Pakistan to stop the movement of Baluch insurgents from Pakistan.[130] A suicide attack carried out by Jundallah in Iran in October 2009 killed more than forty people in Sistan and Baluchestan Province. Those killed included commanders of the IRGC and tribal elders of the province. The attack was condemned by Pakistan.[131] Another suicide attack was carried out by Jundallah in 2010 outside the Imam Hussein Mosque in Chabahar. The bombing targeted a group of worshippers preparing to mark the Shi'a commemoration of Ashura, killing thirty-nine people.[132]

The above attacks prompted Iran to protest against Pakistan, with Iran blaming Pakistan and its intelligence services, the Inter-Services Intelligence (ISI), for the attacks. The then Iranian foreign minister, for example, stated, 'They [terrorist groups] cross into Iran illegally. They are based in Pakistan – and the hands of those behind the crimes in southeast Iran must be cut.'[133] After the second attack in 2010, *Mehr News*, an official media outlet in Iran, published the message that:

> These people [terrorists] are mostly based in Pakistan and especially in the city of Quetta and are backed by the ISI. The responsibility of all terrorist attacks, kidnappings and murders that happen in our eastern border with Pakistan is with the government of Pakistan and Pakistan should be held responsible for these attacks.[134]

It should be noted that other militant Baluch groups have also undertaken terrorist attacks in Sistan and Baluchestan. For instance, Jaysh al-Adl claimed responsibility for killing twenty-seven and hurting more than three hundred people in one deadly attack in the province's capital Zahedan in July 2010.[135] In October 2018, Jaysh al-Adl abducted twelve Iranian security personnel near Zahedan along the Iran–Pakistan border.[136] In a deadly suicide attack in February 2019, Jaysh al-Adl killed

---

[129] Khan, 'Towards Harmonization of Pak–Iran Relationship', 95.
[130] Zahid Ali Khan, 'Balochistan Factor in Pak–Iran Relations: Opportunities and Constraints', *South Asian Studies* 27(1) (2012): 133.
[131] Khan, 'Towards Harmonization of Pak–Iran Relationship', 90–1.
[132] Mark Tran and Saeed Kamali Dehghan, 'Iran Mosque Bombing Kills Dozens', *The Guardian*, 15 December 2020, https://www.theguardian.com/world/2010/dec/15/iran-chahbahar-suicide-bombing-mosque.
[133] Khan, 'Towards Harmonization of Pak–Iran Relationship', 93.
[134] Tran and Dehghan, 'Iran Mosque Bombing Kills Dozens'.
[135] Basit, 'Explaining the Impact of Militancy on Iran–Pakistan Relations', 1047.
[136] 'Jaish al-Adl Claims Responsibility for Abducting Iran's Security Officials', *Dawn*, 22 October 2018, https://www.dawn.com/news/1440649.

twenty-seven IRGC members and wounded thirteen others.[137] The government in Pakistan has often denied its involvement in these attacks and has assured Iran that it would help to trace those responsible for them if they are found inside the Pakistani border. For example, after the 2009 terrorist attack, an assurance was given by Pakistan's president Asif Ali Zardari to Iranian president Mahmoud Ahmadinejad that his country does not allow terrorist groups to use Pakistan to facilitate attacks against Iranian civilians and security forces. Zardari also noted that the terrorist attack was 'gruesome and barbaric and bore the signatures of a cowardly enemy on the run' and expressed sympathy with the government and people of Iran and prayed for the dead.[138] Like Zardari, the foreign office spokesperson of Pakistan, Abdul Basit, stated that 'there are forces which are out to spoil our relations with Iran. But our ties are strong enough to counter these machinations.'[139] Along similar lines, Pakistani foreign minister Shah Mehmood Qureshi stated, 'We have a good relationship with Iran and are committed in the fight against extremists. Why would we do anything that would damage and jeopardize our relationship?'[140] To assure Iran that Pakistan was never involved in the terrorist attacks undertaken by Jundallah and that the country is not a safe haven for Jundallah members, Pakistan handed over six militants, including Hamid Rigi, the brother of Jundallah head Abdolmalik Rigi. Further, in February 2010, Abdolmalik Rigi was arrested while en route from Dubai to Kyrgyzstan. It was argued at the time that Pakistani intelligence had assisted Iran in arresting Rigi.[141]

Despite these efforts by Pakistan, Iran continues to view Pakistan as a place from where Jundallah and Jaysh al-Adl militants operate and pose a threat to Iran's security. As noted by Saikal, 'Tehran continues to see Pakistan as responsible for the rise of what it considers to be designated terrorist organizations. This has considerably affected Iranian–Pakistani relations.'[142] More importantly, Iran has alleged several times that Pakistan collaborates with Saudi Arabia and the United States, claiming that these countries provide logistical support for Jundallah and Jaysh al-Adl on the Iran–Pakistan border. For instance, following a terrorist attack in 2009, General Mohammad Pakpour, then head of the IRGC ground forces, said that: 'The terrorists were trained in the neighbouring country by the Americans and British. The enemies of the Islamic Republic of Iran are unable to tolerate the unity in the country.'[143] Likewise, then head of the IRGC, Mohammad Ali Jafari stated, 'The group of Rigi has direct contact with the American and British intelligence services and, unfortunately, the Pakistani intelligence service . . . He is supported by them

---

[137] Solhdoost and Pargoo, 'Iran's Nontraditional Security Challenges', 149.
[138] 'Iran Blames US and Pakistan for Attack', *Dawn*, 20 October 2009, https://www.dawn.com/news/497566/iran-blames-us-and-pakistan-for-attack.
[139] Cited in Khan, 'Towards Harmonization of Pak–Iran Relationship', 93.
[140] Ibid.
[141] Ibid.
[142] Saikal, *Iran Rising*, 183.
[143] 'Iran Blames US and Pakistan for Attack'.

and without doubt he is acting under their orders and plans.'[144] In a similar fashion, after Jaysh al-Adl's suicide attack in February 2019, Jafari stated that the terrorist attack was conducted with the assistance of Saudi Arabia, the United States and the UAE, and warned Pakistan to take stronger security measures to crack down on the terrorists: 'If Pakistan fails to punish them in the near future, Iran will do so based on international law and will retaliate against the terrorists.'[145]

As already discussed, Iran views Pakistan as a potential threat to its security on the basis that it harbours anti-Iranian and anti-Shi'a terrorist organisations. It should be noted that the border between Iran and Pakistan (areas stretching along the Sistan and Baluchestan Province) is rough terrain which makes surveillance of the area extremely difficult. Smugglers use this area to transfer weapons and drugs into Iran. In addition, 'because of the inhospitable terrain, Pakistani border guards might not have been able to monitor the activities of . . . [Jundallah]'.[146] Among our research participants, very few spoke about the rise of sectarian Baluch militant groups such as Jundallah and their presence in Pakistan as a factor hindering good relations between Iran and Pakistan. Indeed, our research participants did not consider the presence of such groups inside Pakistan as a key factor that could cause the Iran–Pakistan relationship to deteriorate. One participant stated that 'Jundullah is operating in Balochistan as well as in Karachi, [and] Iran is also angry' about it, but this does not play an important role in the Iran–Pakistan relationship.[147] According to a former ambassador, 'the terrorists go from Pakistan to Iran and from Iran to Pakistan as well. Therefore, border cooperation between the two countries is ascending.'[148] The cross-border movement of militants has been a source of tensions for both sides, often leading to border skirmishes. One interviewee shared that, 'If any operation is done on the Pakistani side of the border, Iranians blame Pakistan and vice versa. This affects the relationship between the two countries.'[149] Despite this latter view, most research participants, as stated above, did not consider issues arising from border-related matters and the presence of some terrorist groups in Pakistan to be a serious challenge to the relationship between the two countries, but emphasised the impact of Pakistan's closeness to Saudi Arabia as the key challenge to Iran–Pakistan relations. Iran has serious reservations about Pakistan in relation to several issues, and one of them is indeed Pakistan's long-established relationship with Saudi Arabia, Iran's major regional rival. In addition to the fact that Iran views Pakistan as being responsible for harbouring terrorist organisations such as Jundallah, Iran has alleged that the strong relationship between Pakistan and Saudi Arabia has facilitated logistical

---

[144] Ibid.
[145] Ted Regencia, 'Iran Warns Pakistan to Crack Down on Jaish al-Adl', *Al-Jazeera*, 16 February 2019, https://www.aljazeera.com/news/2019/2/16/iran-warns-pakistan-to-crack-down-on-jaish-al-adl.
[146] Khan, 'Towards Harmonization of Pak–Iran Relationship', 95.
[147] P30, interviewed on 20 May 2019, Peshawar.
[148] P24, interviewed on 2 June 2019, Islamabad.
[149] P2, interviewed on 2 May 2019, Islamabad.

support to terrorist organisations. The Pakistan–Saudi Arabia relationship has had an undesired and negative impact on relations between Iran and Pakistan.

Another point of concern from Tehran's perspective is that Saudi Arabia considers Pakistan as a strategic balance against Iran. Pakistan's trade with Saudi Arabia significantly outweighs trade between Iran and Pakistan. The balance of trade between Iran and Pakistan was US$191.478 million in 2003–2004, whereas the amount of trade between Saudi Arabia and Pakistan was much higher, at US$2,125.664 million in the same period. In 2007–2008, the balance of trade between Iran and Pakistan was worth US$333.188 million, while that between Saudi Arabia and Pakistan was US$3,229.597 million in the same period.[150]

Many of our Pakistani participants mentioned the Saudi factor as a key obstacle to improving Iran–Pakistan relations. While Iran has often had tense relations with Saudi Arabia, Pakistan and Saudi Arabia have enjoyed cooperation in a variety of areas, including security. One interviewee, an assistant professor at Quaid-i-Azam University, stated that 'the first and the foremost cause of the trust deficit between Pakistan and Iran is Saudi Arabia'.[151] Another interviewee, who is a former ambassador and lieutenant general in the Pakistan Army, shared that 'Since the Saudis have an old and long linkage and relationship with Pakistan, Pakistan was looked upon with suspicion by Iran.'[152] Similarly, another interviewee from the Centre for Research and Security Studies and a prominent local analyst, explained the nature of the relationship between Pakistan and Saudi Arabia: 'Since 1998, Pakistan has got financial support from Saudi Arabia. Also, Pakistan and Saudi Arabia both are Sunni dominated states. So, Pak–Saudi relations contribute to the Pak–Iran trust deficit.'[153] The trust deficit is 'two ways', as another research participant from the International Islamic University Islamabad shared, 'Iran always remains concerned about Pakistan's relations with Saudi Arabia.'[154] Likewise, another participant argued that the 'over-influence of Saudi Arabia in Pakistan' is a key factor which 'irritates Iran'.[155]

Some of our interviewees stated that Pakistan has been, at times, neutral regarding the Iranian–Saudi rivalry. For example, one participant shared that 'although it is a bit difficult for Pakistan to strike a balance in maintaining good relations with Iran and Saudi Arabia simultaneously, it [Pakistan] tried its best to not intervene in Saudi conflict regions.'[156] Another interviewee from the Institute of Strategic Studies in Islamabad defended Pakistan's neutrality in the Iran–Saudi Arabia rivalry, and considered it a good strategy adopted by the Pakistani government: 'Refusing to join

---

[150] *Challenges and Opportunities in the Iran–Pakistan Relationship* (Islamabad: National University of Sciences and Technology, 2015), 9.
[151] P17, interviewed on 29 May 2019, Islamabad.
[152] P18, interviewed on 30 May 2019, Islamabad.
[153] P11, interviewed on 30 May 2019, Islamabad.
[154] P1, interviewed on 16 May 2019, Islamabad.
[155] P30, interviewed on 20 May 2019, Peshawar.
[156] P17, interviewed on 29 May 2019, Islamabad.

the coalition with Saudi Arabia is a huge step and then maintaining cordial diplomatic relations with Iran . . . Joining the military alliance would have been stupidity but we have not done that and still have remained neutral.'[157]

Conclusion

Besides the fact that both Afghanistan and Pakistan are Iran's neighbours and home to a sizeable Shi'a minority, Iran has several concerns driving its desire for more influence in both states. As examined in this chapter, Iran's relationship with each state has included elements of instability due to water-sharing disputes and the issue of Afghan refugees with Afghanistan, and concerns about Pakistan providing refuge and/or support to Baluch insurgents who continue to attack border regions in Iran. As demonstrated, our research participants identified several key sources of tensions in terms of Iran's relations with Afghanistan and Pakistan. Our Afghan interviewees were very critical of Tehran's attitude towards the Afghan refugees living in Iran and also considered the water dispute as a key pending dispute between Afghanistan and Iran. Our Pakistani interviewees mentioned the Saudi factor and border/security issues between Iran and Pakistan as sources of mistrust and tension, but most of them considered the former issue a more significant problem. In addition to these issues, which are largely bilateral, Iran has ongoing worries concerning the geoeconomic and geopolitical dynamics that involve multiple actors in Afghanistan and Pakistan.

---

[157] P20 interviewed on 23 May 2019, Islamabad.

4
Geostrategic Interests

Both Afghanistan and Pakistan are significant for Iran's geoeconomic and geopolitical interests in South and Central Asia. While for rich countries, economic strength is central to the projection of soft and hard power, Iran's case is somewhat different due to economic constraints. Still, like economically strong countries, Iran also has geopolitical and geostrategic interests that influence its engagement with Afghanistan and Pakistan. As we argue in this chapter, these interests do not just revolve around trade and connectivity as Iran itself is a participant in bigger geopolitical realities involving other players, such as India and China. New Delhi and Beijing have long desired greater connectivity with the energy-rich Central Asian republics, which is why India has been investing in the Chabahar Port and China has built a deep-sea port in Gwadar, Pakistan. It is therefore important to see Iranian interests in Afghanistan and Pakistan through the lens of geopolitics. This chapter examines a variety of factors to provide a better understanding of Tehran's geostrategic interests involving Afghanistan and Pakistan. We will also discuss how security issues influence Iranian policymakers' perspectives concerning Iran's relationship with Afghanistan and Pakistan. As in the previous chapters, we will reflect the ideas of our research participants in our discussion.

The case of Afghanistan

Afghanistan is of great significance to Iran's national security. Carter argues that Iran views Afghanistan 'as an extension of its traditional sphere of economic and political influence' and as 'an integral buffer zone for its national security'.[1] Historical factors have further increased the importance of Afghanistan for Iran's geopolitical objectives. During the Cold War, for example, a proxy war in Afghanistan involving the Soviet Union and the United States posed a serious threat to Iran's national security. At that time, Tehran condemned the military occupation of Afghanistan by the Soviet Union and felt threatened by the influence of communism on its eastern neighbour.[2] This was in line with Iran's position that the presence of great powers

---

[1] S. Carter, 'Iran's Interests in Afghanistan and Their Implications for NATO', *International Journal* 65(4) (2010): 980.
[2] Haji-Yousefi, 'Iran Foreign Policy in Afghanistan', 66.

in Afghanistan should be taken into serious consideration due to Afghanistan's geostrategic significance for Tehran.

According to many of our Afghan interviewees, Afghanistan's geographical position plays a significant role in its attraction to other countries, including Iran, China and Pakistan. To reflect the ideas of few participants, one noted that 'Afghanistan is situated geographically and politically in a sensitive situation due to its neighbours like China, Pakistan, and Iran. And each country is trying somehow to maintain its interest in Afghanistan.'[3] Similarly, another participant acknowledged that Afghanistan is situated in a special geographical location, which has sparked the interests of big regional and world powers, including Iran and the United States.[4] Likewise, another participant from the Afghan High Peace Council stated that 'a country's strategic position and its geographical location establish the platform for other countries to influence it. Big countries can use this position according to their own interests.'[5] Indeed, Afghanistan's geostrategic location is a significant factor prompting other states to seek influence there.

The occupation of Afghanistan by the Soviet Union coincided with the birth of the Islamic Republic in Iran. Despite Iran's opposition to the United States, with anti-Western sentiment emerging during and after the Iranian Revolution of 1979, communism was perceived to be far more dangerous than the United States by the Islamic Republic. The Islamic Republic's slogan 'Neither East, Nor West' demonstrated that Iran had no preference for either superpower. Thus, the Islamic Republic opposed the Soviet occupation of Afghanistan. For its part, the communist government in Kabul had a negative outlook towards Iran and perceived the Islamic Republic as a serious threat. In this hostile environment, the two countries deported each other's diplomats and cancelled many of their bilateral agreements.[6] Iran's foreign policy on Afghanistan during much of the 1980s was affected not only by the presence of Soviet troops on its eastern border, but also by the involvement of rival states such as the United States and Saudi Arabia in Afghanistan. The Islamic Republic considered the external involvement through proxies as threats to its national security.[7]

Iran was also concerned about the internal conflict and turmoil experienced in Afghanistan and sought to support certain non-state actors. After the withdrawal of Soviet troops from Afghanistan in 1989, Pakistan, Saudi Arabia and the United States – which had backed Sunni mujahideen in Afghanistan during the 1980s – sought to instal Sunni leaders in the future interim government. In the late 1980s, the Peshawar Alliance – a group of seven Sunni mujahideen factions in Peshawar in Pakistan – announced a 'government-in-exile' which included only

---

[3] A6, interviewed on 22 May 2019, Kabul.
[4] A11, interviewed on 9 June 2019, Kabul.
[5] A4, interviewed on 20 May 2019, Kabul.
[6] Haji-Yousefi, 'Iran Foreign Policy in Afghanistan', 66.
[7] Ibid.

Sunni leaders.[8] In response, Iran supported the Hazaras and other factions under the Northern Alliance, stressing that they had been among the first ethnic groups in Afghanistan that had resisted the communist regime. This showed Iran's interest in, and support of, the political representation of Shi'as in Afghanistan. The fact that most Shi'a *maraja-e taqlid* (Sources of Emulation) for Afghans were Iranian facilitated the intensification of Iran's relationship with Shi'a Afghans at that time.[9] However, Iran's support of Shi'a groups was a response to the further involvement of other countries in the region in Afghanistan's armed conflict, mainly Saudi Arabia and Pakistan, which were supporting Sunni groups. In addition to Shi'a groups, Iran attempted to broaden its engagement to include Dari-speaking factions, a language that was seen by Iran as a point of cohesion for diverse Afghan groups, as well as the Sunni Pashtun leader of the Islamic Party, Gulbuddin Hekmatyar.[10]

During the first Taliban administration (1996–2001), Tehran intensified its relationship with both Shi'a Islamist groups and the anti-Taliban United Front and supplied arms to the anti-Taliban opposition. Between 1997 and 2001, a number of conferences were convened in Iran to which key Afghan resistance members were invited.[11] During these years, Iran emphasised the illegitimacy of the Taliban regime, stressing that the Taliban's control over Afghanistan posed a threat not only to Iran's security, but also to regional security and global peace.[12] The rise of the Taliban regime was considered by Tehran as one of the most important challenges and security threats given its anti-Shi'a and anti-Iranian nature. The support that the Taliban received from Saudi Arabia, one of Iran's key regional rivals, provided further grounds for Iran's insecurities. In addition, the presence of the Taliban in Afghanistan allowed Saudi Arabia access to Afghanistan and Central Asia at Iran's expense, and this was detrimental to Iran's influence in Afghanistan. The massacre of Shi'as in Mazar-i-Sharif and the murder of Iranian diplomats in 1998 (an incident which led the two countries to the threshold of war) intensified Tehran's security concerns.[13]

The US invasion of Afghanistan in 2001 led to US forces gaining a significant presence along Iran's eastern borders with Afghanistan. This intensified the challenges in the relationship between Iran and the United States because Iran perceived the presence of US forces as part of Washington's strategy to strengthen its own strategic position in Central and South Asia, as well as the Persian Gulf, at the expense of Iran's national and security interests.[14] Although Iran provided the

---

[8] Asta Olesen, *Islam and Politics in Afghanistan* (London: Curzon, 1995), 291.
[9] Vanessa Martin, *Creating an Islamic State: Khomeini and the Making of a New Iran* (London: I. B. Tauris, 2000), 194.
[10] Koepke, *Iran's Policy on Afghanistan*, 5.
[11] Ibid., pp. 5–6.
[12] Haji-Yousefi, 'Iran Foreign Policy in Afghanistan', 67.
[13] Barzegar, 'Iran's Foreign Policy in post-Taliban Afghanistan', 123.
[14] Ibid., 119.

United States with intelligence on al-Qaeda and the Taliban, US president George W. Bush included Iran in the 'axis of evil' in 2002. Referring to Iran, Iraq and North Korea, Bush stated that 'states like these, and their terrorist allies, constitute an axis of evil, arming to threaten the peace of the world'.[15] This statement was a significant source of concern for Iran's policymakers who interpreted it as meaning that Iran could be the next target of the US-led 'War on Terror'.

In the post-Taliban era, Iran demonstrated a desire for stability in Afghanistan, given the potential for insecurity in Afghanistan to translate into insecurity in Iran. According to a senior Iranian diplomat, 'Iran has to try to create a stable Afghanistan. The more insecurity this country experiences, the more harm Iran would face from Afghanistan.'[16] For this reason, Iran sought to assist in Afghanistan's reconstruction. At the Donor Conference held in 2002, Iran pledged US$650 million for the reconstruction of Afghanistan.[17] In the same year, Iran pledged US$500 million in economic assistance to Afghanistan – funds spent on roads, energy infrastructure and schools, seeking to make Afghanistan more stable.[18] In 2002, during his visit to Afghanistan, then president of Iran, Mohammad Khatami, stated that 'today, the Afghan nation has a government that is based on its own will ... the stability and security of Afghanistan is the same as our own security and stability'.[19] It should be noted that Iran's influence was important in the establishment of the Karzai government after the collapse of the Taliban regime. Initially, the Northern Alliance, dominated by Tajiks with close ties to Iran, was reluctant to share power with President Hamid Karzai, but Iranian political pressure on the Northern Alliance during the first round of negotiations in Bonn led to an agreement on the formation of the new government.[20]

Since 2002, Iran has sought to help the Afghan government by providing aid in various fields, such as the economy, transportation, trade and energy, as well as matters related to Afghanistan's social structure. During the London Conference on Afghanistan Reconstruction in 2006, Iran pledged an additional US$100 million in aid to Afghanistan, and also declared that an instalment of its original US$650 million aid would be delivered to the Afghan government by the end of 2006.[21] The establishment of a friendly government in Afghanistan was strategically important for Iran and strengthened Iran's position not only in Afghanistan but also in Central Asia. This could also be considered part of Iran's attempt to extend its economic interests and to ease the isolation imposed by the United States through economic

---

[15] George W. Bush, 'Address Before a Joint Session of the Congress on the State of the Union', *Compilation of Presidential Documents*, 29 January 2002, https://www.govinfo.gov/content/pkg/WCPD-2002-02-04/pdf/WCPD-2002-02-04-Pg133-3.pdf, 135.
[16] Cited in Akbarzadeh, 'Iran's Policy towards Afghanistan', 68.
[17] Haji-Yousefi, 'Iran Foreign Policy in Afghanistan', 69.
[18] Nader et al., 'Iran and Afghanistan: A Complicated Relationship', 19.
[19] Milani, 'Iran's Policy Towards Afghanistan', 249.
[20] Nader and Laha, *Iran Balancing Act in Afghanistan*.
[21] Milani, 'Iran's Policy Towards Afghanistan', 251.

sanctions. Extending its economic sphere of influence in Afghanistan enabled Iran to become a hub for the transit of goods between the Persian Gulf, Afghanistan, India and China.[22] This substantially increased Iran's trade and investment in Afghanistan.

From mid-2007, Iran began to call repeatedly for a timetable for the US withdrawal from Afghanistan. Iran viewed US efforts to stabilise Afghanistan with suspicion and gradually advocated the complete withdrawal of foreign troops and the closure of all US military bases. The United States, at times, claimed that Iran sought to escalate instability in Afghanistan and accused it of having a dual policy in the country. The United States asserted that, on the one hand, Iran supports stability in Afghanistan, but, on the other hand, it is wary of Afghanistan's stability representing a success for the United States. Some reports were released by the United States and its Western allies claiming that Iran escalated tensions in Afghanistan by providing support to the Taliban. According to one report, UK forces operating on the Iran–Afghanistan border had documented proof that Iran was supplying the Taliban with ammunition.[23] Indeed, although Iran viewed the Taliban regime as a security threat, it did initiate a limited relationship with the group. According to another report authored by US General Stanley A. McChrystal, Iran provided aid to the Afghan government, but at the same time allowed weapons to pass into the hands of the Taliban:

> Iran plays an ambiguous role in Afghanistan, providing developmental assistance and political support to GIRoA [Government of the Islamic Republic of Afghanistan] while the Iranian Quds Force is reportedly training fighters for certain Taliban factions and providing other forms of military assistance to insurgents. Iran's current policies and actions do not pose a short-term threat to the mission, but Iran has the capability to threaten the mission in the future.[24]

Similarly, George Tenet, Director of the CIA, said:

> While Iran's officials express a shared interest in a stable government in Afghanistan, its security forces appear bent on countering the US presence. This seeming contradiction in behaviour reflects deep-seated suspicions among Tehran's clerics that the US is committed to encircling and overthrowing them.[25]

Later, in private conversations with US officials, senior Afghan officials alleged that Iran had supported the Taliban in order to 'counter Western influence' in

---

[22] Ibid.
[23] Mark Townsend, 'Special Forces Find Proof of Iran Supplying Taliban with Equipment to Fight British', *The Guardian*, 22 June 2008, http://www.guardian.co.uk/uk/2008/jun/22/military.afghanistan.
[24] Cited in Sajjan M. Gohel, 'Iran's Ambiguous Role in Afghanistan', *CTC Sentinel* 3(3) (2010): 13–16, https://ctc.usma.edu/irans-ambiguous-role-in-afghanistan.
[25] Milani, 'Iran's Policy Towards Afghanistan', 248.

Afghanistan.²⁶ According to some reports, the Iranian Quds Force provided weapons, roadside bombs, explosives and other forms of support to the Taliban during the second half of the 2000s.²⁷ For example, armour-piercing bullets, C-4 plastic explosives and anti-tank mines of Iranian origin are reported to have appeared in Afghanistan in 2007.²⁸ In addition, shipments of Iranian-made arms, including low-altitude surface-to-air missiles, were discovered in 2009 in Helmand.²⁹ Iran is also claimed to have sent rocket-propelled grenades to rural Afghanistan where the Taliban dominated during the late 2000s.³⁰

The policy to support the Taliban can be viewed in the light of Iran's opposition to the long-term presence of US troops in Afghanistan in any form (especially in the form of occupied military bases) due to its security concerns.³¹ As Koepke notes, although the Iranian government opposed the reinstallation of Taliban rule in Afghanistan, it followed a strategy that aimed to create 'a major headache in Afghanistan' for the United States.³² Barzegar also notes 'From Iran's perspective, the presence of U.S. troops in the region is in line with U.S. policy to strengthen its strategic position in broader Central and South Asia as well as the Persian Gulf', which in turn threatened Iran's national and security interests during the second half of the 2000s, and it was in this sense that Iran 'routinely encouraged [the Afghan] parliament to support anti-coalition policies and to raise anti-American talking points during debates'.³³ Iran's opposition to the presence of the United States in Afghanistan intensified with the increase in US attempts to minimise Iran's economic, political and security role in Afghanistan – a trend which continued under the Obama administration.³⁴ In this respect, Iran criticised the 2012 US–Afghanistan Strategic Partnership Agreement (SPA), which provided the framework for relations between the United States and Afghanistan, stating that such an agreement would create distrust among regional states.³⁵

Iran's strategy in Afghanistan, which has been oriented around the withdrawal of US troops, has been stressed by many Iranian political authorities, whether they belong to the reformist camp or the conservative one. The Iranian police chief

---

[26] Koepke, *Iran's Policy on Afghanistan*, 18.
[27] Gohel, 'Iran's Ambiguous Role in Afghanistan', 12.
[28] Chris Zambelis, 'Is Iran Supporting the Insurgency in Afghanistan', *Terrorism Monitor* 7(33), https://jamestown.org/program/is-iran-supporting-the-insurgency-in-afghanistan.
[29] Gohel, 'Iran's Ambiguous Role in Afghanistan', 12.
[30] See Lara Logan, 'Cooperation Rises between Iran and Taliban', *CBS News*, 7 October 2009, https://www.cbsnews.com/news/cooperation-rises-between-iran-and-taliban.
[31] It should be noted that US military bases in Afghanistan include the Bagram military base to the north of Kabul and the Shindand base in the west of Afghanistan, in the province of Herat
[32] Koepke, *Iran's Policy on Afghanistan*, 17.
[33] Ibid., 18.
[34] Barzegar, 'Iran's Foreign Policy in post-Taliban Afghanistan', 131.
[35] Ibid., 119. For Iran's security concern and its link to Tehran's regional influence, see Ali Akbar, 'Iran's Regional Influence in Light of Its Security Concerns', *Middle East Policy* 28(3/4) (2021): 186–202.

Brigadier General Esma'il Ahmadi-Moqaddam, stated that the presence of the US forces in Afghanistan is a great threat to Iran.³⁶ In 2006, the former Iranian president, Akbar Hashemi Rafsanjani, accused the United States of attempting to 'make a nest for themselves here' in Afghanistan and Central Asia.³⁷ Later, at the second Bonn Conference on 5 December 2011, Ali Akbar Salehi, Iran's then foreign minister, highlighted Iran's opposition to the presence of US forces in Afghanistan and also to US–Afghanistan agreements, emphasising Iran's preference for the complete withdrawal of US forces from Afghanistan.³⁸ Similarly, Hossein Sheikholeslam, adviser to the speaker of Iran's parliament on international affairs and former deputy foreign minister, stressed the importance of the withdrawal of US forces from Afghanistan, stating that 'If foreign security forces completely withdraw from Afghanistan, Iran will be ready to talk with the United States on Afghanistan's developments in the presence of Afghan authorities.'³⁹ President Rouhani, who rose to power in 2013, clearly stressed the importance of the US withdrawal from Afghanistan, stating that: '[Iran] is opposed to the presence of any foreign force in the region, the Middle East, the Persian Gulf and particularly the Islamic country of Afghanistan ... They should all leave [Afghanistan] and leave the security of Afghanistan to its own people.'⁴⁰

To summarise, although establishing security and stability in Afghanistan is one of the key features of Iran's geopolitical interests in Afghanistan, a key focus for Iran has also been to implement policies that could ultimately lead to the withdrawal of US forces from Afghanistan. From Iranian policymakers' perspective, even though the collapse of the Taliban regime was beneficial to its national interests, the presence of foreign forces in its neighbourhood (in this case Afghanistan) would not bring peace and security to Iran and to the region.

Our Afghan participants explained that Iranian leaders and policymakers considered the presence of US troops in Afghanistan to be a great threat to Iran's national security. The perceived threat due to the presence of US troops in Afghanistan and Iran's subsequent heightened interest in Afghan affairs was highlighted by the majority of our research participants. According to some participants, the presence of US troops in Afghanistan scared Iran and created challenges that led Tehran to desire the failure of the United States in Afghanistan. It was also argued by some of our participants that issues of trade, for instance, were secondary to Iran's security concerns vis-à-vis US troops in Afghanistan.⁴¹

Some of our interviewees also linked Iran's support for the Taliban to Iran's security concerns. In the opinion of one interviewee, who was a political analyst from Kabul, Iran provided intermittent support to the Taliban in Afghanistan since it

---

³⁶ Akbarzadeh, 'Iran's Policy towards Afghanistan', 71.
³⁷ Cited in Milani, 'Iran's Policy Towards Afghanistan', 248.
³⁸ Barzegar, 'Iran's Foreign Policy in post-Taliban Afghanistan', 123.
³⁹ Ibid., 133.
⁴⁰ Ibid., 126.
⁴¹ A22, interviewed on 29 May 2019, Kabul; A21, interviewed on 22 June 2019, Kabul.

needed to keep the United States 'busy in Afghanistan' and 'to shift their [the United States'] attention' away from Iran.[42] This participant noted that Tehran's support of the Taliban should be understood within broader Iranian security concerns and the threat perception of Iranian leaders and policymakers. Iran's relationship with the Taliban in Afghanistan, including its relationship after the Taliban's coming to power in August 2021, will be discussed in detail in Chapter 6 where we explore Iran's political influence in Afghanistan.

The case of Pakistan

Pakistan's strategic importance for Iran began with its emergence as an independent state after its partition from the British India in 1947. Mohammad Reza Shah Pahlavi was the first Iranian head of state to visit Pakistan, and this visit in March 1950 was followed by the signing of a Treaty of Friendship in the same month.[43] The relationship between Iran and Pakistan during the Shah's regime was focused primarily on the convergence of strategic interests. Both countries were US allies and members of the anti-Soviet Baghdad Pact. Under the Shah, Iran offered gas and oil to Pakistan on generous terms and the two countries cooperated to suppress rebel movements in Baluchestan.[44] Although Pakistan sought closer ties with Arab states in the 1970s in order to gain support for its own position in the Kashmir dispute with India, the relationship between Iran and Pakistan remained cordial until 1979 when the Iranian Revolution toppled the Shah's regime.

After the emergence of the Islamic Republic, Pakistan initially tried to balance its foreign policy with Iran and the United States. Pakistan was among the first countries to recognise the Islamic Republic of Iran and remained neutral during the Iran–Iraq War (1980–1988). During the 1980s, both Iran and Pakistan opposed the Soviet invasion of Afghanistan, but Pakistan's support to the Taliban regime between 1996 and 2001 affected Iran–Pakistan relations, since Iran viewed the Taliban as a threat to its national interest, as discussed earlier. Indeed, Pakistan supported the Taliban, whereas Iran backed non-Pashtun groups such as the Tajiks, Uzbeks, Turkmens and Hazaras.[45] Accordingly, from a strategic perspective, Pakistan became more important for Iran in the second half of the 1990s.

Among other sources of friction in the Iran–Pakistan relationship is the latter's closeness to Saudi Arabia. In the 1980s, the Pakistani military regime under General Zia-ul-Haq cooperated fully with Saudi Arabia, and both countries emerged as frontline states in the US struggle to expel Soviet forces from Afghanistan. During this time, Pakistan became the transit point for weapons, facilitating the transfer

---

[42] A6, interviewed on 22 May 2019, Kabul.
[43] Shah Alam, 'Iran–Pakistan Relations: Political and Strategic Dimensions', *Strategic Analysis* 28(4) (2004): 526.
[44] Harsh V. Pant, 'Pakistan and Iran's Dysfunctional Relationship', *Middle East Quarterly* 16(2) (2009): 43–50.
[45] Ahmed and Akbarzadeh, 'Understanding Pakistan's Relationship with Iran', 88.

of arms to mujahideen in their fight against the Soviet army.[46] Indeed, the war in Afghanistan brought Pakistan and Saudi Arabia much closer. As Pant notes, 'Tehran did not want to cede the advantage to Islamabad [in the 1980s] . . . and continued to fight for influence in Afghanistan, even as the Pakistani- and Saudi-backed Taliban consolidated control over 90 percent of the country. This proxy fight, however, polarized Afghanistan and brewed further Pakistan–Iran mistrust.'[47]

After the rise of the Taliban in Afghanistan in the 1990s, some elements of the Pakistani government, in particular ISI, supported the Taliban, hoping to achieve their own goals.[48] ISI is also believed to have supported other extremist and violent groups in Afghanistan such as the Haqqani Network and the Islamic Party, which seek to create instability in Afghanistan.[49] This influenced Iran–Pakistan relations as well and threatened Iran's interests, since it potentially challenged development and stability in South Asia and the transit route between Iran and southern Asia. In 1998, after the Taliban attacked an Iranian consulate at Mazar-i-Sharif and murdered six Iranian diplomats, Iran blamed Pakistan for the incident.[50]

The establishment of the Taliban regime in most parts of Afghanistan in 1996 led to a deterioration in relations between Iran and Pakistan. However, owing to this, the relationship with Pakistan became more important for Iran from a strategic point of view. Iran therefore maintained some economic relations with Pakistan, as will be discussed in the following chapters. After 11 September 2001, Pakistan became an active ally of the United States in the 'War on Terror'. Iran, on the other hand, sought to pursue a policy of neutrality instead of support for NATO and ISAF-led forces inside Afghan territory.[51] Indeed, one more tension between Iran and Pakistan since 1979 has been that while the 'War on Terror' brought the United States and Pakistan closer, it contributed to further distrust between Iran and Pakistan.

The US factor and its negative impact on the Iran–Pakistan relationship were also mentioned by some of our Pakistani interviewees. According to one viewpoint, Pakistan's cooperation with the United States since 2001 reflects its position 'under America's shadow', which makes Iran uncomfortable.[52] Another participant from the Pak Institute for Peace Studies noted that the US factor, which significantly influences Iran–Pakistan relations, should be viewed in the light of Iran's anti-American policy after the Iranian Revolution of 1979:

> The trust deficit [between Iran and Pakistan] started from the Iranian revolution when Iran's relations with the US worsened . . . Before the revolution, Pakistan and Iran were

---

[46] Pant, 'Pakistan and Iran's Dysfunctional Relationship'.
[47] Ibid.
[48] Barzegar, 'Iran's Foreign Policy in post-Taliban Afghanistan', 129.
[49] Ibid., 130.
[50] Ahmad Rashid, *Taliban* (London: Yale University Press, 2000), 203.
[51] *Challenges and Opportunities in the Iran–Pakistan Relationship*, 5.
[52] P19, interviewed on 28 May 2019.

both allies of the US. After that, the situation changed and till now, the trust deficit between Iran and Pakistan has not lessened.[53]

As we discussed in Chapter 3, the Saudi factor also influences the relationship between Iran and Pakistan. While Iran and Pakistan have never directly articulated concerns over geoeconomic competition, for example, involving the ports in Chabahar and Gwadar, such competition is quite natural as both ports aim to achieve connectivity with Central Asia. Pakistan's security establishment looks at Chabahar Port through a security lens, and, as argued by Ahmed and Bhatnagar, this India-funded port 'is a significant irritant for the military establishment' in Pakistan.[54] In the following section, we expand our analysis of how the two ports have become a source of mistrust between Iran and Pakistan.

Chabahar vs Gwadar

Chabahar Port, located in the town of Chabahar, a coastal town in the Sistan and Baluchestan Province in southeastern Iran, next to the Gulf of Oman, is a strategically and economically valuable port. It is an important port providing Iran with easy access to the Indian Ocean and South Asian states, since it is closer to India than Iran's Bandar Abbas Port.[55] The port – which is on the Makran coast of the Indian Ocean about 100 km west of the Pakistan border – is being developed by India, Iran and Afghanistan. India assisted with the building of Chabahar Port to obtain access to Afghanistan and Central Asia and to reduce Afghanistan's dependence on Pakistan, as will be discussed below.

Chabahar Port began as a joint venture between India and Iran. The idea of developing a port at Chabahar was initiated by Mohammad Reza Shah Pahlavi. The Shah proposed investing US$ 8 billion in the project, but because of rivalry between members of the Organisation of the Petroleum Exporting Countries (OPEC) with the United States in the 1970s, Iran did not pursue it.[56] In the 1990s, Iran employed Indian contractors to begin work on Chabahar Port, but the project was suspended due to a lack of funding from Iran.[57] In 2003, India's prime minister, Atal Bihari Vajpayee, signed a deal with Iran to renew the Chabahar Port project, which provided India with the opportunity to access Afghanistan and send supplies to Kabul.[58] In 2004, a consortium of Indian building companies signed an agreement with Iran

---

[53] P6, interviewed on 28 May 2019.
[54] Zahid Shahab Ahmed and Stuti Bhatnagar, 'The India–Iran–Pakistan Triad: Comprehending the Correlation of Geo-economics and Geopolitics', *Asian Studies Review* 42(3) (2018): 531.
[55] 'India, Iran Talk Chabahar Funding', *Hindustan Times*, 5 May 2013, https://www.hindustantimes.com/world/india-iran-talk-chabahar-port-funding/story-wThJi3190IRnZdoQUG7o1N.html.
[56] Harsh V. Pant and Ketan Mehta, 'India in Chabahar', *Asian Survey* 58(4) (2018): 662.
[57] Shawn Amirthan, 'What are India, Iran and Afghanistan's Benefits from the Chabahar Port Agreement?' *Strategic Analysis* 41(1) (2017): 88.
[58] Ibid., 88.

to develop Chabahar, but after sanctions were imposed on Iran due to its nuclear programme, the project stalled and ultimately crumbled again.[59] In 2012, before the visit of Indian prime minister Manmohan Singh to Tehran, Iran and India agreed to establish a joint working group on Chabahar, and Iran approved the establishment of a Free Trade-Industrial Zone (FTZ) around Chabahar.[60]

In May 2016, during the visit of Indian prime minister Narendra Modi to Iran, the 'Trilateral Transit Agreement' (known as the Chabahar Agreement) was signed between India, Iran and Afghanistan. Modi described the agreement as 'a new foundation of convergence between three nations'.[61] In December 2017, Iran's president Rouhani inaugurated the development of the first phase of Chabahar Port.[62] A crucial part of the agreement is the role of Afghanistan, which benefits in terms of renewing its ties with India as well as reducing its trade dependence on Pakistan.[63] This is particularly noteworthy when it comes to the increase in Afghanistan's trade capacity because 'Pakistan does not allow India overland transit access, [and this is] a major obstacle for critical trade between Afghanistan and India.'[64] Considering this, India has been exploring alternatives to help ease Afghanistan's trade dependence on Pakistan, and this was a shared goal of India and the erstwhile government of Ashraf Ghani. For example, in November 2017, Kabul said that it was no longer dependent on Pakistan after receiving its first shipment of wheat from India via Chabahar Port.[65] The Chabahar project was therefore significant from a geoeconomic perspective for all three countries involved. As Indian officials stated in November 2017, 'The reason for cooperation between India and Iran to help Afghanistan was to find an alternate route for trade between the three countries.'[66] For Iran, the presence of Afghanistan in the deal is in line with its geoeconomic and geostrategic interests since it establishes a connection between Iran and South Asia.

According to the 2016 Chabahar agreement among Iran, India and Afghanistan, Indian commodities moving to Afghanistan 'will be given preferential handling with much reduced tariff at Chabahar Port'.[67] According to the Chabahar deal, the berths, which are to be operated for ten years by India Ports Global, will be

[59] Ibid., 89.
[60] Pant and Mehta, 'India in Chabahar', 668.
[61] Cited in Vinay Kaura, 'India's Aims in Central Asia and India–Afghanistan–Iran Triangular Relationship', *Journal of Central Asian Studies* 24(1) (2017): 30.
[62] Nazim Rahim and Asghar Ali, 'The Sino-Indian Geo-Strategic Rivalry: A Comparative Study of Gwadar and Chabahar Ports', *The Dialogue* 13(1) (2018): 95.
[63] Amirthan, 'What are India, Iran and Afghanistan's Benefits from the Chabahar Port Agreement?' 87.
[64] Asha Sawhney, 'Chabahar Port: Unlocking Afghanistan's Potential', *Center for Strategic and International Studies*, 8 April 2019, https://www.csis.org/chabahar-port-unlocking-afghanistans-potential.
[65] Ayaz Gul, 'Indian Wheat Makes History, Arriving in Afghanistan via Iran', *Voice of America*, 11 November 2017, https://www.voanews.com/a/indian-wheat-makes-history-arriving-in-afghanistan-via-iran/4110774.html.
[66] Rahim and Ali, 'The Sino-Indian Geo-Strategic Rivalry', 99.
[67] Muhammad Uthman, 'Indian Outreach in Iran and Afghanistan: Regional Implications with Focus on Pakistan', *The Dialogue* 13(1) (2018): 58.

developed at a cost of US$85 million over the course of eighteen months. Upon completion of upgrade works mentioned in the agreement, Chabahar's capacity will be increased to 8 million tonnes from its previous 2.5-million tonne capacity. India also allowed the development of two terminals at Chabahar Port that permit Indian goods to reach Afghanistan via Iran.[68] For India, Chabahar Port provides access not only to the energy resources of Iran but also to those of Central Asia. Its investment in Chabahar Port is also aimed as a counter to Chinese investment in the Gwadar Port in Pakistan, as will be discussed below.

The Chabahar project is of particular importance to Iran for several reasons. It is Iran's only port with direct access to the Indian Ocean, one of the 'maritime highways of the world' that offers a pathway for the global movement of resources.[69] Chabahar Port is more beneficial for Iran than Bandar Abbas Port, as Chabahar is able to handle a cargo capacity of 250,000-tonne vessels, while Bandar Abbas can only handle up to 100,000-tonne vessels.[70] As Ryan Mitra notes, 'upon completion, Chabahar would be able to host 82 million metric tonnes annually, far exceeding the cargo-capacity of Bandar Abbas'.[71] As a result, developing Chabahar allows Iran not only to receive larger ships but also to increase its exports, thereby opening up further avenues for international trade. It should be noted that Bandar Abbas Port is not fully efficient since most shipping is conducted via 150,000-tonne vessels, and cargo destined for Bandar Abbas must first be offloaded in the UAE and then transferred onto smaller ships which can move through Bandar Abbas. Chabahar would solve this problem and reduce Iran's reliance on the UAE.[72] Hence, it can be stated that Chabahar Port has a political importance for Iran given Tehran's troubled relationship with the UEA.

Another significant aspect of the project is to develop a trade corridor and free trade zone. Chabahar has been declared a Free Trade and Industrial Zone by the Iranian government, a status that has enhanced the city's international trade significance. Chabahar Port therefore can be 'the focal point of Iran for the development and expansion of transit routes among countries situated in the northern part of the Indian Ocean and Central Asia'.[73] Chabahar Port has the potential to absorb massive foreign investment for Iran in general, and the Sistan and Baluchestan region, in particular, contributing to its prosperity. The trade corridor provided through Chabahar Port is likely to reduce transportation times by 50 per cent and

---

[68] Amirthan, 'What are India, Iran and Afghanistan's Benefits from the Chabahar Port Agreement?' 87.
[69] Rorry Daniels, 'Strategic Competition in South Asia: Gwadar, Chabahar, and the Risks of Infrastructure Development', *American Foreign Policy Interests* 35(2) (2013): 93
[70] Paras Ranta, 'Why Chabahar Agreement is Important for Iran?' *Observer Research Foundation*, 17 July 2017, https://www.orfonline.org/expert-speak/why-chabahar-agreement-important-for-iran.
[71] Ryan Mitra, 'India's Persian Desire: Analyzing India's Maritime Trade Strategy vis-à-vis the Port of Chabahar', *Maritime Affairs: Journal of the National Maritime Foundation of India* 15(1) (2019): 46.
[72] Amirthan, 'What are India, Iran and Afghanistan's Benefits from the Chabahar Port Agreement?' 91.
[73] Zahid Ali Khan, 'China's Gwadar and India's Chahbahar', *Strategic Studies* 32(4) (2013): 91.

transportation costs by 60 per cent compared with using Bandar Abbas Port, given that the port is an FTZ.[74]

Chabahar Port allows Iran to strengthen its ties with India and gives Iran an opportunity to establish strong economic connections with other countries (beyond China and Russia). At the time it was signed, when the United States was still in the JCPOA, the Chabahar Agreement provided Iran with an appropriate opportunity to reintegrate back into the global economy and strengthen its ties with other countries in 'a bid to overcome its isolation and spur foreign investment and trade'.[75] It was also expected to enable Iran to ease the heavy dependence on China that it developed during the sanctions period.

From a geostrategic perspective, Chabahar Port provides better economic security for Iran since it is not located within the Strait of Hormuz, thus leaving it less vulnerable to international pressure in times of tensions between Iran and the United States.[76] Indeed, the port removes the risk of large-scale disruption caused by a possible blockade of the Strait of Hormuz. Further, the Iranian government has sought to connect Chabahar with Iran's main rail and road network to Central Asia and Afghanistan. With the assistance of India, Iran has spent a great deal of money on its railway project to connect Chabahar Port to Central Asia, Afghanistan and Central Iran. This project includes the development of three road infrastructure projects, namely, the Iranshahr–Fahraj, Iranshahr–Zahedan–Mashhad and Iranshahr–Zahedan–Milak roads, which also connected Chabahar city to Dubai in December 2010.[77] As noted by Stobdan, 'Chabahar–Iranshahr–Zahedan–Mashhad can be linked to the existing Eurasian railway line which connects other parts of Central Asia. Similarly, this route can hook onto ongoing corridor plans and programmes like Transport Corridor Europe–Caucasus–Asia (TRACECA), Central Asia Regional Economic Cooperation (CAREC) and other multilateral transport initiatives in the region.'[78] In addition, India plans to construct a 900-km long railway track that would connect Chabahar Port to the mineral-rich Hajigak region of Afghanistan.[79]

During Rouhani's visit to India in February 2018, India reiterated its commitment to complete the Chabahar–Zahedan railway line and signed an agreement with Iran giving India Ports Global Private Limited the rights to one port terminal of

---

[74] Ranta, 'Why Chabahar Agreement is Important for Iran?': Iran has also offered the establishment of an elaborate FTZ. The FTZ is divided into nine functional zones, with 26 per cent of the territory being allocated to the trade and service sector, 49 per cent to industry, and 25 per cent to tourism and residential activities.
[75] Pant and Mehta, 'India in Chabahar', 661.
[76] Mitra, 'India's Persian Desire', 42.
[77] Khan, 'China's Gwadar and India's Chahbahar', 92.
[78] P. Stobdan, 'To make Chabahar a "Game Changer" Central Asian States Need to be Roped In', *IDSA Comment*, 12 December 2017, https://idsa.in/idsacomments/to-make-chabahar-a-game-changer-central-asian-states_pstobdan_121217.
[79] Stobdan, 'To Make Chabahar a "Game Changer" Central Asian States Need to be Roped In'.

Chabahar for eighteen months.[80] Despite the fact that Chabahar is the only Iranian port with exemptions from economic sanctions reimposed by the United States in 2018, US sanctions on Iran have had some negative impacts on the Chabahar project. For instance, the sanctions led to the refusal of Swiss and Finnish firms to bid for contracts to supply necessary equipment.[81] In December 2019, Iran and India agreed to accelerate the development of the port. President Rouhani emphasised the importance of the project in boosting trade in the region, stating, 'completing the Chabahar–Zahedan railway and connecting it to Iran's national railway can elevate the position of Chabahar port, revolutionise regional commerce and help transport goods on a cheaper and shorter route'.[82] The Indian-built, 193-km road from Delaram, in Afghanistan's Nimruz Province, to Zaranj, on the Iranian border, links Chabahar to Zaranj; this will benefit Iran from a geostrategic perspective, strengthening Iran's influence in Afghanistan. In addition, India is involved in a Chabahar–Faraj–Bam rail link and in a railway line from Chabahar to Zahedan on the Iran–Afghan border.[83] This is part of a grand land road network in Afghanistan which connects Herat and Kabul via Mazar-i-Sharif in the north and Kandahar in the south, ultimately connecting Afghanistan to Uzbekistan.[84] This demonstrates the geostrategic importance of the Chabahar project.

Before proceeding to explain the Gwadar Port project, it is important to address Pakistan's concerns with regard to Chabahar Port. Considering that these two ports are 100 nautical miles away from each other, competition for trade may arise, but Pakistan is more concerned about India being a key player in Chabahar, and this could potentially affect the Iran–Pakistan relationship.[85] India's status as a key financer of Chabahar Port has increased its influence in Iran. India's arch-rival Pakistan has been concerned about the potential for Chabahar to be used by India for intelligence gathering and clandestine operations against Pakistan, as will be explained later.[86] Another important concern for Pakistan is that Chabahar Port could become an Indian military base,[87] even though the likelihood of this, given that India has expressed no such interest, is slim. The heightened concerns of Pakistan's military leadership can be observed in frequent articles published in *Hilal* – the magazine of the Pakistani armed forces. In one such article, Iran is criticised for 'overlooking the subversive activities of the Indian consulate in Zahidan'.[88] Pakistan has alleged

---

[80] Pant and Mehta, 'India in Chabahar', 668.
[81] Ibid., 677
[82] 'Iran and India Agree to Speed Up Chabahar Port Project', *Livemint*, 25 December 2019, https://www.livemint.com/news/india/iran-and-india-agree-to-speed-up-chabahar-port-project-11577117807733.html.
[83] Brahma Chellaney, 'Chabahar: Gateway to Afghanistan and Central Asia', *Hindustan Times*, 26 April 2018, https://chellaney.net/2018/04/26/chabahar-gateway-to-afghanistan-and-central-asia.
[84] Khan, 'China's Gwadar and India's Chahbahar', 94.
[85] Ahmed and Akbarzadeh, 'Understanding Pakistan's Relationship with Iran', 91.
[86] Ibid.
[87] Ahmed and Bhatnagar, 'The India–Iran–Pakistan Triad', 528.
[88] Ibid., 529.

that India's consulate in Zahidan is being used to fuel unrest and insurgency in Balochistan. In 2016, the Pakistani foreign office summoned India's high commissioner in Islamabad to lodge an official protest, expressing 'deep concern on the illegal entry into Pakistan by a RAW [India's Research and Analysis Wing] officer and his involvement in subversive activities in Balochistan and Karachi'.[89] This happened after Pakistani authorities claimed that they had arrested an Indian spy, Kulbhushan Jadhav, who had travelled to Pakistan from Iran.[90]

Despite both Iran and India denying these allegations strongly, this episode is indicative of Pakistan's concerns regarding the Chabahar project and the activities of the Indian intelligence service in Iran. Similar concerns were raised by Pakistani officials during President Rouhani's visit to Pakistan in 2016, when Inter-Services Public Relations – the media centre associated with Pakistan's armed forces – shared the text of the army chief's meeting with Rouhani: 'There is one concern that RAW is involved in Pakistan, especially in Balochistan, and sometimes it also uses the soil of our brother country Iran.'[91] During the meeting with Rouhani, Pakistani General Raheel Sharif asked Rouhani to tell RAW that 'they should stop these activities and allow Pakistan to achieve stability'.[92] Rouhani denied the allegation, stating, 'Whenever Iran comes closer to Pakistan such rumours are spread.'[93] To sum up, an increasing Indian presence in the region through Chabahar Port is a source of concern for Pakistan, creating tensions for the Iran–Pakistan relationship.

Gwadar Port

Gwadar is a deep-water port in Pakistan that China has developed to achieve economic and strategic objectives. China invested US$248 million in Phase 1 of Gwadar Port and plans to invest US$1.02 billion in Phase 2 of the project.[94] Gwadar Port is situated in the province of Balochistan, close to the Strait of Hormuz. It serves as an energy corridor from western China through Pakistan to the Persian Gulf.[95] China initiated the project with the help of the Pakistan government in 2008. Gwadar Port is important for Pakistan from geostrategic and geo-economic perspectives. First, it raises the capacity of Pakistan's navy to 'a level that rivals regional powers'.[96] This is due to the fact that before the development of Gwadar Port, Pakistan's largest naval port was at Karachi, a location considered to be too

---

[89] 'Pakistan Says It Captures Indian Spy, Summons Envoy to Protest', *Reuters*, 25 March 2016, https://www.reuters.com/article/us-pakistan-india-idUSKCN0WR0VC.

[90] Iftikhar A. Khan, 'Iran Responds to Letter about Indian Spy', *Dawn*, 16 June 2016, https://www.dawn.com/news/1265187.

[91] 'Rouhani Denies Discussing "RAW's involvement in Balochistan" with Pakistani Leadership', *Dawn*, 27 March 2016, https://www.dawn.com/news/1248078.

[92] Ibid.

[93] Ibid.

[94] Amirthan, 'What are India, Iran and Afghanistan's Benefits from the Chabahar Port Agreement?' 89.

[95] Ali Zaman Shah, 'Geopolitical Significance of Balochistan', *Strategic Studies* 37(3) (2017): 134.

[96] Daniels, 'Strategic Competition in South Asia', 95

close to the dominant Indian navy and its bases in Gujarat and Mumbai.[97] That is, for Pakistan, Gwadar Port provides its navy with strategic depth since it is situated farther away from Karachi Port, and from India's naval bases. Secondly, the Gwadar project boosts the local economy of Pakistan, generating billions of dollars in revenue and creating at least 2 million job opportunities. Thirdly, the port will launch additional infrastructure projects, connecting Pakistan to greater Central Asia.[98] Finally, Gwadar provides an opportunity for Pakistan to increase its military connections and cooperation with China.

Since 2019, Iran has showed an interest in connecting Chabahar Port with Gwadar Port.[99] Iran's view of the Gwadar and Chabahar projects is different from that of Pakistan. While Pakistan sees the two ports as competing projects, and the latter a threat to its security, Iran considers the two as 'sister ports'. In an address given at the Institute of Strategic Studies Islamabad (ISSI) in May 2016, Iran's ambassador to Pakistan, Mehdi Honerdoost, noted that Gwadar and Chabahar are sister ports, not rival ports.[100] In the same year, when Iran and India were finalising the Chabahar agreement, Honerdoost stated that the 'Chabahar Port agreement between Iran, India and Afghanistan is "not finished" and "not limited to these three countries"'. Honerdoost also asserted that 'We are waiting for new members. Pakistan, our brotherly neighbour, and China, a great partner of the Iranians and a good friend of Pakistan, are welcomed.'[101] It should be noted that Pakistan also hinted at its desire to connect Gwadar and Chabahar, with Sartaj Aziz, the prime minister's adviser on foreign affairs, stating that this would be possible through road and rail links.[102] The fact that Tehran tried to dispel the idea that Chabahar is designed to rival Gwadar demonstrates that Iran's aim is mainly oriented towards boosting trade. Honerdoost declared, 'We are ready for any rapprochement between regional countries which directly impact the interests of the people of our countries. Trade and business is business, and politics is politics. We should separate them.'[103] Iran's interest in balancing its relations with both Pakistan and India was also reflected in Rouhani's statement during his visit to Pakistan in 2016: 'India, like Pakistan, is Iran's friend.'[104]

In May 2019, Iran showed further interest in connecting Pakistan's Gwadar Port with Chabahar Port to promote trade and commerce in the region. The proposal

---

[97] See Hasan Yaser Malik, 'Strategic Importance of Gwadar Port', *Journal of Political Studies* 19(2) (2012): 57–69.
[98] Daniels, 'Strategic Competition in South Asia', 95
[99] Syed Fazl-e-Haider, 'Shifting Alliances in the Gulf a Boon to China', *The Interpreter*, 18 November 2019, https://www.lowyinstitute.org/the-interpreter/shifting-alliances-gulf-boon-china.
[100] Mir Sherbaz Khetran, 'Gwadar and Chabahar', *Strategic Studies* 38(2) (2018): 53.
[101] Mateen Haider and Mahnoor Bari, 'Chabahar Not a Rival to Gwadar, Iranian Envoy Tells Pakistan', *Dawn*, 27 May 2016, https://www.dawn.com/news/1261006.
[102] Khetran, 'Gwadar and Chabahar', 53–4.
[103] Haider and Bari, 'Chabahar Not a Rival to Gwadar'.
[104] Malik Muhammad Ashraf, 'Pak–Iran Relations', *The News*, 5 April 2016, https://www.thenews.com.pk/print/110365-Pak-Iran-relations.

was introduced by Iranian foreign minister Mohammad Javad Zarif, who met Pakistan's civil–military leadership in Islamabad: 'I've come here with a proposal for the government of Pakistan for connection between Chabahar and Gwadar . . . We believe that Chabahar and Gwadar can complement each other.' Zarif continued: 'We can connect Chabahar and Gwadar, and then through that connect Gwadar to our entire railroad system, from Iran to the North Corridor, through Turkmenistan and Kazakhstan, and also through Azerbaijan, Russia, and through Turkey.'[105] In September 2019, Iran expressed an interest in the China–Pakistan Economic Corridor. Members of the Indian Association of Foreign Affairs said Iran seeks to develop a 'Liquefied Natural Gas (LNG) pipeline to China along the China–Pakistan Economic Corridor (CPEC)'.[106]

Iran's interest in investing in the Gwadar project and in linking Chabahar to Gwadar is connected to a number of objectives. First, it would allow Iran to export natural gas to Pakistan via Gwadar. Iran has already completed its part of a gas pipeline to Pakistan under an earlier agreement, but due to the US pressure and the lack of funding, Pakistan did not complete its portion. Furthermore, Iran's interest in participating in the Gwadar Port project is rooted in its desire to balance the growing Saudi Arabian influence in the China–Pakistan Economic Corridor.[107] From a strategic perspective, Gwadar Port is important for Iran because it is situated near Chabahar Port and is close to the Strait of Hormuz.[108] In addition, it increases the potential for Iran–Pakistan trade and the two countries' economic relationship. Finally, Iran could use Gwadar Port as a transit terminal for crude oil exports to China, in particular Xinjiang Province.[109] While some of our Pakistani research participants focused on differences between Iran and Pakistan's perspectives with respect to Gwadar Port,[110] our analysis identified numerous convergences of interest between the two states and those will likely grow after Iran's partnership with China. Facing a problem in the shape of a lack of investment from India, Iran invited China and Pakistan to participate in the Chabahar project. In 2020, Iran and China signed a twenty-five-year agreement through which Beijing plans to invest US$400 billion in Iran in various projects, including Chabahar Port.[111]

---

[105] 'Iran Ready to Connect Gwadar Port with Chabahar', *Pakistan Today*, 25 May 2019, https://www.pakistantoday.com.pk/2019/05/24/iranian-fm-zarif-calls-on-pm-qureshi-amid-rising-tensions-with-us.

[106] Nader Habibi and Hans Yue Zhu, 'What CPEC Means for China's Middle East Relations', *The Diplomat*, 22 January 2020, https://thediplomat.com/2020/01/what-cpec-means-for-chinas-middle-east-relations.

[107] Andrew Korybko, 'Iran's Interest in CPEC Strengthens Regional Integration', *CGTN*, 16 September 2019, https://news.cgtn.com/news/2019-09-16/Iran-s-interest-in-CPEC-strengthens-regional-integration-K2ybECc94A/index.html.

[108] Rahim and Ali, 'The Sino-Indian Geo-Strategic Rivalry', 87.

[109] Khan, 'China's Gwadar and India's Chahbahar', 81.

[110] P2, interviewed on 2 May 2019, Islamabad.

[111] Farnaz Fassihi and Steven Lee Myers, 'Defying U.S., China and Iran Near Trade and Military Partnership', *New York Times*, 11 July 2020, https://www.nytimes.com/2020/07/11/world/asia/china-iran-trade-military-deal.html.

While it is too early to tell how this partnership will unfold, it is quite likely that China's investment in Chabahar Port will also secure its investment in Gwadar Port and indirectly bring Iran and Pakistan closer.

Conclusion

This chapter examined the geostrategic significance of Afghanistan and Pakistan to Iran. We looked at both historical and contemporary drivers of Iran's foreign policy vis-à-vis Afghanistan and Pakistan. As it was threatened by the presence of Soviet troops along its borders with Afghanistan, Iran expanded its influence in Afghanistan. Similarly, the presence of US forces on Iran's eastern borders after 2001 became a national security concern for Tehran, leading to an upscaling of Iran's influence in Afghanistan. As Tehran had not recognised the Islamic Emirate of Afghanistan, the Taliban government's collapse offered it an ideal opportunity to expand its cultural, economic and political influence. While Iran historically supported the Northern Alliance in Afghanistan, it also established connections with the Taliban. As some of our Afghan research participants stated, a key objective of its support for the Taliban and the US–Taliban peace deal has been to ensure the withdrawal of US troops from Afghanistan. With withdrawal of US troops in August 2021, that concern has been addressed but there remain other challenges, some of which were discussed in the final chapter and others will be discussed in Chapter 6. Iran and Pakistan are locked in a geoeconomic and geopolitical competition between India and China. Since the 1990s, India has been the main funder of Chabahar Port, which raised eyebrows in Pakistan and led to Islamabad accusing India of using Iranian soil for covert operations inside Pakistan. Officially, however, Iran and Pakistan look at the ports at Chabahar and Gwadar as complementary. China's involvement in Chabahar Port may address Pakistan's concerns or those of its military establishment, which views the port as a national security threat. In the following chapters, Iran's influence in both countries will be examined through cultural, ideological, political and economic lenses.

5
Cultural and Ideological Influences

Owing to historical factors such as the Persian colonial legacy and the Persian language being the *lingua franca* of the Indian subcontinent before the British Empire, today's Iran enjoys some advantages in terms of promoting its positive image through soft power strategies in both Afghanistan and Pakistan. Iran also holds an important position for millions of Shi'as in both Afghanistan and Pakistan, which Tehran actively draws upon to achieve its ideological and political goals in both countries. This chapter presents an analysis of Iranian soft power resources and instruments in connection with its efforts to leverage its ideological and cultural characteristics to promote its goodwill in Afghanistan and Pakistan. Leaning on our interview data, we demonstrate how Iranian efforts to wield ideological and cultural influence have been received in both countries.

Engagement in Afghanistan

The collapse of the Islamic Emirate of Afghanistan in 2001 provided Iran with an opportunity to expand its cultural influence. Iran's conflictual relationship with the Taliban, and its backing of anti-Taliban factions under the Northern Alliance during the early 1990s had limited its role in Afghanistan previously, preventing Tehran from expanding its cultural influence in Afghanistan. The post-9/11 dynamics therefore provided Iran with a viable opportunity to expand its influence through its international commitments towards the reconstruction of Afghanistan. As Nader argues, 'Iran's cultural and religious bonds allow it to exercise influence over key ethnic and religious groups, including the Tajik and Hazara.'[1] It should be noted that the relationship between Iran and the Hazara community in Afghanistan significantly increased after the Iranian Revolution in 1979. In the 1980s, for instance, when some Afghan Shi'a clerics were arrested by the communist regime in Kabul, they established stronger connections with Iranian *maraja-e taqlid*.[2] Iran continues to share ethnic and religious links with Afghanistan's Shi'a minority Hazara community, which resides in the central and northern regions of Afghanistan.

---

[1] Nader and Laha, *Iran's Balancing Act in Afghanistan*.
[2] Martin, *Creating an Islamic State*, 194, 232.

Language and culture are valuable soft power assets that can be used by states to exercise influence in other countries.[3] Iran uses its language and culture to enhance its soft power in Afghanistan. As mentioned in Chapter 1, Iran's ICRO has established cultural centres (*Khana-e-Farhang*) and liaison offices in Kabul, Mazar-i-Sharif and Herat. The ICRO has also appointed a cultural attaché in the Iranian consulate in Jalalabad.[4] Through these cultural centres, Tehran seeks to promote the teaching and study of Persian language and literature to help increase cultural awareness of the shared traditions of the Iranian and Afghan peoples.[5]

In terms of its public diplomacy strategy and to promote its own positive image in Afghanistan, Iran has invested in Afghanistan's media landscape by setting up TV channels that broadcast programmes in Dari and Pashto. Mass media plays a crucial role in promoting a country's goodwill, and many countries use that as an important soft power tool. This particularly is the case of Turkey's increasing soft power as a result of its historical television series that are very popular particularly across the Muslim world.[6] Some scholars have examined Iran's engagement in the media sector in Afghanistan and argued that the pro-Iran media outlets in Afghanistan receive substantial funding from Tehran.[7] A *Reuters* report in 2012 claimed that roughly a third of Afghanistan's media outlets were either receiving content or financial support from Iranian sources.[8] According to a 2012 estimate, Tehran invested US$100 million annually in media, civil society and religious programmes across Afghanistan.[9] This is significant because television is more popular than newspapers in Afghanistan. According to Nader et al., 'Iranian influence in Afghan media is so substantial that Persian words are often used in Pashto-language media.'[10] Regarding this, an Afghan businessman described Iran's investment in Afghan media in the following manner: 'To me their biggest influence is cultural and educational.

---

[3] Alexandre Rabêlo Neto, José Milton de Sousa-Filho, Áurio Lúcio Leocádio and João Carlos Hipolito Bernardes do Nascimento, 'Internationalization of Cultural Products: The Influence of Soft Power', *International Journal of Market Research* 62(3) (2020): 335–49.

[4] See a list of Iranian cultural centres and liaison offices abroad at: 'Raiznan-e farhangi Iran dar kharej az keshvar', Regional Information Centre for Science and Technology (n.d.), https://ricest.ac.ir/branch.

[5] Richard Weitz, 'Iran and Afghanistan: More of the Same', *Central Asia-Caucasus Analyst*, 7 February 2014, https://www.cacianalyst.org/publications/analytical-articles/item/13002-iran-and-afghanistan-more-of-the-same.html. It is important to note that Tehran's extensive cultural soft power campaign began in the pre-revolution era under the Shah, when Tehran distributed Persian-language books, newspapers and Iranian films in the region. See Vatanka, *Iran and Pakistan*, 96.

[6] Senem B. Çevik, 'Turkish Historical Television Series: Public Broadcasting of neo-Ottoman Illusions', *Southeast European and Black Sea Studies* 19(2) (2019): 227–42.

[7] See Nader et al., 'Iran and Afghanistan: A Complicated Relationship'.

[8] Ferris-Rotman, 'Insight. Iran's "Great Game" in Afghanistan'.

[9] Ibid.

[10] Nader et al., 'Iran and Afghanistan: A Complicated Relationship', 14.

When I watch most of the TV channels, I do not understand them because they use Iranian expressions.'[11] We recorded similar statements from our other Afghan participants. For example, a member of the Afghanistan Analysts Network mentioned that some of the TV shows and series produced in Iran and broadcast through Afghan channels have a considerable following in Afghanistan.[12] Other interviewees expressed caution towards Iran's use of the media in Afghanistan. One political analyst explained 'they [Iranians] tried to influence some of our media channels to mix their language, terms, words and phrases with our language, but it didn't work as they were expecting'.[13] Another participant from Afghanistan's State Ministry of Parliamentary Affairs expressed concern about Iran's cultural influence being expanded to the media sphere, stating that 'if Iran is making good movies and TV series, we will be attracted automatically. But if they want to gain political influence through spreading their culture [via media], this is not a good thing.'[14] This means that some research participants considered that the Iranian presence in the Afghan media is designed to boost Tehran's cultural and political influence in Afghanistan.

As stated in Chapter 1, scholars of soft power emphasise the importance of educational engagement to increase a country's soft power. After the collapse of the Taliban regime in 2001, Iran pursued a top-down approach to cultural and educational engagement in Afghanistan. According to the department of culture at the Iranian embassy in Kabul, Tehran gifted 7,000 books to scientific, academic and cultural centres in Afghanistan in 2002. Iran justified this by stating that many libraries in Afghanistan were destroyed during the civil war in Afghanistan.[15] In 2006 and 2007, Iran's activities at Kabul University included the establishment of 'the first national teacher training centre, construction of a centre for religious affairs, provision of education scholarships, construction of a vocational training centre', and a programme to 'send experts to train Afghan teachers'.[16] During the past two decades, Iran's supply of books to Afghan schools has been an important mechanism for increasing its overall influence in the country. The number of books published in Iran and then sent to Afghan universities is so large that, according to an Afghan leader, 'If the books that are published in Iran are taken away, Kabul University won't have anything else.'[17] Needless to say, some of these books reflect a certain political and religious agenda in line with Iran's official position, including

---

[11] Ibid.
[12] A18, interviewed on 16 June 2019, Kabul.
[13] A10, interviewed on 2 June 2019, Kabul.
[14] A17, interviewed on 16 June 2019, Kabul.
[15] 'Iran Gifts 7000 Books to Afghan Scientific, Cultural Centers', *Tehran Times*, 24 July 24 2002, https://www.tehrantimes.com/news/85117/Iran-Gifts-7-000-Books-to-Afghan-Scientific-Cultural-Centers.
[16] Frederick W. Kagan, Kimberly Kagan and Danielle Pletka, *Iranian Influence in the Levant, Iraq, and Afghanistan* (Washington, DC: American Enterprise Institute, 2008), 38.
[17] Nader, et al., 'Iran and Afghanistan: A Complicated Relationship', 13.

Shi'a teachings.[18] For example, in May 2009, the Ministry of Culture and Information of Afghanistan declared that it had found 25 tonnes of books transferred by a private publisher from Iran to Afghanistan.[19] Among these books were the *Nahjul-ul-Balagha*, a collection of letters and speeches attributed to Imam Ali, and another important Shi'a book, namely, *Usul-e-Kafi*.[20]

The idea that Iran's educational influence in Afghanistan grew significantly after the fall of the first Taliban government was also highlighted by our Afghan interviewees. According to an Afghan analyst, 'Iran has research organizations in Afghanistan and publishes or translates books from other languages into Persian which are being used in Afghanistan especially by Afghan students.'[21] According to another insight, Iran's construction of libraries and focus on book publication in Afghanistan is aimed at influencing 'our new generation ... and youth'.[22] An Afghan economic and political expert explained that, 'in academic environments like Kabul University or in universities in which the language of instruction is Persian, 60–70% of the academic, social and arts-related books are written or translated in Iran'.[23] Likewise, an academic from Kabul University revealed that 'most of our resources [in Afghanistan], especially educational and academic, come from Iran'.[24] He noted that Afghanistan lacks adequate in-country resources for the publication of a sufficient number of books for educational purposes, and that Iran uses this opportunity to publish books for Afghan students which naturally increases and deepens Tehran's influence in Afghanistan.[25]

Additionally, Iran has also enhanced its cultural activities in Herat. In 2018, Iran and Afghanistan signed a Memorandum of Understanding (MoU), according to which the two countries committed to establishing cultural centres affiliated with the Iranian consulates in Mashhad and Herat. They agreed to hold events such as book fairs and art exhibitions, as well as events to promote the shared cultural heritage of both countries.[26] Such cultural and educational events are considered crucial in terms of soft power and this is particularly what the UK's British Council does with its branches globally.[27] In October 2019, Iran opened its first *Khana-e-Farhang* in Herat. On this occasion, Iran's ambassador to Afghanistan hosted a ceremony

---

[18] Ibid.
[19] Here is a source in Persian: 'Afghan-Authored Books Among Those Thrown into the River' [in Dari], *Afghan Paper*, 26 May 2009, http://www.afghanpaper.com/nbody.php?id=846.
[20] Rustam Ali Seerat, 'Iran and Saudi Arabia in Afghanistan', *The Diplomat*, 14 January 2016, https://thediplomat.com/2016/01/iran-and-saudi-arabia-in-afghanistan.
[21] A7, interviewed on 29 June 2019, Kabul.
[22] A10, interviewed on 2 June 2019, Kabul.
[23] A22, interviewed on 29 May 2019, Kabul.
[24] A13, interviewed on 11 June 2019, Kabul.
[25] Ibid.
[26] 'Iran, Afghanistan to Establish Cultural Centers in Mashhad, Herat', *IRNA*, 16 September 2018, https://en.irna.ir/news/83035434/Iran-Afghanistan-to-establish-cultural-centers-in-Mashad-Herat.
[27] James Pamment, *British Public Diplomacy and Soft Power: Diplomatic Influence and the Digital Revolution* (Cham: Palgrave Macmillan, 2016).

in which he talked about the growing cultural cooperation between the two countries. Noting the importance of Herat in cultural matters, the Iranian ambassador to Afghanistan underscored 'the need to reach common ground in the field of culture'.[28]

Some of our Afghan research participants also noted that Iran not only supports religious ceremonies, but also other types of activities in Afghanistan, which in turn increases its soft power in certain regions of Afghanistan. These include traditional Iranian ceremonies, the celebration of Ayatollah Khomeini's birthday, the anniversary of the birth of the Islamic Republic of Iran and Quds Day (an occasion established by Ayatollah Khomeini as a day of Muslim solidarity with the Palestinian people).[29] One participant noted that ceremonies such as 'the celebration of Imam Khomeini's birthday and Quds Day' are 'followed by many Afghans'.[30] This emphasis on promoting key elements of the Islamic Republic's ideology was also noted by interviewees. A professor at the University of Herat noted that some Shi'a Afghan refugees in Iran are trained in the Iranian cities of Qom and Mashhad, transferring the fundamental principles of the Islamic Revolution to Afghanistan.[31] He further noted that some Afghan refugees, upon their return to Afghanistan, commemorate the anniversary of Imam Khomeini's death and continue to celebrate other political occasions such as Iran's Islamic Revolution day in Afghanistan.[32]

With regard to Iranian influence in education, Tehran has been using a variety of methods, such as student exchange programmes and scholarships for Afghan students. To this end, a few Iranian universities have opened campuses in Afghanistan. These include the Islamic Azad University, MIU and Payame Noor University, all of which specialise in distance learning.[33] According to Abdul Waheed Khan, former assistant director general for communication and information at UNESCO, 'Iran has a large pool of human resources in science and technology to produce quality educational content for cross-border education and has long experience of open and distance learning, such as Payame Noor University.'[34] In 2013, Iran declared the establishment of a branch of the Ferdowsi University of Mashhad (FUM) in the Afghan city of Herat, to be called Khajeh Abdollah Ansari University.[35] In 2017, Allameh Tabataba'i University, a major public university in Tehran, launched a Pashto-language programme in Iran in cooperation with the Faculty of Literature

---

[28] 'Iran's House of Culture Inaugurated in Herat', *IRNA*, 6 October 2019, https://en.irna.ir/news/83505991/Iran-s-House-of-Culture-inaugurated-in-Herat.

[29] The Quds Day is held on the last Friday of the fasting month of Ramadan each year, the day is marked by events and protests in Iran.

[30] A6, interviewed on 22 May 2019, Kabul.

[31] A23, interviewed on 25 June 2019, Kabul.

[32] Ibid.

[33] Wagdy Sawahel, 'Iran, Saudi Arabia Vie for Influence over Afghan HE', *University World News*, 15 December 2017, https://www.universityworldnews.com/post.php?story=20171212141208319.

[34] Wagdy Sawahel, 'Overseas Campuses Expanded in Drive for "Soft Power"', *University World News*, 19 January 2013, https://www.universityworldnews.com/post.php?story=2013011813380699.

[35] Sawahel, 'Overseas Campuses Expanded in Drive for "Soft Power"'.

and Languages at Kabul University.³⁶ According to one estimate, there were 38,000 Afghan students in Iran as of January 2019.³⁷ Iran's humanitarian/charity organisations, such as the Imam Khomeini Relief Committee, which are operating in various parts of Afghanistan including the provinces of Kabul, Herat, Balkh and Nimruz, provide scholarships to Afghans to study in Iran. Afghan scholarship recipients are often postgraduate students studying science and technology. Iran has also established centres in Afghan universities in which Persian language and literature as well as Islamic studies are taught.³⁸ Salem argues that 'cross-border universities will help in improving Iran's image and enhancing mutual understanding, along with spreading [Iranian] culture'.³⁹ The idea that Iran grants scholarships to Afghan students was acknowledged by many of our research participants. They viewed scholarships as an important soft power instrument employed by Tehran in addition to its cultural centres in Afghanistan.⁴⁰ A participant from Afghanistan's Ministry of Justice asserted that Iran has a broader strategy behind its scholarship scheme because those opportunities are not merely limited to Hazara or Shi'a students from Afghanistan, showing that Tehran aims to influence other ethnic groups as well.⁴¹ He further added that this strategy also helps Iran avoid being labelled as promoting its ideological agenda in Afghanistan.⁴²

As explained in Chapter 1, one strategy Iran pursues to exercise influence outside its borders is the establishment of strong connections with, and support for, Shi'a groups of other countries and the promotion of Shi'a teachings. Since the 1980s, Iran has been supporting Shi'a groups in Afghanistan, although as discussed in previous chapters, Iran, has at times, supported Sunni groups too. According to Mohammad Omar Daudzai, former Afghan ambassador to Iran, some Afghan Shi'a religious leaders receive funds from Iran.⁴³ In line with promoting Shiism, Iran's aid included funding religious institutions such as Shi'a religious seminaries and higher education in Afghanistan. Iran supports the Khatam al-Nabyeen Islamic University, the most prestigious religious seminary in Afghanistan. Iranian donations are claimed to cover 80 per cent of its library costs. Most students at this university are Shi'a Hazaras, and the curriculum at the university largely resembles that of religious seminaries in Iran.⁴⁴ The university itself is run by Grand Ayatollah Asif Mohseni, a former Shi'a leader and the spiritual leader of Afghanistan's Shi'a minority, who has close ties to the clerical establishment in Iran. Khatam-al

---

[36] Ahmad Quraishi, 'Iranian University Launches Pashtu Faculty', *Pajhwok Afghan News*, 3 March 2017, https://www.pajhwok.com/en/2017/03/03/iranian-university-launches-pashtu-faculty.

[37] 'IRNA Roundtable: Afghan University Students in Iran and their Educational Problems' [in Persian], *IRNA*, 2 January 2019, https://www.irna.ir/news/83155937.

[38] Sawahel, 'Overseas Campuses Expanded in Drive for "Soft Power"'.

[39] Ibid.

[40] A8, interviewed on 8 May 2019, Kabul.

[41] A21, interviewed on 22 June 2019, Kabul.

[42] Ibid.

[43] Filkins, 'Iran is Said to Give Top Karzai Aide Cash by the Bagful'.

[44] Kagan, Kagan and Pletka, *Iranian Influence in the Levant, Iraq and Afghanistan*, 81

Nabyeen Islamic University has signed a few MoUs with Iranian universities. For example, in 2019, it signed an agreement with the Tehran University of Medical Sciences (TUMS).[45] It is also important to note that with Iranian financial and technical assistance, Mohseni runs a private TV channel and a radio station called *Tamadon* (Civilization). TV personnel are reported to receive training by Iranian advisers. *Tamadon* covers various programmes about the Israeli–Palestinian conflict and the US occupation of Iraq and Afghanistan.[46]

Iran also uses the Khatam-al Nabyeen Islamic University to disseminate its ideology. According to one of the students at the university, 'Our teachers are all Afghans who studied in Iran and other foreign countries.'[47] The university is also known as a centre for boosting Iranian influence in Afghanistan, including through the promotion of the theory of the Guardianship of the Jurist (*velayat-e faqih*).[48] The books used as teaching materials include 'the same sort of lessons' that are taught in Iran with regard to the concept of *velayat-e faqih*. Ayatollah Khamenei is considered in these books to be the *vali-e faqih* [supreme religious expert with authority to rule] and the representative of the twelfth Shi'a Imam Mahdi.[49]

In addition to Tehran's activities to promote its cultural norms and the Islamic Republic's official policies as well as Shi'a teachings, Iran has engaged in the provision of various types of social services to Afghan civilians. Iranian institutions such as the Iranian Red Crescent Society and the IKRC have also provided financial assistance to Afghans. In particular, the IKRC provides assistance to orphans, the physically disabled and the elderly. It distributes food aid, blankets and fuel, interest-free loans, and marriage assistance to young people.[50] The IKRC seeks to influence village leaders and poorer segments of Afghan society. It has more than 30,000 people on its payroll in Afghanistan.[51] As is often claimed, the goal of the IKRC is not merely oriented around charity work. It also sponsors events at the Iranian embassy in Kabul to promote the official policies of the Islamic Republic such as organising Quds Day rallies in major Afghan cities.[52] Kamal and Ra'ees have carried out a detailed case study of the IKRC's work in Afghanistan and argue

---

[45] '40,000 Afghans Enrolled in Iranian Universities', *Outlook Afghanistan*, 28 August 2019, http://www.outlookafghanistan.net/national_detail.php?post_id=24402.

[46] See Baresh Roshangar, 'Mohseni: Prozha-e Bast Salta-e Iran dar Manteqa' ['Mohseni: The Project of Iran's Expansion of Hegemony in Region'], *Kabul Press*, 19 April 2009, https://www.kabulpress.org/article3319.html.

[47] Zarif Nazar and Charles Recknagel, 'Controversial Madrasah Builds Iran's Influence in Kabul', *Radio Free Europe*, 6 November 2010, https://www.rferl.org/a/Controversial_Madrasah_Builds_Irans_Influence_In_Kabul/2212566.html.

[48] Nazar and Recknagel, 'Controversial Madrasah Builds Iran's Influence in Kabul'.

[49] Ibid.

[50] Ahmad Majidyar and Ali Alfoneh, 'Iranian Influence in Afghanistan: Imam Khomeini Relief Committee', *Middle Eastern Outlook*, July 2010, https://www.aei.org/research-products/report/iranian-influence-in-afghanistan.

[51] Kagan, Kagan and Pletka, *Iranian Influence in the Levant, Iraq and Afghanistan*, 81.

[52] Ibid.

that the organisation acts as a key tool for Iran to export its Islamic revolution. They further add that, 'the IKRC is tasked to nurture Afghan sympathizers for the Islamic Republic of Iran to enhance this country's soft power in Afghanistan'.[53] Another Iranian humanitarian organisation in Afghanistan is the *Moaseseh Hemayat Sabz-e Parsiyan*, which provides health services in the provinces of Kabul, Herat and Takhar.[54] As Afghanistan has fallen deeper into humanitarian and economic crisis since the Taliban's takeover, Tehran has continued to provide humanitarian aid in the shape of medicine and food.[55]

Many of our Afghan research participants stated that factors such as shared linguistic and cultural heritage, as well as religion, play a significant role in the expansion of Iranian influence in Afghanistan. Most participants indicated that Iran uses its common language of Persian and its culture to expand its influence in Afghanistan. Also noteworthy was Iran's greater influence in areas such as Herat where Dari Persian is the predominant language. An Afghan political analyst noted for instance that 'if this cultural relationship that we have based on the Persian language did not exist, we would not have experienced such influence by Iran'.[56] Another participant claimed that Iran's linguistic influence in Afghanistan is so vast that the Afghan language can be said to be 'Iranised' in one way or another.[57] He revealed that many Afghan students who studied in Iran use Iranian expressions and slang upon their return to Afghanistan, and that this is particularly observable when they start working in the media in Afghanistan.[58] One interviewee stated that shared language is a factor used by Iran to exercise its influence over non-Shi'a groups in Afghanistan.[59]

Iran's use of religion, particularly Shi'a Islam, as an instrument to exercise influence in Afghanistan was also widely noted among our research interviewees. Iran's support of Shi'a groups, especially the Hazara community in addition to other ethnic or religious groups, was also highlighted by some participants. Several participants noted that the existence of cultural and religious proximity is one of the main factors that helps Iran to increase its soft power in Afghanistan. For a few interviewees, Iran's ideological influence in Afghanistan extends beyond Tehran's cultural influence. Iran's influence over Shi'a populations was also viewed by several interviewees as an ideological tool that suits Iran's interests.[60] One participant

---

[53] Abdol Moghset Bani Kamal and Wahabuddin Ra'ees, 'Iran's Aid Diplomacy in Afghanistan: The Role of Imam Khomeini Relief Committee', *Contemporary Review of the Middle East* 5(4) (2018): 308.

[54] 'Chahar muaseseh ghair entefai irani dar Afghanistan faaliat darand', *Radio Azadi*, 15 May 2014, https://da.azadiradio.com/a/25385293.html.

[55] 'Iran Sends Humanitarian Aid to Needy Afghan People', *Iran Press*, 4 May 2022, https://iranpress.com/content/58293/iran-sends-humanitarian-aid-needy-afghan-people.

[56] A11, interviewed on 9 June 2019, Kabul.

[57] A13, interviewed on 11 June 2019, Kabul.

[58] Ibid.

[59] A1, interviewed on 8 May 2019, Kabul.

[60] A6, interviewed on 22 May 2019; A1 interviewed on 8 May 2019, Kabul; A9, interviewed on 30 May 2019.

from Afghan civil society stated that owing to its centrality to Shiism in the Muslim world, Iran's ideological influence is not limited to Afghanistan.[61] He explained that Iran exercises influence on Shi'a populations in other parts of the Muslim world, including in Pakistan, Central Asian countries and Turkey.[62] As already noted, some participants stated that Shi'a Afghans who have studied in Iran contribute to the spread of Iranian ideology in Afghanistan upon their return. The data we received through our interviews with research participants indicated that Afghan students, particularly in areas such as Kandahar, Herat, Nimruz, Farah and Ghor, play a significant role in spreading the ideology of the Islamic Republic of Iran. One interviewee stated that the Iranian university system requires students, even in the field of engineering, to study certain courses related to Shiism and language, which naturally leads international students including Afghans studying in such fields to become familiar with Iranian cultural and religious norms and values.[63]

In relation to other religious activities conducted by Tehran, our research participants also noted that Iran supports and funds Afghan Shi'a religious scholars through the establishment of various Shi'a centres in Afghanistan.[64] Iran's religious influence in Afghanistan arguably increased following the Soviet withdrawal from the country in 1989, but stopped during the first Taliban administration (1996–2001).[65] Following the Soviet withdrawal, one interviewee noted, Iran established Shi'a mosques in Afghanistan and also facilitated the movement of Shi'a religious scholars from Qom to Afghanistan, which has had a significant influence on Afghans.[66] Some people in Afghanistan also celebrate traditional Iranian ceremonies and religious performances, as explained by one interviewee.[67] This is particularly visible in Muharram (the month in which commemorations for the Shi'a Imam Hussein are held) ceremonies held every year in Afghanistan: 'The 10th of Moharram is being celebrated in a different way now [compared to the past]. This shows Iran's influence.'[68] One interviewee claimed that Iran funds many Afghan Shi'as in Afghanistan to 'perform Moharram'.[69]

Engagement in Pakistan

Prior to the Iranian Revolution of 1979, the Shah of Iran sought to expand Persian culture in Pakistan through publicising Iranian literature, art and language. In 1956, Iran signed a cultural agreement with Pakistan, according to which the two

---

[61] A9, interviewed on 30 May 2019.
[62] Ibid.
[63] A22, interviewed on 29 May 2019, Kabul.
[64] A1, interviewed on 8 May 2019, Kabul; A18, interviewed on 16 June 2019, Kabul.
[65] A17, interviewed on 16 June 2019, Kabul.
[66] Ibid.
[67] A25, interviewed on 29 June 2019, Kabul.
[68] A20, interviewed on 28 June 2019, Kabul.
[69] A1, interviewed on 8 May 2019, Kabul.

countries agreed to increase their cultural cooperation.[70] Later, when then president of Pakistan, Field Marshal Ayub Khan, visited Tehran in 1959, both the Shah and Khan emphasised cultural commonalities between the two countries. Referring to these commonalities, Khan stated, 'We embrace the same faith and have a common cultural heritage. Your language and literature have been the fountainhead of inspiration for us for us for centuries . . . Your literature is our literature, your historic heroes are our heroes.'[71] Long before the revolution, the Shah had launched Iranian cultural centres (*Khana-e-Farhang*) across Pakistan to spread awareness of *Iran Zamin* (the Land of Iran) in Pakistan, and to promote the cultural influence of Persia from ancient times, as we discussed in Chapter 2.[72]

After the establishment of the Islamic Republic in 1979, Iran expanded its cultural centres in Pakistan to increase its influence but still focused on the promotion of Persian language and literature. In 1992, a Persian-language research institute was established in Pakistan.[73] Also, the number of *Khana-e-Farhangs* significantly increased during the post-Revolution era, and currently there are *Khana-e-Farhangs* in various Pakistani cities, including Karachi, Peshawar, Lahore, Rawalpindi and Quetta. Persian is often taught at these cultural centres, although there are other universities and institutions in Pakistan offering Persian-language classes. According to Salahuddin, the vice chairman of Gandhara Hindko Board, 'The Khana-e-Farhang efforts for the promotion of Persian language are not confined to the centre as these extend to public and private universities in Peshawar and other cities.'[74] There are reports indicating that some primary and high schools have employed at least one Persian teacher to teach the language.[75] This is reminiscent of Nye's theory that language represents an important aspect of soft power.[76] In one of its latest efforts to promote the Persian language in Pakistan in 2022, the Iranian cultural centre in Rawalpindi announced the inauguration of a Persian-language course with online and face-to-face classes. In this ceremony, a Persian-language teacher said, 'Persian language is a reliable cultural bridge between Iran and Pakistan.'[77]

---

[70] Aisha Rafique, Tahir Maqsood and Asima Naureen, 'Pak–Iran Cultural and Historical Ties', *IMPACT: International Journal of Research in Applied, Natural and Social Sciences* 2(11) (2014): 149.
[71] Vatanka, *Iran and Pakistan*, 27–8.
[72] Ibid., 171
[73] Rafique, Maqsood and Naureen, 'Pak–Iran Cultural and Historical Ties', 149.
[74] 'Poets and Writers Praise Services of Khana-e-Farhang', *The News*, 19 August 2018, https://www.thenews.com.pk/print/357168-poets-and-writers-praise-services-of-khana-e-farhang.
[75] Rafique, Maqsood, and Naureen, 'Pak–Iran Cultural and Historical Ties', 146.
[76] Nye, *Soft Power: The Means to Success in World Politics*.
[77] 'New Persian-Language Course in Pakistan with the Aim of Strengthening Cultural Relations between the Two Countries', *IRNA*, 13 May 2022, https://www.irna.ir/news/84751482/%D8%AF%D9%88%D8%B1%D9%87-%D8%AC%D8%AF%DB%8C%D8%AF-%D8%A2%D9%85%D9%88%D8%B2%D8%B4-%D8%B2%D8%A8%D8%A7%D9%86-%D9%81%D8%A7%D8%B1%D8%B3%DB%8C-%D8%AF%D8%B1-%D9%BE%D8%A7%DA%A9%D8%B3%D8%AA%D8%A7%D9%86-%D8%A8%D8%A7-%D9%87%D8%AF%D9%81-%D8%AA%D9%82%D9%88%DB%8C%D8%AA-%D8%B1%D9%88%D8%A7%D8%A8%D8%B7-%D9%81%D8%B1%D9%87%D9%86%DA%AF%DB%8C.

The vast majority of our research participants from Pakistan acknowledged the influence of the Persian language in Pakistan over the course of history and in the contemporary era. According to a participant at the Iqbal International Institute for Research and Dialogue (IRD), the Persian language has provided a strong tool for Iranians to exert influence in Pakistan: 'Their language, i.e., Persian, has a special relation with the entire region. I think this is their success.'[78] A researcher at the International Islamic University in Islamabad added that, 'for long, the Persian language remained the identity of Muslims of the subcontinent. Our religious literature was in the Persian language. Our national poet Muhammad Iqbal has written in Persian. In his poetry, he called Iran an important state of the East.'[79] The use of the Persian language 'as a tool of communication in the Mughal Emperor's court' was also noted.[80] Owing to the influence of the Persian language, another participant explained, Iran's influence in Pakistan which predated the Iranian Revolution of 1979 is 'normal and natural'.[81] Along similar lines, a professor at Quaid-i-Azam University in Islamabad emphasised that the influence of Iran in Pakistan did not begin with the birth of the Islamic Republic in Iran, but has its roots in the historical connections between the two countries.[82] The argument was also made that if 'we did not have Urdu, Persian would be the national language of Pakistan'. Urdu as a language is also greatly influenced by Persian; according to one participant, this influence can be seen in more than 50 per cent of Urdu vocabulary.[83] According to another participant, the Persian language was 'more attractive for Shi'as and the Barelvi school of Islamic thought, but not for the Deobandi school', and it was argued that through the language Iran has been able to attract those who subscribe to either the Barelvi or Shi'a schools of thought.[84] Participants often noted that the Persian influence on Pakistani culture is observable in poetry and architecture. One participant stated that, 'Iranian influence can be seen in architecture, music and poetry as well. Alama Iqbal's great work in the Persian language has made common people think he was a Persian.'[85] Other participants also emphasised the importance of the Iranian influence on Pakistani literature and poetry.[86]

It is important to note that the Iranian cultural centres have sponsored the publication of books written about Persian literature in Pakistan. For example, Syed Ghayoor Hussain, who has been teaching Persian language and literature at *Khana-e-Farhang*, wrote a book in 2016 about Persian literature titled *Qand-e Parsi* (*The Sweetness of Persia*) – sponsored by *Khana-e-Farhang*. In parts of this book,

---

[78] P1, interviewed on 16 May 2019, Islamabad.
[79] P12, interviewed on 27 May 2019, Islamabad.
[80] P16, interviewed on 27 May 2019, Islamabad.
[81] P4, interviewed on 9 May 2019, Islamabad.
[82] P5, interviewed on 14 May 2019, Islamabad.
[83] Ibid.
[84] P15, interviewed on 29 May 2019, Islamabad.
[85] P5, interviewed on 14 May 2019, Islamabad.
[86] P7, interviewed on 10 May 2019, Islamabad.

the poems of Hafiz and Saadi, two prominent classical Persian poets, are quoted. Some poems by Pakistan's national poet, Muhammad Iqbal, are also included in the book.[87] As mentioned earlier, several prominent poets of Pakistan or the Indian subcontinent, such as Mirza Asadullah Ghalib and Muhammad Iqbal, composed poetry in Persian. Iranian cultural centres have benefited from this legacy by offering courses on Iqbal's poetry. For example, the *Khana-e-Farhang* in Pakistan's northwestern city of Peshawar began classes on Iqbal's Persian masterpiece titled *Javed Nama* in 2018. These classes were claimed to have been launched in response to the significant demand of 'Persian lovers in the city'.[88] This Iranian cultural centre has also been active in offering classes in Persian art and calligraphy.[89]

Iran's cultural influence in Pakistan is not limited to the areas of language and literature, but also, as in the case of Afghanistan, extends to student exchange programmes. In November 2004, on the occasion of the visit of Hussein Amini, the governor of Iran's Sistan and Baluchestan Province, and Owais Ghani, the governor of Balochistan Province in Pakistan, an agreement was signed on student and teacher exchange programmes between the two provinces.[90] In addition to student exchange programmes, delegations from official Iranian media outlets also frequently visit Pakistan. Iranian journalists, some of whom are affiliated with government organisations, have also settled in various cities of Pakistan.[91] Despite these efforts, Iran's influence on the Pakistani media is far less significant than its media influence in Afghanistan. A few of our Pakistani participants believed that the media and some magazines in Pakistan are influenced by Iran; for instance, according to a researcher from the International Islamic University in Islamabad, 'If you read "Express" in Pakistan, an article in favour of Iran is scheduled to be published daily. The other media channels can also be seen promoting the same.'[92] Most participants, however, did not believe that the influence of Iran on the Pakistani media is significant.

During recent years, Iran has increased its cultural activities in Pakistan through the *Khana-e-Farhang* network. An MoU was signed in 2019 between Pakistan's Institute for Art and Culture (IAC) and the *Khana-e-Farhang* in Lahore to enhance collaboration between the two institutions. Matters such as cultural exchange programmes for artists and students as well as conducting joint research and other collaborative projects were discussed in the meeting between the director of Lahore's *Khana-e-Farhang* and IAC's vice chancellor. The IAC also committed to convene an Iranian film festival and invite some professionals to deliver talks. *Khana-e-Farhang*

---

[87] 'All-in-one Book Published for Persian learners', *The News*, 23 August 2016, https://www.thenews.com.pk/print/144596-All-in-one-book-published-for-Persian-learners.

[88] 'Iran Cultural Centre to Arrange Classes on Iqbal Lahori', *Islamic Culture and Relations Organization*, 24 December 2018, http://islamabad.icro.ir/index.aspx?pageid=11661&newsview=720543.

[89] 'Iran Cultural Centre to Arrange Classes on Iqbal Lahori'.

[90] Rafique, Maqsood and Naureen, 'Pak–Iran Cultural and Historical Ties', 147.

[91] Ibid., 149.

[92] P12, interviewed on 27 May 2019, Islamabad.

announced that it would set up a place at the IAC where books and documents about Iranian culture and art would be displayed.[93] *Khana-e-Farhang*'s activities did not stop during the coronavirus outbreak; from mid-2020 *Khana-e-Farhang* has been offering virtual Persian-language classes to Pakistani students.[94]

It should be noted that Quetta, the provincial capital of Pakistani Balochistan and home to a significant number of Shi'a and ethnic Hazaras, hosts an Iranian cultural centre. As Vatanka notes, 'In Quetta, Iran's religious and cultural influences are perhaps more visible in this area than elsewhere in Pakistan.'[95] The cultural centre in Quetta seeks to enhance and promote sociocultural relations between the citizens of the two countries in various ways, including the exchange of scholars, intellectuals, businessmen and students. It offers Persian courses as well as courses in various fields such as calligraphy and classical Persian music.[96] The Hazara community of Quetta has regular interaction with Shi'a religious figures, for example, from Qom, and often organises lectures involving Qom-based scholars in Quetta.[97] Some Pakistani research participants highlighted that Iran's influence is greater in certain Shi'a majority areas and border regions in Balochistan.[98] The existence of the Baloch population in both countries has been considered a key factor that can enhance Iran's influence in Pakistan. According to a former senator who was interviewed in Islamabad, the Baloch population should never be ignored when speaking about Iran's influence in Pakistan.[99] Likewise, an interviewee from the Pak Institute for Peace Studies (PIPS) stated that 'there is a significant influence of Iran in Balochistan primarily because of trade. That region's dependence is on Iran.'[100]

When it comes to Iran's religious influence on Shi'as in Pakistan, many participants mentioned Iran's influence in areas such as Khuram Agency and Quetta as being significant.[101] Iranian influence was also observed to be 'greater in Shi'a majority regions of Pakistan like Hazara, Karachi, Chakwal, Bhakkar', with a strong 'pro-Iran sentiment' visible in these regions.[102] Iran's influence was also argued to be significant in areas such as Gilgit-Baltistan.[103] Indeed, several participants stated that Iranian influence is more observable in those areas of Pakistan with significant Shi'a populations, which some considered 'natural', stating that the 'people

---

[93] 'IAC, Khana-i-Farhang Sign MoU to Forge Cultural Linkages', *Dawn*, 20 December 2019, https://www.dawn.com/news/1523202.
[94] 'Virtual Persian Language Course to be Held in Pakistan', *Islamic Republic News Agency*, 12 June 2020, https://en.irna.ir/news/83818833/Virtual-Persian-language-course-to-be-held-in-Pakistan.
[95] Vatanka, *Iran and Pakistan*, 239.
[96] Rafique, Maqsood and Naureen, 'Pak–Iran Cultural and Historical Ties', 147.
[97] Ibid.
[98] P8, interviewed on 20 May 2019, Islamabad.
[99] P25, interviewed on 20 June 2019, Islamabad.
[100] P6, interviewed on 24 May 2019, Islamabad.
[101] P8, interviewed on 20 May 2019, Islamabad.
[102] P16, interviewed on 27 May 2019, Islamabad.
[103] P19, interviewed on 28 May 2019, Islamabad.

of those areas have a soft corner for Iran'.[104] A former general in the Pakistan army mentioned other Shi'a communities in Pakistan, including the Agha-Khanis and the Noorbukhshis, noting that the former, in particular, 'look towards Iran and have an affinity with them'.[105] The connections between Iranian and Pakistani Shi'as were also considered as a kind of 'spiritual link'.[106] Despite the Iranian influence in parts of Pakistan with significant Shi'a populations, one of our participants explained that such influence was also somewhat visible in other parts of Pakistan, such as 'Gilgit Baltistan, Kohat, Parachinar, the old city in Peshawar [and] Punjab as well'.[107]

With regard to Iran's religious soft power in Pakistan, it should be noted that Iran hosts many Pakistani Shi'a pilgrims annually. The shrine of Imam Reza, located in the Iranian city of Mashhad, is the key location visited by Pakistani Shi'a pilgrims, and has presented a great opportunity for Iran to enhance its goodwill. This was indicated in President Ebrahim Raisi's meeting with the Pakistani foreign minister in June 2022. Raisi, who is a former custodian of Astan-e Qods-e Razavi, stated in the meeting that: 'The majority of the foreign pilgrims [coming] to the shrine of Imam Reza are Pakistanis and their love for the *ahl al-bayt* is well-known.' Raisi also said that the visits of Pakistani Shi'a pilgrims to Iran contributes to the close relationship between Iran and Pakistan. Several key Pakistani politicians have visited the shrine, including former prime ministers Benazir Bhutto and Imran Khan. To increase its attractiveness, a key goal of soft power strategies,[108] Iran provides unique services to Pakistani Shi'a pilgrims. Most prominently, Iran has constructed the Imam Reza Pilgrimage House at the Mirjaveh–Taftan border crossing, which is the key road connection between Iran and Pakistan. The Pilgrimage House facilitates Pakistani pilgrims' travel to Iran and it has a capacity of more than 2,000 beds and provides various free services to pilgrims.[109] Further, Astan-e Quds also plans to establish free hostels for Pakistani pilgrims in Mashhad to facilitate their travel.[110]

Iran often emphasises other aspects of its identity and cultural norms, such as Nowruz, a New Year festival that falls on the spring equinox, in its diplomatic engagement with countries in which Nowruz is celebrated. In Pakistan, Nowruz is celebrated in areas such as the northern Gilgit-Baltistan region, parts of the Khyber Pakhtunkhwa Province bordering Afghanistan, and in some parts of Balochistan like Quetta. Iranian presidents send felicitations on the occasion to many countries, especially Pakistan, as a means of emphasising their intimate cultural

---

[104] P7, interviewed on 10 May 2019, Islamabad.
[105] P18, interviewed on 30 May 2019, Islamabad.
[106] P13, interviewed on 17 May 2019, Islamabad.
[107] P27, interviewed on 4 May 2019, Islamabad.
[108] Nye, 'Soft Power', 167.
[109] *Hawza News*, '30 Million Pilgrims Visit the Holy Shrine of Imam Reza Annually'.
[110] 'With the Cooperation of Āstān-e Quds-e Razavī, a Pakistani Pilgrimage House Will be Built in Mashhad', *Qudsonline*, 19 September 2019, https://www.qudsonline.ir/news/671042.

connections.¹¹¹ Iranian cultural centres in Pakistan also host Nowruz celebrations, and many locals – mainly Shi'as – attend such events held at their nearby *Khana-e-Farhang*.¹¹² One such Nowruz celebration in Pakistan was attended by Pakistani president Arif Alvi in March 2019, at which he met with the Iranian ambassador to Pakistan and praised the Iranian cultural adviser's efforts in convening the event.¹¹³ Some of our Pakistani interviewees explained that Nowruz is being celebrated in several Pakistani regions, which is another sign of Iran's soft power in Pakistan.¹¹⁴

Another key activity of Iranian cultural centres in Pakistan has been the offering of courses on the history of Shiism and the theory of *velayat-e faqih*. Shi'a scholars from Iran often attend Iranian cultural centre activities, and, at times, these scholars have been targeted by Sunni extremist groups in Pakistan.¹¹⁵ Since the Iranian Revolution, as Zahab notes, 'Iranian cultural centres (*khana-e farhang*) in Pakistan became very active, distributing works by prominent ulama translated into Urdu as well as anti-Wahabi literature'.¹¹⁶ In addition, hundreds of scholarships are granted by the Islamic Republic to Pakistanis for religious studies in Iran, for example, facilitating their enrolment in certain courses at Qom seminaries. According to one estimate, about 4,000 Pakistani students received scholarships in the 1980s and attended courses introducing them to the doctrine of the Guardianship of the Jurist. Upon their return to Pakistan, these students introduced *velayat-e faqih* to other Pakistani Shi'as.¹¹⁷ This was important in the 1980s given that many Pakistani Shi'as were followers of Iraqi Ayatollah al-Khoi, who was against the theory of *velayat-e faqih*, and argued that the clergy have no significant place in running the government during the era of the occultation of Imam Mahdi.¹¹⁸ Iran's use of scholarships to entice Pakistani students to study in Iran has continued during the first decades of the twenty-first century. In 2016, the Islamic Republic of Iran's Ministry of Science, Research and Technology stated that it would seek to foster stronger ties with Pakistan through higher education, and thus declared that it would

---

¹¹¹ Shahram Akbarzadeh and James Barry, 'State Identity in Iranian Foreign Policy', *British Journal of Middle Eastern Studies* 43(4) (2016): 617.

¹¹² 'Jashn e Nowruz Celebrations', *The Nation*, 25 March 2018, https://nation.com.pk/25-Mar-2018/jashn-e-nowruz-celebrations1?show=previewutm_medium=Politic.

¹¹³ 'Nowruz Celebrated in Pakistan with Iran's Active Participation', *Islamic Republic News Agency*, 25 March 2019, https://en.irna.ir/news/83253459/Nowruz-celebrated-in-Pakistan-with-Iran-s-active-participation.

¹¹⁴ P5, interviewed on 14 May 2019, Islamabad.

¹¹⁵ See, e.g., 'Shia Scholars among Four Killed in "Sectarian" Attack', *The News*, 25 February 2014, https://www.thenews.com.pk/archive/print/487302-shia-scholar-among-four-killed-in-%E2%80%98sectarian%E2%80%99-attacks.

¹¹⁶ Mariam Abou Zahab, 'The Politicization of the Shia Community in Pakistan in the 1970s and 1980s', in Alessandro Monsutti, Silvia Naef and Farian Sabahi (eds), *The Other Shiites: From the Mediterranean to Central Asia* (Bern: Peter Lang, 2007), 101.

¹¹⁷ Zahab, 'The Politicization of the Shia Community', 101.

¹¹⁸ See Naser Ghobadzadeh, *The Religious Secularity: A Theological Challenge to the Islamic State* (New York: Oxford University Press, 2015), 153.

award scholarships to Pakistani students in fields such as geosciences, electrical and hydrocarbon engineering.[119]

Iran's educational influence in Pakistan was also acknowledged by some of our participants.[120] Some noted that education is a key instrument enabling Iran to attract Shi'a students from Pakistan. For instance, one interviewee from the International Islamic University Islamabad, stated that, 'around 35,000 Pakistani students are studying in Iran and at the National University of Modern Languages (NUML), the last semester of a masters in Persian includes Iranian literature [courses] and a visit to Iran'.[121] The impact of Iran's soft power has also been noted in Shi'a Pakistani students who travel to Iran to study. It has been argued that 'many students from Pakistan go there [Iran] for study. It is obvious that they get influenced by the *fatwas* and teachings or Iranian thought' while studying there.[122] Another participant noted that 'Iran is an important destination for Shi'a pilgrims [including Pakistani Shi'as]. Many Shi'a students go to Iran to pursue their education. This social interaction has enhanced bilateral affiliation and coordination.'[123]

Iran has often sought to support cultural ceremonies associated with Shi'a ideology in Pakistan. In particular, the Hazara community in Quetta has engaged in ceremonies such as the celebration of Ashura in the month of Muharram. During such activities, colourful posters of Ayatollah Khomeini are often visible.[124] Popular slogans initiated by the Islamic Republic, including those against the United States and Israel, are also known to have been chanted after Friday prayers in many Pakistani Shi'a mosques.[125] In the subsequent discussion, we explore prominent Shi'a groups in Pakistan that have had close ties with Iran and have been influenced by Iran's political ideology, including its anti-American agenda since the 1980s. These groups represent Iranian ideological influence in Pakistan. We do not explain Iranian influence in Pakistan's formal politics in this section, but will discuss it in Chapter 6.

Tehrik-i-Nifaz-i-Fiqah-i-Jafria (TNFJ)

Tehrik-i-Nifaz-i-Fiqah-i-Jafaria (TNFJ) is a Shi'a political party in Pakistan with close ties to Iran. Under the leadership of Allamah Jaffer Hussein, the TNFJ was

---

[119] 'Iran Higher Education Scholarships for Pakistani Nationals', *Islamic Republic of Iran: Ministry of Science, Research and Technology*, http://www.unesco.org/new/fileadmin/MULTIMEDIA/FIELD/Tehran/images/PAKISTANFINAL.pdf.
[120] P13, interviewed on 17 May 2019, Islamabad.
[121] P12, interviewed on 27 May 2019, Islamabad.
[122] P20, interviewed on 23 May 2019, Islamabad.
[123] P21, interviewed on 24 May 2019, Islamabad.
[124] Zahab, 'The Politicization of the Shia Community', 101; Hassan Abbas, 'Shiism and Sectarian Conflict in Pakistan: Identity Politics, Iranian Influence, and Tit-for-Tat Violence', *Combating Terrorism Center*, 22 September 2010, https://ctc.usma.edu/wp-content/uploads/2011/05/CTC-OP-Abbas-21-September.pdf, 29.
[125] Abbas, 'Shiism and Sectarian Conflict in Pakistan', 28–9.

inspired by Ayatollah Khomeini and the Iranian Islamic revolution.[126] After Hussein's death in 1984, the TNFJ split into two groups: one led by Arif Hussaini, the other by Hamid Moosavi. Although these two groups had different approaches and strategies – Moosavi's ideas were oriented around the traditional mould (more religiously inclined), while Hussaini's ideas reflected the modern reformist tendency (more politically inclined) within Shiism – both leaders considered themselves to be followers of Khomeini.[127] Hussaini, originally from Khurram Agency, had studied at Shi'a seminaries in Najaf and Qom, and was strongly supported by Ayatollah Khomeini.[128] Some sources report that Ayatollah Khomeini himself appointed Hussaini as his representative in Pakistan after the death of Allamah Jaffer Hussein.[129] In turn, Hussaini supported the Iranian Revolution and Khomeini's agendas. According to Rieck, 'Hussaini was probably the most ardent admirer of Khomeini among Pakistan's Shi'a *'ulama* of his generation and status.'[130] Hussaini preached Khomeini's ideas to Pakistani Shi'as and encouraged his followers to emulate Khomeini's political and religious thought. Hussaini also introduced the observance of Quds Day in Pakistan in 1984, later adding a 'Death to America Day'.[131]

In one interview, Hussaini stated that an Islamic system of government based on the Iranian political system could 'serve as a working model' for his country.[132] In this interview, Hussaini supported the agenda of the Iranian Revolution, stating that this revolution gave Muslims, especially those living in Islamic countries, the impression that 'a life of dignity is possible only under the protection of Islam'.[133] According to Hussaini, the Iranian Revolution had an anti-imperialist message – a message that Hussaini considered a necessity for many nations in the world: 'The Iranian revolution has destroyed the belief that governments or nations must look towards either the USA or the Soviet Union for their existence. It has demonstrated that nations can live safely under the protection of Islam even if they defy both superpowers.'[134] Hussaini also supported Iran in the 1987 Mecca incident where a clash occurred between Shi'a pilgrims and the Saudi Arabian security forces. For Hussaini, 'Iranian Muslims were raising slogans in Mecca on the occasion of *haj* against America and the Soviet Union. God has permitted Muslims to rise

---

[126] Maleeha Lodhi, 'Pakistan's Shia Movement: An Interview with Arif Hussaini', *Third World Quarterly* 10(2) (1988): 806.

[127] Ibid.

[128] Rieck, *The Shias of Pakistan*, 221.

[129] Ahmad K. Majidyar, 'The Shiites of Pakistan?: A Minority Under Siege', *American Enterprise Institute*, 2014, https://www.aei.org/research-products/report/the-shiites-of-pakistan-a-minority-under-siege 129.

[130] Rieck, *The Shias of Pakistan*, 220.

[131] Ibid.

[132] Lodhi, 'Pakistan's Shia Movement: An Interview with Arif Hussaini', 811.

[133] Ibid.

[134] Ibid.

against the infidels and to get rid of them.'¹³⁵ In November 1987, Hussaini participated in the 'International Congress on Safeguarding the Sanctity and Security of the Holy *Haram*' in Tehran, which 'demanded to put the holy places of Islam under international Muslim supervision'.¹³⁶

Tehrik-e-Jafaria Pakistan (TJP)

The TJP, or Tehrik-e-Islami, another influential Shi'a political party in Pakistan, is an offshoot of the TNFJ led by Allamah Sajid Ali Naqvi. This party was strongly influenced by the Iranian Revolution and promotes the Shi'a legal system, *fiqh Jafariyya*, to Pakistani Shi'as to 'prevent imposition of the Sunni school of thought' in the country.¹³⁷ Tehrik-e-Islami was banned twice times during the presidency of the former president of Pakistan Pervez Musharraf. More recently, the party has been one of the supporters of the Iranian government in Pakistan. For example, once the result of the 2009 presidential election in Iran was declared, Naqvi announced his support for Ahmadinejad's re-election, stating that Ahmadinejad enjoyed the trust and support of Iranians. He expressed hope that Iran and Pakistan would extend their relationship during Ahmadinejad's second term.¹³⁸ Later in September 2011, Naqvi attended the 'First International Islamic Awakening Conference' in Tehran. At this conference, Naqvi supported Tehran's regional policy, stating that Iran under the leadership of Ayatollah Khamenei would 'transform' the entire region after the political upheaval in a few Arab countries.¹³⁹

Majlis Wahdat-e-Muslimeen (MWM)

The MWM (Council of Unity of Muslims) also maintains a strong relationship with Tehran. It was founded in April 2008 in Punjab.¹⁴⁰ The group supports Iran's foreign policy, has organised rallies in Pakistan against the US presence in the region, and has often asked Pakistani policymakers to strengthen Pakistan's ties with Iran. The ideas of the group's secretary general, Allama Raja Nasir Abbas, reflect Iran's anti-American ideology. In 2012, Abbas termed the US embassy and consulates as 'the real centers of terrorism in Pakistan' and warned that the Shi'as would 'expel the Americans from Pakistan if the state institutions failed to do so'.¹⁴¹

---

[135] Ibid., 816.
[136] Rieck, *The Shias of Pakistan*, 230.
[137] 'TJP and TNFJ'.
[138] Ariel Farrar-Wellman, 'Pakistan–Iran Foreign Relations', *Critical Threats*, 5 July 2010, https://www.criticalthreats.org/analysis/pakistan-iran-foreign-relations#_ftn1.
[139] Alex Vatanka, 'The Guardian of Pakistan's Shia', *Hudson Institute*, 1 June 2012, https://www.hudson.org/research/9863-the-guardian-of-pakistan-s-shia.
[140] Rieck, *The Shias of Pakistan*, 311.
[141] Ibid.

The influence of Iran on the MWM has been visible from the very beginning of its establishment. Three years after the formal establishment of the MWM, Abbas revealed that before the establishment of his group, he had contacted the office of Iran's supreme leader for advice and received the message that the 'inaction of Shi'as should end in Pakistan'. He also stated at one point that 'he considered those believing in the guardianship of the Islamic jurisprudence part of the MWM'.[142] Nasir Abbas' connection to Tehran is confirmed by his strong support of *velayat-e faqih*. According to him, 'Islam is a complete and perfect religion and code of life and it has a political system in the form of guardianship of Islamic jurisprudence.'[143]

Senior leaders of the MWM often express their support of the Iranian Revolution and leaders including Khomeini and Khamenei on the anniversary of the Islamic Revolution of 1979. In a seminar held in the port city of Karachi, Pakistan, in February 2014, in connection with the thirty-fifth anniversary of the Islamic Revolution, Abbas praised the Iranian Revolution of 1979, and spoke about Iran's role in resisting imperialism. He stressed that Ayatollah Khomeini's policy vis-à-vis the United States should be emulated in Pakistan.[144] He also emphasised that the Iranian Revolution was a 'revolution against tyranny', stating that the 'Islamic Revolution was not limited to Iranians; rather it was a world revolution against tyranny', which should be emulated by many people in the region including Pakistanis, Iraqis, Syrians, Palestinians, Lebanese, Yemenis and Egyptians.[145] Other members of the party made speeches in this seminar and criticised US foreign policy in the region and demanded that the government of Pakistan should base its relations with the United States solely on the value of mutual respect.[146]

When a terrorist attack was carried out in the Iranian city of Ahvaz in 2018, the deputy secretary general of Pakistan's MWM, Allamah Sayyed Ahmad Iqbal Razavi, visited the Iranian consulate in Karachi and offered his condolences to Ahmad Mohammadi, the consul general of the Islamic Republic of Iran.[147] In his meeting with Mohammadi, Razavi supported Iran and condemned US policy in the region, stating that 'the Ahvaz terrorist attack is a sign of the weakness of the United States and the Arab countries who are trying to take action against the Iranian people by resorting to Daesh'.[148] MWM's secretary had condemned the terrorist attack

---

[142] 'A Particular Mindset is Trying to Push Shia Muslims to Wall', *Shiite News*, 7 June 2012, http://shiitenews.org/shiitenews/pakistan-news/item/1338-a-particular-mindset-trying-to-push-shia-muslims-to-wall.

[143] 'A particular mindset is trying to push Shia Muslims to wall'.

[144] 'Imam Khomeini Aroused Oppressed People of the World: Raja Nasir Jafari', *Islam Times*, 12 February 2014, https://www.islamtimes.org/en/news/350753/imam-khomeini-aroused-oppressed-people-of-the-world-raja-nasir-jafari.

[145] Ibid.

[146] Ibid.

[147] 'Pakistan's Majlis Wahdat-e-Muslimeen Condemns the Terrorist Attack in Ahvaz', *Rasa News Agency*, 28 September 2018, https://en.rasanews.ir/en/news/440720/pakistan%e2%80%99s-majlis-wahdat-e-muslimeen-condemns-the-terrorist-attack-in-ahvaz.

[148] Ibid.

in Ahvaz prior to this meeting, suggesting that it had been orchestrated by certain Arab states.[149]

In May 2018, Allama Raja Nasir stated that the United States puts pressure on Pakistan to stay away from Iran even though Iran is the only country that can address Pakistan's energy needs. The pressure from the United States and its allies, he stressed, causes Pakistan to lose many opportunities to enhance its trade with Iran – an issue that will be discussed in details in Chapter 6.[150] Further, in a meeting with Pakistani prime minister Imran Khan, Nasir stressed the importance of enhancing Pakistan–Iran relations.[151] Seeking to influence Pakistan's foreign policy, he told Imran Khan that 'the enemies are trying to weaken the country but this challenge can be effectively overcome through national unity', and asked the prime minister to strengthen Pakistan's relations with Tehran.[152]

This organisation has also organised rallies titled 'Down with USA Day' in Karachi during the past few years.[153] At one of these rallies in which protesters carried banners and placards inscribed with slogans against the United States and Israel, Abbas attended and made a speech which, broadly speaking, was in harmony with many aspects of Tehran's position concerning the United States and Israel. He spoke of the US invasions of Iraq and Afghanistan and its presence in Syria, stating that the United States has violated many international laws. The secretary general of the MWM also addressed Pakistani policymakers, saying that there was 'nothing new in President Trump's slurs against Pakistan. US administration under past presidents too had insulted the Pakistani nation time and again.'[154]

Imamia Students Organisation (ISO)

According to its leader, Syed Nasir Shirazi, the ISO came into existence before the Iranian Revolution in 1972, when secular student organisations were dominating the educational institutes of the country.[155] Before the success of the Islamic Revolution in Iran, the ISO was responsible for the needs of Shi'a students in Pakistani educational institutions and often facilitated Shi'a prayers.[156] After the revolution,

---

[149] Ibid.
[150] 'Wahdat-e-Muslimeen Protest against US', *The Nation*, 14 May 2018, https://nation.com.pk/14-May-2018/wahdat-e-muslimeen-protest-against-us.
[151] 'Top Pakistani Religious Leader Calls for Stronger Regional Ties with Iran', *Newsday24*, 2020, https://www.newsday24.com/iran/top-pakistani-religious-leader-calls-for-stronger-regional-ties-with-iran.
[152] 'Top Pakistani Religious Leader Calls for Stronger Regional Ties with Iran'.
[153] 'Wahdat-e-Muslimeen Protest against US'.
[154] Ibid.
[155] Amir Rana and Waqar Gillani, 'Iran Not Funding ISO: Shirazi', *Daily Times*, November 24, 2003, http://archive.vn/ab3QO.
[156] Husain Haqqani, 'Weeding Out the Heretics: Sectarianism in Pakistan: Sectarianism in Pakistan', *Hudson Institute*, 1 November 2006, https://www.hudson.org/research/9769-weeding-out-the-heretics-sectarianism-in-pakistan.

the ISO expanded its activities. It began to offer scholarships to Shi'a students to study in Iran and engaged in political activities.[157] It should be noted that the ISO organised demonstrations in Pakistan against the Shah before the triumph of the Iranian Revolution, and was the first Shi'a group in Pakistan to publicly accept Ayatollah Khomeini as a *marja*.[158]

Sources indicate that between 50 and 70 per cent of all Shi'a students in Pakistan are members of the ISO.[159] The extent to which Tehran gives financial assistance to this organisation is unclear. In an interview with *Daily Times*, Shirazi stated that his organisation neither receives funds from Iran nor does it politically affiliate itself with Tehran. However, he admitted that his organisation has been ideologically inspired by the 'spiritual guidance' of Ayatollah Khamenei.[160] According to Shirazi, 'the ISO has no political links with Iran. Iran is only the source of ideological inspiration to us.'[161]

The assassination of Qasem Soleimani

The Iranian ideological influence on Pakistani Shi'as, especially Iran's anti-American and anti-Israeli rhetoric, became more noticeable after the assassination of Iranian general Qasem Soleimani by the United States in January 2020. Syed Hamid Ali Shah Moosavi, the leader of the TNFJ, condemned Soleimani's killing, calling the American attack a 'naked aggression'. Moosavi stated that 'America has tarnished the UN constitution by attacking Iran's sovereignty', calling on the Pakistani government to 'condemn the American attack in bold and clear words'. Moosavi called for the unity of Muslims and condemned the 'Zionist powers', which, according to him, 'are putting all efforts to override the Islamic world'.[162] Two other groups, the MWM and ISO, also strongly condemned the killing of Soleimani at a demonstration in Islamabad. The senior members of these Shi'a groups called on the leaders of the Muslim world, especially the Pakistani government, not to remain silent about the assassination of Soleimani and US policy in the region.[163] They also declared solidarity with the Iranians and chanted the 'Death to America' slogan at the demonstration.[164]

The MWM organised a protest and called the killing of Suleimani an 'act of international terrorism'.[165] At the demonstration, MWM's leader Allama Hasan

---

[157] Ibid.
[158] Majidyar, 'The Shiites of Pakistan?', 129
[159] Ibid.
[160] Rana and Gillani, 'Iran Not Funding ISO: Shirazi'.
[161] Ibid.
[162] *Tehreek e Nifaz e Fiqah Jafariya*, 4 January 2020, https://www.tnfj.org/sec/rnd.htm#4jan20.
[163] 'Protests Held in Pakistan to Condemn Assassination of General Suleimani', *Islamic Republic News Agency*, 3 January 2020, https://en.irna.ir/news/83618950/Protests-held-in-Pakistan-to-condemn-assassination-of-General.
[164] 'Protests Held in Pakistan to Condemn Assassination of General Suleimani'.
[165] 'MWM Protests in Karachi against Killing of Soleimani', *The News*, 4 January 2020, https://www.thenews.com.pk/print/593358-mwm-protests-in-karachi-against-killing-of-soleimani.

Zafar Naqvi, stressed his anti-American views. In line with Tehran's anti-American sentiments, he stated that the killing of those who defended Muslim sacred sites in Iraq and Syria, that is, Suleimani and Abu Mahdi al-Muhandis, by the United States shows that it supports the terrorists. He even urged the rulers of Muslim countries to halt their diplomatic relations with the United States.[166] Secretary general Abbas said that the entire Muslim world was grieving and felt anger over the killing of Soleimani.[167]

Further, leaders of several Shi'a groups such as the ISO, Jafaria Alliance, MWM and Ulema-e-Imamia decided to convene on the fortieth day after the killing of Soleimani (on 9 February 2020), in order to observe *Chehlum* for him.[168] Shi'as hold a *Chehlum* ceremony to commemorate the fortieth day after a person's death, and these commemorations are at times political, for example, during the Iranian Revolution. During the celebration, Shi'a groups defended Iranian policy with regard to the United States and Israel was clearly visible. For example, Abbas spoke about Soleimani's activities, stating that he defeated the US plot in the region, and many participants chanted slogans against the United States and Israel.[169] He defended Tehran's anti-US policy, stating that 'the protection and survival of the Ummah lies in staying away from the US, which always stabs from the back and reneges on commitments and promises'.[170] MWM's deputy secretary general Rizvi also made a speech about Soleimani, stating that 'General Suleimani lives on in the hearts of all free people', while condemning the US policy in the region.[171]

According to most of our Pakistani research participants, the Shi'a ideology is a key source of Iranian soft power in Pakistan. They believed that Iran aims to support Shi'a groups in Pakistan to counter Saudi Arabia's influence in the region. Several participants suggested that many local Shi'as are uncomfortable with the growing alignment of Pakistan and Saudi Arabia. Noting that Pakistan has the second largest Shi'a community after Iran and that around 40 million Shi'as live in Pakistan; one participant, for instance, stated that it is natural that Iran uses Shiism to exercise its influence in Pakistan.[172] Participants observed that the vast majority of Shi'as in Pakistan hold the Iranian government in high esteem and that Iran's revolutionary ideology has influenced Shi'as in Pakistan since the birth of Islamic Republic in Iran. For instance, one participant believed that the Iranian Revolution 'inspired people [in Pakistan] … By that time, Sunni militias [had] started emerging in

---

[166] Ibid.
[167] Ibid.
[168] 'Shia Parties Will Observe Chehlum of Qassem Soleimani in Pakistan', *Shiite News*, 21 January 2020, https://shiitenews.org/shiitenews/pakistan-news/item/108498-shia-parties-will-observe-chehlum-of-qassem-soleimani-in-pakistan.
[169] 'Islamic Countries Urged to Stay Away from Imperialist Forces', *The News*, 10 February 2020, https://www.thenews.com.pk/print/611570-islamic-countries-urged-to-stay-away-from-imperialistic-forces.
[170] Ibid.
[171] Ibid.
[172] P21, interviewed on 24 May 2019, Islamabad.

Pakistan and [they were] supported by Saudi Arabia. And there is talk that Shi'a militias originated [in Pakistan] were supported by Iran.'[173]

Iranian funding of Shi'a groups was also highlighted by several participants. Indeed, they believed that Shi'as in Pakistan are not only 'spiritually' supported by Tehran, but also receive significant funding from Tehran.[174] There is, however, no concrete evidence available to back up such claims. Some participants noted the influence of groups supported by Tehran, such as the TJP and TNFJ, especially in areas such as Multan, Lahore and Faisalabad during the 1980s and 1990s; however, as other participants noted, the influence of these groups has lessened since the 2000s.[175]

Even though most interviewees indicated that Iran exercises a significant level of influence on areas of Pakistan with large Shi'a populations, a few participants noted that Iran has a certain degree of influence over Pakistani Sunnis too.[176] Iran's influence on Sunni populations in Makran was argued to be related to the fact that people's 'economic activities heavily depend on Iran'.[177] Similarly, another participant mentioned that Iran's influence is not often restricted to one particular area or region: 'Apart from Upper Kurram, Iran's ideological influence is scattered because the Shi'a population in Pakistan is scattered.'[178] It was also acknowledged that Shi'a groups in Pakistan are not only supported by Iran, but also by Shi'a organisations in other countries of the region. For example, one interviewee noted the support of Kuwait-based Shi'a organisations and charities. He further added:

> It cannot be ruled out that Iran and such Shi'a organisations are on the same page but at the same time, they are different as they are coming from different countries. There might be some coherence and understanding on a policy-level, but it is not just Iran. The effect of the Shi'a revival can be seen from different sources.[179]

Conclusion

While Iran has similar interests in terms of the promotion of its soft power through ideological and cultural interventions in Afghanistan and Pakistan, for example, through its cultural centres and links with and influence on Shi'a groups, different dynamics are evident in each case. Iran enjoys certain advantages, including a demographic advantage in the form of a sizeable Shi'a population in both countries, and a historical advantage in the deep imprint of the Persian colonial legacy. Using

---

[173] P28, interviewed on 20 May 2019, Islamabad.
[174] P27, interviewed on 4 May 2019, Islamabad.
[175] P11, interviewed on 16 May 2019, Islamabad.
[176] P24, interviewed on 2 June 2019, Islamabad; P13, interviewed on 17 May 2019, Islamabad.
[177] P6, interviewed on 24 May 2019, Islamabad.
[178] P28, interviewed on 20 May 2019, Islamabad.
[179] P19, interviewed on 28 May 2019, Islamabad.

these levers, Iran has employed a variety of instruments, including Persian heritage and the promotion of Shiism, to create a positive image in both countries.

The impact, however, varies in each state. Iran enjoys much greater influence in Afghanistan than in Pakistan because Tehran has been able to invest in infrastructure, particularly through the creation of educational and media institutions, to pursue its national interest. This was particularly the case in Afghanistan during the period 2001–2021, when Iran's economic, political and cultural influence increased significantly in the country. As far as educational cooperation is concerned, Tehran's strategy is not only limited to targeting Afghan Shi'as, that is, Hazaras, as it has also been offering scholarships to Sunnis and Afghans of all ethnicities. In contrast, Iran's influence in Pakistan is not so multifaceted and is largely limited to the country's Shi'a population, especially in the Shi'a majority areas of Gilgit-Baltistan and Parachinar in the northwest of Pakistan. Iran's cultural and ideological influence in both countries is visible in Shi'as' celebration of Nowruz and the anniversary of Imam Khomeini's death. In terms of how Iran's ideological and cultural influence is received in both these states, our research participants largely reflected on Iran's influence over Shi'a populations in both countries for political gain, although, as stated, Iran's influence on Sunnis in both countries was also acknowledged to a certain degree by some of our research participants. In Chapter 6 we examine further the degree to which Iran has managed to gain political influence in both Afghanistan and Pakistan.

6
Iran's Political Influence

Focusing on Iran's political influence in Afghanistan and Pakistan in this chapter, we explore how Tehran has employed a variety of soft and hard power tools to gain influence over certain political groups in both countries. Subsequent to the discussion in Chapter 5 on Iran's support of Shi'a groups in Afghanistan and Pakistan, this chapter analyses whether Tehran has used its soft power to influence domestic politics in these two neighbouring states. The chapter provides a brief history of Iranian political influence after the establishment of the Islamic Republic and then proceeds to examine this influence in the contemporary period. Its main focus is the evolution of the Iranian influence on domestic politics in Afghanistan and Pakistan. In Afghanistan, we also examine Tehran's reaction to the Taliban's return to power in August 2021. In Pakistan, we focus particularly on the PPP, which has been viewed as a pro-Iran political party. After analysing Iran's political influence in both countries, we examine the role of the Quds Force and how its recent change of leadership is likely to influence Iran's soft power especially in Afghanistan.

The case of Afghanistan

After the emergence of the Islamic Republic in Iran in 1979, Tehran began to support Shi'a groups in Afghanistan, especially those that followed Khomeini's political ideology. Several Afghan Shi'a groups formed Afghanistan's Hazara-dominated Hezb-e Wahdat political party.[1] During the Afghan–Soviet War, Iran supported Shi'a mujahideen, while the majority Sunni mujahideen received support from Saudi Arabia, Pakistan and the United States.[2] During the 1990s, Iran's involvement in Afghan politics and its support of certain groups increased for two reasons. First, the Iran–Iraq War ended in 1988, and this allowed Tehran to expand more resources in Afghanistan. Secondly, as explained in Chapter 4, with the rise of the Taliban to power in 1996, Iran was confronted by the strong presence of an anti-Shi'a regime in Afghanistan, which encouraged Iran to invest more funding to support anti-Taliban factions under the Northern Alliance.[3]

---

[1] Nader et al., 'Iran and Afghanistan: A Complicated Relationship'.
[2] Ibid., 8.
[3] Saikal, *Iran Rising*, 179.

Iran's influence on domestic politics in Afghanistan increased following the fall of the Taliban government in 2001. During President Karzai's government, Tehran exercised significant influence on Kabul. The Northern Alliance, dominated by Tajik commanders, was reluctant to share power with Karzai, but Iranian political pressure on Northern Alliance leaders during negotiations in Bonn persuaded them to reach an agreement, which led to the formation of the new Afghan government.[4] As explored in Chapter 3, Iran played a significant role in Afghanistan's reconstruction programme. In December 2005, in a meeting with Iran's foreign minister in Kabul, Karzai explicitly highlighted Tehran's support for development projects in Afghanistan.[5] In 2010, Karzai confirmed that his office had received money from Iran, but stated that the United States made similar payments. Karzai said in October 2010 that, 'The government of Iran assists (my) office with five or six or seven hundred thousand euros once or twice a year, which is official aid.'[6] Some funds received from Tehran, according to Karzai, were used for presidential office expenses and staff salaries. Karzai stated, 'Cash payments are done by various friendly countries to help the presidential office, to help expenses in various ways, [and] to help the employees around here, and people outside ... We will continue to ask for cash from Iran.'[7] When asked about the reason why the assistance was provided in cash, Karzai said, 'because of the nature of the Afghan financial system, there have been times where assistance has come into Afghanistan in the form of cash'.[8] According to some reports, payments were made to senior officials in the Karzai's government who were pursuing an anti-American policy.[9] The payments were made by Iran in order to enhance its influence and to create a significant gap between the Afghans and their American and NATO allies. One of our interviewees from Afghanistan confirmed that Karzai 'was given a box of money' during his visit to Tehran, which, for him, demonstrated how Iran influenced the Afghan government.[10] According to another interviewee, 'Iran provided Karzai with a full package of intelligence information against the US'.[11] This participant pointed to a video showing 'when the US ambassador asks Karzai to come with him, he does not [show any interest] but when Iran's ambassador asks him, he goes and [even] takes selfies with him'.[12] The overall perception of our participants was that the Karzai government was financially supported by Tehran, and Tehran, at times, paid Karzai funds in cash.

---

[4] Nader and Laha, *Iran's Balancing Act in Afghanistan*.
[5] 'Karzai: Iran's Help has Contributed to Afghanistan Development', *Iran News*, 27 December 2005, http://payvand.com/news/05/dec/1216.html.
[6] 'Karzai Says His Office Gets "Bags of Money" from Iran', *Reuters*, 25 October 2010, https://www.reuters.com/article/us-afghanistan-karzai-idUSTRE69O27Z20101025.
[7] Ibid.
[8] Ibid.
[9] Filkins, 'Iran is Said to Give Top Karzai Aide Cash by the Bagful'.
[10] A7, interviewed on 27 May 2019, Kabul.
[11] A6, interviewed on 22 May 2019, Kabul.
[12] Ibid.

There are other reports that confirm this allegation. The *New York Times* reported in 2010 that then Iranian president Mahmoud Ahmadinejad brought two boxes of cash to Kabul during a visit to Afghanistan. Ahmadinejad gave one box of cash to Daudzai – Karzai's chief of staff – and the other to the palace of Karzai. Daudzai – himself an anti-Western figure – belonged to Hezb-i Islami, which had fought the Soviet Union in the 1980s. Daudzai was the Afghan ambassador to Iran in 2005, but returned to Afghanistan in 2007 and began to work closely with Karzai. He maintained a close relationship with Iran's ambassador to Afghanistan and frequently received funds from Iran.[13]

In terms of its political influence in Afghanistan, Iran has maintained relationships with both Shi'a and non-Shi'a groups and individuals. As stated earlier, Iran has supported Shi'a Hazaras in Afghanistan. Hazara politicians occupied important government positions after the collapse of the first Taliban administration. These political groups or senators affiliated with Hazaras (in the Afghan parliament) were often supported by Tehran. According to one source, up to fifty-five members of the Afghan parliament in 2013 were Shi'as and had connections to Iran.[14] Iran's use of Shi'a groups to enhance its interests in Afghanistan was also highlighted by some of our Afghan interviewees. According to one participant, 'Iran is using ideological means to approach our Shi'a people; the main aim behind this support is to provide a superior political position for Shi'as and to use them as a shield to protect their interest.'[15] The idea that Iran approached Shi'a politicians, and sought to use them for its own political interest was a common view among our Afghan participants. Iran's outreach to Sunni political groups in Afghanistan was also highlighted by some interviewees. As stated by a former member of Afghanistan's parliament, Iran supported other communities, such as Tajiks and Pashtuns, and thus Tehran's support is not confined to Hazaras alone:

> When I was a member parliament, one of the Hazara members said that once he asked Iran to support him and Iran rejected his request, saying that we support Pashtun, Uzbek or Tajik members . . . This shows that Iranians think very strategically and they don't want to [only] support Shi'as but want to use other communities [as well].[16]

It is important to note that Tehran has also established connections with Pashtun groups. Iran has long maintained a relationship with Gulbuddin Hekmatyar's Hezb-e Islami. When the Taliban took over Kabul in 1996, Hekmatyar sought refuge in Iran and remained there until 2002. It is reported that Hekmatyar received Iranian support in his battle against US forces during the 2000s.[17] Alireza Nader states that an influential Afghan told him in an interview that 'Afghanistan's ex-ambassador to

---

[13] Filkins, 'Iran is Said to Give Top Karzai Aide Cash by the Bagful'.
[14] Nader et al., 'Iran and Afghanistan: A Complicated Relationship', 7.
[15] A6, interviewed on 22 May 2019, Kabul.
[16] A10, interviewed on 2 June 2019, Kabul.
[17] Nader et al., 'Iran and Afghanistan: A Complicated Relationship', 7.

Iran was also a previous member of Hezb-e Islami and was so close to the Islamic Republic that we all know about the bags of money that he was receiving.'[18]

As we explained in Chapter 4, reports emerged about Iran's engagement with the Taliban. Prior to the Taliban's takeover in August 2021, Iran had developed links with some Taliban leaders. For example, in 2012, it was reported that Iranian officials had allowed a member of the Taliban's leadership council to open a liaison office in Zahedan in Iran.[19] Some sources suggest that a Taliban leader, Mullah Akhtar Mansour, had travelled to Iran several times. His final visit to Iran was in May 2016 before he was killed in a US drone strike inside Pakistan after crossing the border from Iran.[20] In September 2018, *Le Figaro* reported that Taliban commanders were receiving strong financial and military support from Iran after the Trump administration's withdrawal from the nuclear deal.[21] By the end of 2018, Iranian officials began to publicise Tehran's relationship with the Taliban. For example, Iranian foreign minister Mohammad Javad Zarif confirmed Iran's contact with the Taliban, although he stressed that his country did not seek to undermine Afghanistan's National Unity government.[22]

Many of our Afghan participants agreed that Iran had supported the Taliban in Afghanistan and established strong relations with Taliban leaders before its return to power in August 2021. According to one interviewee, 'Iranians support the Taliban in Farah in Helmand in Nad-e Ali district [and] you can find the Taliban equipped with modern weapons there; all are being supported by Iran.'[23] Another participant mentioned that 'Iran is supporting the Taliban in Nimruz and Helmand and Farah, militarily and financially; our security department has discovered guns and other weapons [in these areas] that belong to Iran.'[24] The broadening of Iran's relationship with the Taliban after the fall of its first administration was also noted.[25] One participant from the Afghanistan Analysts Network explained that after the fall of the Taliban regime in 2001, Iran 'had a very bad relationship with the Taliban', but this policy gradually changed in a way that 'today they [Iranian officials] host the Taliban [leaders] in Tehran and talk to them'.[26]

Some participants reported that Iran met with and hosted Taliban leaders. One participant noted that Iran had hosted some Taliban leaders and that 'Iranian officials including Iran's foreign minister said that peace in Afghanistan is not possible without the Taliban's participation in the peace process.'[27] Another participant pointed

---

[18] Ibid.
[19] Ben Farmer, 'Taliban Opens Office in Iran', *The Telegraph*, 1 August 2012, https://www.telegraph.co; uk/news/worldnews/middleeast/iran/9444402/Taliban-opens-office-in-Iran.html.
[20] Saikal, *Iran Rising*, 179.
[21] Akbarzadeh and Ibrahimi, 'The Taliban', 769.
[22] Saikal, *Iran Rising*, 179.
[23] A6, interviewed on 22 May 2019, Kabul.
[24] A21, interviewed on 22 June 2019, Kabul.
[25] A9, interviewed on 30 May 2019, Kabul.
[26] A18, interviewed on 16 June 2019, Kabul.
[27] A21, interviewed on 27 May 2019, Kabul.

out that Iran's 'foreign minister openly confessed that they have relation with Taliban leaders ... It is always openly said that Iran has relations with the Taliban.'[28] Other participants noted that Iran held a conference in 2019 which was attended by some Taliban leaders and that some Taliban leaders live in Iran.[29]

It is important to understand why Iran established links with the Taliban. As Nader notes, one reason for cooperation between Iran and the Taliban is that Tehran realised that the Taliban were likely to be a major factor in Afghanistan following the US withdrawal, therefore, it made sense from Iran's perspective to avoid a complete reliance on its traditional partners, namely Shi'as and Tajiks.[30] Indeed, envisaging the likely instability of the US-backed government in Kabul after the withdrawal of US forces from Afghanistan, Iran developed a relationship with the Taliban. This is evident from Mohammad Javad Zarif's claim in January 2019 that 'it would be impossible to have a future Afghanistan without any role for the Taliban'.[31] Tehran seems to have displayed a realistic policy vis-à-vis the Taliban. Like most other regional actors,[32] Iran too has recognised the Taliban as a reality of Afghanistan. Hence, Tehran fully supported the peace deal between the United States and the Taliban which was signed in Doha in February 2021. A statement from the Iranian Ministry of Foreign Affairs stated, 'The Islamic Republic of Iran believes lasting peace will be established in Afghanistan only through intra-Afghan talks attended by the country's political groups, including the Taliban, while taking into account the considerations of Afghanistan's neighbouring countries.'[33] Further, in July 2021, approximately one month before the Taliban's takeover of Afghanistan, Tehran hosted a meeting between the Taliban and the Ashraf Ghani government to facilitate an intra-Afghan peace process.[34]

Further, it is important to note that the relationship between Iran and the Taliban improved in the context of Saudi Arabia's harsh stance against Qatar, where the Taliban's political office was located. Qatar's improved relations with Iran have helped Iran and the Taliban come closer. Another reason for Tehran's relationship with the Taliban is that Iran could potentially use this group to counter the US presence in Afghanistan. Tehran's cooperation with the Taliban could demonstrate to the

---

[28] A22, interviewed on 29 May 2019, Kabul.
[29] A21, interviewed on 22 June 2019, Kabul; A24, interviewed on 27 June 2019, Kabul.
[30] Nader et al., 'Iran and Afghanistan: A Complicated Relationship', 7.
[31] Cited in Akbarzadeh and Ibrahimi, 'The Taliban', 769.
[32] Zahid Shahab Ahmed, Abbas Farasoo and Shahram Akbarzadeh, 'The Taliban Develops Regional Relationships as It Makes Territorial Gains in Afghanistan', *Melbourne Asia Review*, 10 September 2020, https://melbourneasiareview.edu.au/the-taliban-is-actively-developing-relationships-with-regional-powers-as-it-makes-territorial-gains-in-afghanistan.
[33] 'Statement on Agreement Signed between US, Taliban', *Iran's Ministry of Foreign Affairs*, 1 March 2020, https://en.mfa.ir/portal/newsview/576903/Statement-on-Agreement-Signed-between-US-Taliban.
[34] 'Intra-Afghan Dialogue Summit Kicks Off in Tehran', *Iran's Ministry of Foreign Affairs*, 7 July 2021, https://en.mfa.ir/portal/newsview/644305/Intra-Afghan-Dialogue-Summit-Kicks-Off-in-Tehran.

United States and its allies the ability of Iran to exercise influence in Afghanistan. One of our research participants stated, 'Iran is supporting the Taliban . . . to show to the US that we have the situation under control in Afghanistan.'[35] Another interviewee's explanation was that closer relations with the Taliban were part of Tehran's broader strategy to counter the US influence on its eastern border with Afghanistan. This means that Tehran's relations with the Taliban should be understood in the light of the former's security concerns.[36] It was highlighted by this interviewee that Iran's ambassador to Afghanistan once indicated that he told a European ambassador that Iran supports the Taliban in Afghanistan in order to obtain information and to 'know what they [Americans] are going to do'.[37]

These perspectives are also reflected in some scholarly works. According to Akbarzadeh and Ibrahimi, 'the Taliban can be one of several proxies that Iran uses to hurt the US and its interests. An escalation in tensions between Iran and the United States . . . has the real potential to increase the relevance of the Taliban for Iran.'[38] The final reason for further cooperation between Iran and the Taliban is their common animosity towards the Islamic State of Khorasan Province (ISKP) in Afghanistan. Although some Taliban elements have been attracted to ISIS (Islamic State of Iraq and Syria), the Taliban view the ISKP as 'a rival that must be prevented from carving out a niche on the Taliban's turf in Afghanistan'.[39] The Taliban's hostility towards the ISKP increased when some of its former members pledged allegiance to Abu Bakr al-Baghdadi, the ISIS chief, in 2015. Hence, Iran's closeness to the Taliban is partly a product of Tehran's view that the Taliban can counter the ISKP. A few research participants, including an official from the Office of the President of the Islamic Republic of Afghanistan, presented this convergence as a key reason for cooperation between Iran and the Taliban.[40]

Another view expressed by some of our Afghan research participants was that Iran played an important role in Afghan politics by supporting certain candidates in elections and governments between 2002 and 2021. A military affairs analyst stated, 'Iran could maintain its interest in Afghanistan by supporting [certain] Afghan politicians and governors to have control over private information about Afghanistan's security and international partners' meetings.'[41] Another interviewee stressed that the most important influence Iran exercises in Afghanistan is in domestic politics. To this end, Iran reached out to local governments in some regions to gain influence in Afghanistan.[42] For example, Iran is reported to have provided

---

[35] A13, interviewed on 11 June 2019, Kabul; A8, interviewed on 8 May 2019, Kabul.
[36] A8, interviewed on 8 May 2019, Kabul.
[37] Ibid.
[38] Akbarzadeh and Ibrahimi, 'The Taliban', 766.
[39] Saikal, *Iran Rising*, 180.
[40] A14, interviewed on 12 June 2019, Kabul; A13, interviewed on 11 June 2019, Kabul.
[41] A20, interviewed on 18 June 2019, Kabul.
[42] A26, interviewed on 27 May 2019, Kabul.

significant support to Atta Muhammad Noor, the governor of Balkh Province in Afghanistan. In an interview, Noor reportedly said that 'Iran had always helped us and supported us with weapons and funding.'[43] It was also pointed out by several interviewees that after the collapse of the Taliban regime in 2001, Iran had an ambiguous policy in Afghanistan, maintaining links with both the Taliban and the government in Kabul. Some of our Afghan interviewees were critical of this policy. For example, one interviewee stated that Iran 'is the only country that has supported the government from one side while trying to harm our security from the other side; Iran has always played a double role'.[44]

Overall, Iran's political influence in Afghanistan is perceived in a number of ways in Afghanistan. Although some participants noted that Tehran's cooperation with the Taliban should be understood in the light of Iran's national security, the dominant viewpoint presented by our research participants is that by investing in relations with non-state actors such as the Taliban, Iran contributes to Afghanistan's instability and insecurity. This latter view is critical of Iran's overall political influence in Afghanistan, claiming that Iran often neglects Afghanistan's national interest. One participant noted that, 'We want what will work in our country's interest and benefit and we want to maintain good relations with other countries too', but Iran seeks to influence Afghanistan's political system and intelligence without considering Afghanistan's own national interest and security.[45] Likewise, a participant from the Peace Training and Research Organisation (PTRO) stated that 'Iranians always claim that we are a good friend of Afghanistan and we have always helped the Ghani government to stand on its feet, but . . . they [Iranians] only want what is in their own interest.'[46] Participants often argued that the Afghan government should have taken a stronger position to diminish Iranian influence, although the inability of the Afghan government to manage this was acknowledged by many participants.

The return of the Taliban

Before proceeding to explain Iranian political influence in Pakistan, it is worth exploring Tehran's reaction to, and concerns about, the Taliban's return in August 2021. The initial reaction of Tehran to the Taliban's return was that the US withdrawal from Afghanistan represented the defeat of US policies in the region. Iranian president Ebrahim Raisi welcomed the withdrawal of foreign troops from Afghanistan, saying 'The defeat of the United States in neighbouring Afghanistan should be transformed into an opportunity to "revive life, security and lasting peace" in

---

[43] A25, interviewed on 29 June 2019, Kabul.
[44] A6, interviewed on 22 May 2019, Kabul; A18, interviewed on 16 June 2019, Kabul.
[45] A6, interviewed on 22 May 2019, Kabul.
[46] A24, interviewed on 27 June 2019.

the country.'⁴⁷ This statement was linked to other reactions seeking to present a relatively positive image of the Taliban.⁴⁸ Indeed, Iran refrained from criticising the Taliban directly, although, as will be discussed, Tehran has not officially recognised the Taliban government and has at times raised concerns over its rise to power. Iran's supreme leader Ayatollah Khamenei stated in late August 2021 that: 'We support the nation of Afghanistan. Governments come and go. What remains is the Afghan nation. The nature of our relations with governments depends on the nature of their relations with us.'⁴⁹ The fact that Tehran refrained from criticising the Taliban is also reflected in a speech by Hassan Kazemi Qomi, special representative of the Islamic Republic of Iran to Afghanistan. During a meeting with the Taliban's foreign minister in November 2021, Kazemi Qomi stated, 'Iran and Afghanistan have strong historical ties and the Islamic Republic of Iran will not leave the Afghan people alone under any circumstances.'⁵⁰ It should be noted that the Taliban similarly sought to maintain peaceful relations with Iran, refraining from increasing tensions, with Taliban spokesman Zabihullah Mujahid stating upon its return to power that 'Currently, we do not have a problem with Iran and we seek to develop our relations with Iran.'⁵¹ Dealing with multiple crises, including an ever-growing economic crisis, the Islamic Emirate of Afghanistan is not in a position to disrupt relations with Iran – the country's leading trading partner. The Taliban understands that Afghanistan's stability is linked to the international recognition of the Islamic Emirate of Afghanistan as it can pave the way for more aid, trade and investment for Afghanistan.⁵²

While refraining from direct moves that could cause tensions with the Taliban, Iranian officials nonetheless stated that they would support an 'inclusive' government which represents Afghan minorities including Shi'as. As explored earlier, Tehran had maintained a close relationship with Afghan Shi'as during the Taliban's first administration (1996–2001) and after the US invasion of Afghanistan. Tehran's

---

⁴⁷ Maziar Motamedi, 'US "Defeat" in Afghanistan a Chance for Peace: Iran President', *Al-Jazeera*, 16 August 2021, https://www.aljazeera.com/news/2021/8/16/raisi-us-defeat-in-afghanistan-should-become-chance-for-peace.
⁴⁸ Solhdoost and Pargoo, 'Iran's Nontraditional Security Challenges', 147.
⁴⁹ Ali Khamenei, 'We Support the Nation of #Afghanistan', *Twitter*, 28 August 2021, https://twitter.com/khamenei_ir/status/1431554721844797442?lang=en.
⁵⁰ 'The Meeting between Representative of the Islamic Republic of Iran and Taliban's Foreign Minister', *Ensaf News*, 16 November 2021, http://www.ensafnews.com/317843/%D8%AF%DB%8C%D8%AF%D8%A7%D8%B1-%D9%86%D9%85%D8%A7%DB%8C%D9%86%D8%AF%D9%87%E2%80%8C%DB%8C-%D8%AC%D9%85%D9%87%D9%88%D8%B1%DB%8C-%D8%A7%D8%B3%D9%84%D8%A7%D9%85%DB%8C-%D9%88-%D9%88%D8%B2%DB%8C%D8%B1.
⁵¹ 'Taliban: We Have No Problem with Iran, We Seek to Develop Our Relation', *Fars News*, 24 September 2021, https://www.farsnews.ir/news/14000702000246.
⁵² Kate Bateman and Asfandyar Mir, 'Taliban Seek Recognition, but Offer Few Concessions to International Concerns', *United States Institute of Peace*, 28 September 2021, https://www.usip.org/publications/2021/09/taliban-seek-recognition-offer-few-concessions-international-concerns.

concern over the composition of the new Afghan government is reflected in Iranian foreign minister Hossein Amirabdollahian's statement that Iran supports the formation of 'an inclusive government with the participation of all people'. Amirabdollahian expressed his hope that the Taliban would facilitate the establishment of such an administration.[53] As of October 2022, the Islamic Emirate of Afghanistan has done little to address the concerns of the international community regarding an inclusive government by providing space for women and ethnic minorities. The Taliban has, however, shown willingness to do that, with the appointment a Hazara deputy minister of economy, Abdul Latif Nazari, in December 2021.[54]

One of the key concerns of Iran vis-à-vis today's Afghanistan is the condition of Shi'as there. Since the rise of the Taliban to power, several attacks against members of the Shi'a minority have taken place in Afghanistan, for which the ISKP has claimed responsibility. In one such attack in October 2021, more than forty people were killed and many injured after an explosion at a Shi'a mosque during Friday prayers in Kandahar.[55] In another attack in April 2022, twelve Shi'as were killed when there was an explosion at a Shi'a mosque in northern Mazar-i-Sharif.[56] These attacks were condemned by the Taliban. Although the Taliban has a history of committing serious abuses against Hazaras in Afghanistan, today's Taliban seems to have pursued an anti-sectarian policy since its return to power in August 2021. In condemning one of the ISKP's attacks against Shi'as, Taliban's deputy prime minister Abdul Salam Hanafi emphasised the importance of unity between Shi'as and Sunnis in Afghanistan.[57]

However, in contrast to this statement, several reports have emerged of escalating tensions between the Taliban and Hazaras. On one occasion, the Taliban forcibly evicted hundreds of Hazara families from southern Helmand and northern Balkh provinces in October 2021.[58] More importantly, clashes between the Taliban and Mawlawi Mehdi, the only Shi'a Hazara commander in the ranks of the Taliban, escalated in Balkhab in June 2022. Mehdi complained that the rights of Hazaras had been significantly violated by the Taliban and that the Hazaras

---

[53] Maziar Motamedi, 'Iran Insists on "Inclusive" Government in Afghanistan', *Al-Jazeera*, 9 September 2021, https://www.aljazeera.com/news/2021/9/9/iran-insists-on-inclusive-afghan-government.

[54] 'Taliban Appoints Abdul Latif Nazari as Deputy Minister of Economy', *Asian News International*, 26 December 2021, https://www.aninews.in/news/world/asia/taliban-appoints-abdul-latif-nazari-as-deputy-minister-of-economy20211226091632.

[55] 'Afghanistan: Suicide Attack Hits Kandahar Mosque During Prayers', *BBC News*, 16 October 2021, https://www.bbc.com/news/world-asia-58925863.

[56] 'IS Claims Deadly Shiite Mosque Bombing in Northern Afghanistan; Several Dead in Other Attacks', *Gandhara*, 21 April 2021, https://gandhara.rferl.org/a/mazar-e-sharif-blast-mosque-afghanistan/31814566.html.

[57] 'A Taliban Authority: Shiites and Sunnis are Members of One Body', *IRNA*, 24 April 2022, https://www.irna.ir/news/84729270.

[58] 'Afghanistan: Taliban Forcibly Evict Minority Shia', *Human Rights Watch*, 22 October 2021, https://www.hrw.org/news/2021/10/22/afghanistan-taliban-forcibly-evict-minority-shia.

have been largely ousted from the government. He also claimed that teaching *Jafari* (Shi'a) jurisprudence has been forbidden in universities and banned from courts, even in Shi'a-majority areas.[59] In turn, the Taliban accused Mehdi of 'embezzling more than $600,000 from the coal mine export business'.[60] Fierce clashes between Taliban and Mehdi's forces erupted after the Taliban deployed 3,000 troops to the Balkhab district of Afghanistan, which resulted in the death of several people including civilians.[61] The World Hazara Council (WHC) condemned the Taliban's attack, expressing its concern that the Taliban may 'target and attack markets, mosques, hospitals and other populated places of the Hazara people'.[62] Iran also reacted to escalated tensions between the Taliban and Hazaras, with Hassan Kazemi Qomi appealing for deescalation from both sides: 'Leaders of all Afghan tribes should distance themselves from the Balkhab conflict. The conflict in Balkhab has benefit for no one and can only result in the bloodshed and destruction of Afghanistan.'[63]

Overall, Iranian political influence in Afghanistan seems to have decreased after the return of the Taliban to power, and despite Iran's efforts to avoid increasing tensions with the Taliban, mainly due to its interest in maintaining peace along its borders, Iranian officials continue to hold concerns vis-à-vis the Shi'a minority in Afghanistan. Whether Iran will be able to enhance or maintain its political influence in Afghanistan under the Taliban, including in Afghan domestic politics, is yet to be seen.

The case of Pakistan

The Iranian Revolution had a significant influence on Shi'a communities in Pakistan. Within months of the Iranian Revolution in 1979, more than 100,000 Shi'as from across Pakistan gathered in Punjab, demanding the recognition of Shi'a laws in the legal system of the country.[64] As discussed in Chapter 5, Arif Hussain Hussaini, the founder of TNFJ, himself had a personal connection with Ayatollah Khomeini. Hussaini was at the forefront of the struggle demanding that Pakistani Shi'as be allowed to follow their own jurisprudence or system of law (based on *Jafari fiqh*).[65]

---

[59] 'Taliban Ousts Its Only Shia Hazara Commander', *Cradle*, 26 June 2022, https://thecradle.co/Article/news/12185.
[60] Ibid.
[61] 'Fierce Fighting Rages between Taliban and Local Forces Led by Mawlawi Mehdi in Balkhab', *Hasht-e Subh*, 23 June 2022, https://8am.af/eng/fierce-fighting-between-taliban-and-mawlawi-mehdis-forces-in-balkhab.
[62] World Hazara Council, 'World Hazara Council Statement on the Situation of Balkhab in Afghanistan', *Twitter*, 25 June 2022, https://twitter.com/WHCOrg/status/1540460439322214400.
[63] 'Kazemi Qomi: The War in Balkhab is American Conspiracy'" *Tasnim News*, 26 June 2022, https://www.tasnimnews.com/fa/news/1401/04/05/2734511.
[64] Majidyar, 'The Shiites of Pakistan?'.
[65] Haqqani, 'Weeding Out the Heretics'.

One year after the Shi'a protest in Punjab, more than 200,000 Shi'as held a further protest rally in Islamabad, which ultimately led the then Pakistani president Zia-ul-Haq exempting Shi'as from paying compulsory *zakat* tax (the Shi'as reasoned that religious tax must be paid to the religious establishment (*marja'iyya*) rather than to the state).[66]

Zia-ul-Haq viewed the rise of Shi'a political activism as a threat. He therefore used diplomatic channels to dissuade Iran from supporting Shi'a groups in Pakistan. Then Pakistani foreign minister Agha Shahi, himself a Shi'a, travelled to Tehran in 1980–1981 to convince Ayatollah Khomeini to refrain from exporting Iranian revolutionary agendas to Pakistan, arguing that Tehran would harm its relations with Pakistan by interfering in Pakistan's internal politics.[67] However, Tehran ignored Pakistan's reservations and continued to support Pakistani Shi'a groups. According to Majidyar, unlike during the pre-revolution era in which Pakistani Shi'a leaders were involved primarily in educational and religious activities, the new government in Iran 'dispatched its revolutionary agents disguised as diplomats and cultural attachés across Pakistan to mobilize and unite the Shi'ite communities'.[68] In the 1980s, Pakistan saw a 'flood of propaganda literature from Iran, high-profile activities of Iranian diplomats and emissaries in Pakistan, exaggerated veneration for Khomeini as the *Imam al-Umma* . . . and huge Shi'a conventions and demonstrations' by various Shi'a groups supported by Iran, such as TNFJ and ISO activists.[69] Urdu translations of the speeches and writings of Khomeini were also distributed on a large scale in Pakistan.[70] Another example of Iran's influence is the observance of the International Quds Day by some Shi'a groups in Pakistan, such as ISO and TNFJ.[71]

During the 1980s, Shi'a groups in Iran and Pakistan had close ties with each other. The number of Pakistani students enrolled at religious schools in Iranian cities, especially in Qom and Mashhad, increased significantly.[72] Upon their return to Pakistan, these students travelled to various Shi'a centres across the country and shared their experiences about attending Iranian universities with other Pakistani Shi'as, familiarising them with the ideas of Iranian religious figures and the theory of *vilayat-e faqih*.[73] Simultaneously, Iranian leaders at times called for support of Shi'a communities in Pakistan. According to a former senior Iranian diplomat to Pakistan, Ali Akbar Omid-Mehr, who defected to the West in the mid-1990s,

[66] Majidyar, 'The Shiites of Pakistan?', 128.
[67] Ibid.
[68] Majidyar, 'The Shiites of Pakistan?', 128.
[69] Rieck, *The Shias of Pakistan*, 231.
[70] Ibid., 234–5.
[71] For a recent report about an Al-Quds Day rally in Pakistan, see 'Al-Quds Rally Rejects "Deal of the Century"', *Dawn*, 1 June 2019, https://www.dawn.com/news/1485881.
[72] Rieck, *The Shias of Pakistan*, 216.
[73] Abbas, 'Shiism and Sectarian Conflict in Pakistan'; see also Zahab, 'The Politicization of the Shia Community', 101.

Ayatollah Khomeini issued a fatwa in 1986 obliging the Iranian state to help the Shi'as of Pakistan.[74] Eventually, by the end of the 1980s, certain Shi'a political groups, such as the TJP, received the backing of Ayatollah Khomeini.[75] Thousands of Pakistani Shi'as, in return, volunteered to serve on the Iranian front during the final years of the Iran–Iraq War.[76] It should be noted that in addition to supporting Shi'a groups, Iran's existing cultural centres in Pakistan were expanded after the Islamic Revolution to incorporate new offerings such as political and ideological education.[77] *Khana-e-Farhangs* themselves played a significant role in distributing the works of leading Iranian *ulema* among Pakistani Shi'as.[78] These cultural centres collaborate closely with prominent Shi'a leaders and regularly organise religious events. For example, the *Khana-e-Farhang* in Karachi organised a convocation ceremony for the Board of Islamic Studies in January 2019. At this event, Hujjat al-Islam (a Shi'a clerical title) Maulana Aqeel Moosa was invited among others, including Maulana Haider Naqvi of Karachi.[79] Iran, however, is not just relying on these cultural centres to promote its religious influence as many Shi'as from Pakistan go to Iran for education, in particular for religious education.[80] In fact, many prominent Shi'a clerics and religious figures from Pakistan have studied in Iran. These include Arif Hussain Hussaini (1946–1988), who studied at the Qom seminary in the 1970s.

During the second half of the 1980s, Iran continued to exercise significant influence on Shi'a groups in Pakistan. When Ayatollah Khamenei, then president of Iran, visited Pakistan in January 1986, many pro-Iran Shi'a activists came to greet him carrying placards that read 'United States is Islam's enemy' and 'Death to American Imperialism'.[81] It is reported that two Shi'a organisations, namely TNFJ and ISO, received funding from the Iranian government and wealthy Pakistani Shi'as to mobilise thousands of their supporters to welcome Khamenei.[82] The pro-Iran posters and anti-American slogans prompted Zia-ul-Haq to order an investigation of the funding and operations of Shi'a organisations in Pakistan.[83] It is important to note that Ayatollah Khamenei, as the supreme leader of Iran, was later supported by many Pakistani Shi'a religious scholars and preachers. For example, Syed Jawad Naqvi, a prominent preacher and the head of a Shi'a seminary in Pakistan, has called

---

[74] In an interview with Vatanka, 'The Guardian of Pakistan's Shia'.
[75] See 'TJP and TNFJ', *Global Security*, https://www.globalsecurity.org/military/world/para/tjp.htm.
[76] Rieck, *The Shias of Pakistan*, 229.
[77] Ibid., 216.
[78] Abbas, 'Shiism and Sectarian Conflict in Pakistan', 29.
[79] 'Convocation Ceremony: Board of Islamic Studies', *Shia TV*, 27 January 2019, https://muharram.shiatv.net/view_video.php?viewkey=1086572882.
[80] P21, interviewed on 24 May 2019, Islamabad.
[81] Vatanka, *Iran and Pakistan*, 178.
[82] Majidyar, 'The Shiites of Pakistan?', 130.
[83] Ibid.

himself a devoted follower of Ayatollah Khamenei.[84] During the rise of the Green Movement in Iran in 2009, Naqvi published various articles and a book in which he denounced Iran's protest movement.[85] With regard to Pakistani Shi'a scholars' support of Ayatollah Khamenei, Vatanka comments:

> [M]any of Pakistan's Shia religious figures have become highly vocal and partisan supporters of Khamenei. Not only do Pakistan's pro-Iran Shia ulema come to Khamenei's defense when he faces his internal Iranian detractors, but they give much publicity and credence to his vision and role as a pan-regional Islamic leader ... Thanks to Iranian funding, this veneration of Khamenei has also become strongly visible in cyberspace. Today, dozens of Pakistani Shia Islamist websites are in operation and they actively engage in propagating the Iranian regime's messages and the teachings of Ayatollah Khamenei.[86]

The sudden increase in sectarian violence in Pakistan, beginning in the late 1980s and reaching a peak in the 1990s, is considered by some to be a result of Iran's influence on Pakistani Shi'as. Sunni and Shi'a militant groups have engaged in multiple conflicts since this time. In 1988, Arif Hussain Hussaini was killed by Sunni terrorists in Gilgit.[87] The incident has often been viewed as the starting point of sectarian violence in Pakistan. Between 1989 and June 2018, there were 3,072 incidents of sectarian violence, leading to the deaths of 5,602 people in Pakistan.[88] Since 2000, sectarian conflict has intensified in Pakistan. In 2009, for example, thirty Shi'as were killed by a suicide bomber in Karachi during the religious observance of Arbaeen.[89] In 2012, a bus headed towards Gilgit was stopped by armed men, and twenty Shi'a passengers were killed.[90] In 2013, a report by PIPS revealed that sectarian attacks across Pakistan had increased by 53 per cent, with more than 85 per cent of them in regions such as Khurram Agency, Quetta, Karachi and Gilgit-Baltistan.[91] In these years, the Iranian media and religious leaders frequently decried the conditions of Shi'as in regions such as Quetta and Parachinar, calling the latter the 'Shiite Gaza' or 'second Gaza' in Pakistan.[92] The rise of anti-Shi'a violence in Pakistan gave Iran an opportunity to provide more support to Shi'a groups. It is reported that a group of Shi'as that defected from the ISO, known as

---

[84] Vatanka, 'The Guardian of Pakistan's Shia'.
[85] Ibid.
[86] Ibid.
[87] 'Pakistan's Sectarian Mire and the Way Forward', *Pak Institute of Peace Studies*.
[88] 'Sectarian Violence in Pakistan', *South Asia Terrorism Portal*.
[89] 'Suicide Bomber Kills 30 on Shia Procession in Karachi', *The Guardian*, 20 December 2009, https://www.theguardian.com/world/2009/dec/28/pakistan-suicide-attack-kills-30.
[90] Taimur Shamil, 'This Muharram, Gilgit Gives Peace a Chance', *Herald*, 12 October 2016, https://herald.dawn.com/news/1153556.
[91] Majidyar, 'The Shiites of Pakistan?', 131.
[92] Ibid., 133.

Sipah-e-Muhammad Pakistan (SMP), engaged in violent acts against Sunni militant groups. In early 2014, Karachi's Criminal Investigation Department arrested two serial killers who had allegedly received 'sectarian terrorism training in Iran'.[93] Since then, however, the Pakistani state has implemented strict security measures, especially with reference to counter-terrorism, which has led to a significant decline in sectarian violence in the country. According to a report by PIPS, the number of incidents of sectarian violence decreased from 220 in 2013 to 12 in 2018.[94] In our data collection, we specifically asked respondents whether there was a relationship between sectarian violence in Pakistan and Iran's support for some Shi'a groups. Some of our interviewees believed that Iran's support of certain Pakistani Shi'a groups increased sectarian violence in the country. It was argued that the resistance of Pakistan and religious parties in Pakistan to the ideas of the Iranian Revolution, 'paved the way to sectarianism'[95] and 'created security problems for both countries [i.e., Iran and Pakistan]'.[96]

This being said, Iran's support of Shi'a groups and its role in the intensification of sectarianism in Pakistan should not be exaggerated. It was noted that Iran did not seek to 'aggressively inflame sectarianism in Pakistan'.[97] Indeed, Iran has sought to continue supporting formal political groups and parties in Pakistan, including those that choose to work within Pakistan's political system, rather than radical Shi'a groups that engage in violent acts. In addition, many Shi'a political groups that received Iranian support, such as TNFJ and MWM – groups whose ideologies were discussed in the last chapter – have been careful to distance themselves from sectarianism, and have, at times, condemned Shi'as using violence against Sunnis.[98] For example, MWM explicitly declared its strategy as 'preventing sectarian infighting and insisting on a united *umma*'.[99] Similarly, other Shi'a groups such as ISO explicitly state that they are not a sectarian organisation, and that their objectives are oriented around protecting the rights of Pakistani Shi'as.[100] Further, it would be a mistake to exaggerate Iran's influence on Pakistani Shi'as. As argued by Majidyar, the majority of Pakistani Shi'as have preserved their political independence.[101] For example, it is worth mentioning that many Pakistani Shi'as have ignored fatwas issued by Khomeini and Khamenei about Muharram rituals.

---

[93] Ibid.
[94] 'Pakistan's Sectarian Mire and the Way Forward', *Pak Institute of Peace Studies*, 8.
[95] P12, interviewed on 27 May 2019, Islamabad.
[96] P27, interviewed on 4 May 2019, Islamabad.
[97] Majidyar, 'The Shiites of Pakistan?', 134.
[98] Weinstein, 'South Asia's Shiites are Eschewing Sectarianism'. It should be noted that some Pakistani officials and senators were Shi'as. For example, the former PPP senator Faisal Raza Abidi is known for plastering posters in Karachi depicting his own name and symbols of Shiism such as Imam Hussein and the Karbala battle.
[99] Rieck, *The Shias of Pakistan*, 312.
[100] Rana and Gillani, 'Iran Not Funding ISO: Shirazi'.
[101] Majidyar, 'The Shiites of Pakistan?', 130.

Despite campaigns run by groups such as ISO in support of fatwas by ayatollahs Khomeini and Khamenei calling for bloody forms of *matam* during Muharram processions, many Shi'as in Pakistan have refused to follow them.[102] In addition, despite the fact that many Shi'as in Pakistan are not hostile towards Iran, there are others who are openly critical of the Islamic Republic. They believe that Iran uses Pakistani Shi'as for its own political interests and that Iran did not sufficiently protect Shi'a communities in Pakistan when they were targeted by Sunni militants.[103]

One of the main political parties engaging in formal politics is the PPP. According to Vali Nasr, the period of the prime ministership of Zulfiqar Ali Bhutto (1971–1977), a Shi'a and the founder of the PPP, 'marked the pinnacle of Shia power in Pakistan and the high point of the promise of inclusive Muslim nationalism'.[104] Pakistani Shi'as have traditionally voted for the PPP. The historic ties between PPP leaders and Iran also led to pro-Iranian policies during the governments of Prime Minister Benazir Bhutto (1988–1990 and 1993–1996) and her widower President Asif Ali Zardari (2008–2013). Iran's connection with the PPP is reflected in the fact that the number of visits to Iran by Pakistani leaders during PPP governments is greater than the number of visits by Pakistani leaders belonging to other parties. For example, during his cumulative ten years in power, Nawaz Sharif only visited Iran three times and no visit took place during his first term as prime minister in 1990–1993.

Zulfikar Bhutto's daughter, Benazir, was elected as Pakistan's prime minister in December 1988. She was, however, removed from office in August 1990 following charges of corruption and abuse of political power. In the interim, Sharif served as prime minister, but Bhutto was re-elected in October 1993 and remained in power until 1996. Unlike Sharif, Bhutto paid several visits to Iran during her prime ministerial terms. She visited the shrine of Imam Reza in Mashhad during her visit in 1990,[105] and in November 1995, Bhutto paid another official visit to Tehran and met Ayatollah Khamenei. Khamenei is reported to have said to Bhutto, 'My daughter, You are a child of Islam, a Muslim and a Shi'a', to which Bhutto is reported to have replied, 'Pray for me that I am forgiven on [the] Day of Judgement.'[106] Bhutto was reported to be loved in Iran as 'Iranian women admired her because she was a woman who was active in politics, and some saw her as a role model for the empowerment of Muslim women.'[107] As we will analyse below, the legacy of Pakistan's governments under Benazir and her father has continued in the form of the PPP's pro-Iran policies.

---

[102] Abbas, 'Shiism and Sectarian Conflict in Pakistan', 45.
[103] Ibid.
[104] Vali Nasr, *The Shia Revival: How Conflicts within Islam Will Shape the Future* (New York: W. W. Norton, 2007), 89.
[105] 'Iran's Affection for Benazir Bhutto', *Payvand*, 2 January 2008, http://www.payvand.com/news/08/jan/1012.html.
[106] Vatanka, *Iran and Pakistan*, 210.
[107] 'Iran's Affection for Benazir Bhutto', *Tehran Times*, 3 January 2008, https://www.tehrantimes.com/news/160545/Iranians-affection-for-Benazir-Bhutto.

Asif Ali Zardari, widower of the assassinated Benazir Bhutto, and successor to President Musharraf in August 2008, is another pro-Iranian Pakistani politician. As the president of Pakistan, he 'was viewed by the Gulf Arabs as a plausible instrument in the hands of Tehran'.[108] From early on, the Saudis stated that they did not trust Zardari since they feared that he had strong ties with Tehran. This idea is reflected in the fact that Riyadh significantly reduced their financial aid to Pakistan in 2008, the year Zardari came to power.[109] The foreign minister of the United Arab Emirates, Sheikh Abdullah bin Zayed Al Nahyan, told US secretary of state Hillary Clinton in 2009 that the Saudis feared 'a triangle in the region between Iran, the [Shi'a] Maliki government in Iraq, and Pakistan under Zardari'.[110] Zardari's connection to Tehran is reflected in his regular visits to Iran in 2009, 2011, 2012 and 2013. In 2011, he made two successive visits to Tehran in June and July, where he met Ayatollah Khamenei.[111] Zardari's pro-Iranian policy was reflected in his siding with Iran in regional conflicts. For example, in conflicts between Tehran and Tel Aviv, after Israel threatened Iran many times that it would launch an attack on Iran's nuclear facilities, Pakistan's high commissioner in London told the *Sun* in February 2012 that: 'Pakistan would be left with no option but to support Iran if Israel attacks it.' In a clear pro-Iranian statement, this senior Pakistani diplomat warned, 'We have a Shia population in Pakistan who will not take it lying down.'[112]

In addition to the PPP, other Shi'a political groups that are influenced by Iran, such as the TNFJ, TJP, MWM and ISO whose ideologies were discussed in the previous chapter, have often advocated for participation in formal politics. This can be observed particularly in the activities of the MWM in the 2010s. In July 2012, Raja Nasir Abbas, MWM's secretary general, announced his organisation's full participation in the upcoming parliamentary elections. He claimed that all Shi'as of Pakistan were now converged to achieve their religious and political rights.[113] He went on to state that in the next election, Shi'as would be represented by 'the biggest political party in the country'.[114] According to Andreas Rieck, the MWM was more successful than many other Shi'a groups in Pakistan at the time in terms of 'mobilising Shias for communal causes'.[115]

In March 2013, the MWM registered with the Election Commission of Pakistan, and its leaders ensured that the party made a strong showing at the 11 May parliamentary elections. Nasir Abbas Shirazi, the secretary of the political wing of the MWM, declared that the party 'would field its own candidates for

---

[108] Vatanka, *Iran and Pakistan*, 250.
[109] Ibid., 251.
[110] Ibid., 250–1.
[111] 'President Zardari Meets Ayatollah Khamenei', *Express Tribune*, 17 July 2011, https://tribune.com.pk/story/211538/president-zardari-meets-ayatollah-khamenei.
[112] Vatanka, *Iran and Pakistan*, 253.
[113] Rieck, *The Shias of Pakistan*, 319.
[114] Ibid., 319.
[115] Ibid., 311.

sixty NA [National Assembly] and forty PA [Provincial Assembly] seats in mostly Shia-dominated areas'.[116] On 21 April, secretary general Abbas presented the party manifesto and proclaimed his readiness to 'join hands with every patriotic, religious or political party which ensured all-out cooperation to eliminate terrorism from the country'.[117] Despite these efforts to engage in formal politics, the MWM failed to achieve many of its objectives. At the end of the election campaign, the number of MWM candidates was reduced to twenty, comprising twelve in Sindh, seven in Punjab and one in Quetta. In addition, the MWM fielded fifty-two candidates for PA seats (twenty-seven in Sindh, twenty in Punjab and five in Balochistan). According to Rieck, 'this fell far short of the number of people mobilised by the MWM at various conventions since 2010, and it stood in huge contrast to the success of Imran Khan's PTI'.[118] The reasons why the MWM failed to achieve success in the election is beyond the scope of this discussion, but its engagement in formal politics in Pakistan demonstrates that it does act in a representative role for the Shi'a community in the country. Although this does not necessarily mean that Iran has a significant role in Pakistani formal politics, at least to the extent of Iran's influence in Afghan politics, it does demonstrate that Shi'a groups have the potential to participate in elections and to challenge other political parties.

This idea was supported by a number of our Pakistani interviewees. Even though many interviewees agreed that Iran supports Shi'a groups in Pakistan, an issue we also addressed in Chapter 5, they believed that Iran currently lacks any significant influence on formal politics in Pakistan. This reflects our earlier observation that even groups like the MWM, which have sought to engage in Pakistan's formal politics, have failed to do so. As one respondent noted, 'Iran does not have much influence on the parliament and political parties'.[119] It is important to highlight that our data was collected during the government of Imran Khan in Pakistan and the collected views could have been different under a PPP government. Another response from participants was that although certain Shi'a groups are supported by Tehran, this does not mean that they share all the political views of the Iranian government. For example, it was noted that some Shi'a groups in Pakistan have not supported Iran's policies'.[120] In addition, with regard to the question of whether Shi'a groups in Pakistan are used as proxies to further Iranian political objectives, some participants responded negatively. For example, a professor from the International Islamic University in Islamabad stated that 'not all Shi'as in Pakistan were used as proxies but there are few that have been used by Iran'.[121] An overwhelming majority of our participants either strongly agreed that Iran's support of Shi'a groups in Pakistan is aimed at countering Saudi influence in the country, but they emphasised that Iranian attempts to influence

[116] Ibid., 323.
[117] Ibid., 324–5.
[118] Ibid., 325.
[119] P12, interviewed on 27 May 2019, Islamabad.
[120] P16, interviewed on 27 May 2019, Islamabad, a journalist at *Dawn*.
[121] P23, interviewed on 20 June 2019, Islamabad.

Pakistan's formal political environment have achieved very limited success. To summarise, Iran's support of Shi'a groups in Pakistan remains limited to its ideological influence and despite Iran's willingness to exercise significant influence in Pakistan's formal politics, Tehran has not yet achieved such an objective.

The Quds Force

The Quds Force is an important Iranian institution that provides it with the capacity to influence other countries. Considering this, we need to pay attention to how a recent IRGC leadership change is likely to impact Iran's influence in Afghanistan and Pakistan. After the death of General Qasem Soleimani in January 2020, General Ismail Qaani was appointed as the head of the IRGC by the supreme leader of the Islamic Republic. A few reports were then released about Qaani's activities in Afghanistan, including the detail that Qaani was the commander of the Fourth Ansar Corps in the 1990s and 'responsible for Guards Corps' activities in Afghanistan, Pakistan, and [the Central] Asian republics'.[122] Qaani supported the Northern Alliance against the Taliban in the 1990s. Photographs of his meeting with Northern Alliance commander Ahmad Shah Massoud in Tajikistan in 1999 have been published by Afghan channel Tolo News.[123] It is important to note that Soleimani himself visited Tajikistan on 21 January 1999, with the purpose of arming the anti-Taliban groups, although other activities of Soleimani including his involvement in combating opium trafficking, are noteworthy.[124] There are also some reports demonstrating that Qaani had strong connections to some Shi'as in Pakistan and became, at times, a central figure in recruiting Pakistani Shi'as to fight in Syria and Iraq.[125]

Further, Qaani has been in contact with Afghan leaders. He is believed to direct certain IRGC activities in Afghanistan, although the details of such activities have not yet been released. He is described as 'someone who knows the Afghan political landscape just as Soleimani knew that of Iraq'.[126] According to Ali Alfoneh, 'it is just as likely that Qaani and Soleimani cooperated with each other in their support to the United Islamic National Front for the Salvation of Afghanistan, known as the Northern Alliance, against the Taliban in the late 1990s'.[127] Alfoneh notes that

---

[122] Mohammad Mohaddessin, *Islamic Fundamentalism: The New Global Threat* (Washington: Seven Locks Press, [1993] 2001), 201.

[123] 'Ismail Qaani was Appointed as the Quds Forces Commander after Soleimani was Killed in US Airstrike', *Tolo News*, n.d., https://tolonews.com/afghanistan/who-soleimani%E2%80%99s-successor-ismail-qaani.

[124] Ali Alfoneh, 'Esmail Qaani: The Next Revolutionary Guards Quds Force Commander?' American Enterprise Institute, 11 January 2012, https://www.aei.org/research-products/report/esmail-qaani-the-next-revolutionary-guards-quds-force-commander.

[125] Umer Karim, 'Death of Qassem Soleimani: What to Expect in Afghanistan and Pakistan', *RUSI*, 24 January 2020, https://rusi.org/commentary/death-qassem-soleimani-what-expect-afghanistan-and-pakistan.

[126] Ibid.

[127] Ibid.

there are a number of reasons for Qaani's connection with Afghan political parties. First, significant numbers of Afghan refugees and immigrants often attended Qaani's speeches in Iran's Khorasan Province. Secondly, Alfoneh cites many references in Iranian press to Qaani's participation in poetry evenings with Afghan mujahideen and Guantanamo Bay detention veterans such as Seyyed Ali-Shah Mousavi Gardizi.[128] Alfoneh concludes, 'That Qaani directs the IRGC QF's activities in Afghanistan, Pakistan, and Central Asia may also provide an indication that he would focus primarily on Afghanistan as IRGC QF commander.'[129]

According to some reports, Qaani travelled to Afghanistan several times before the death of Soleimani. For example, it was revealed that in 2018, Qaani visited Kabul and held talks with government leaders President Ashraf Ghani and Chief Executive Abdullah Abdullah.[130] In the same year, Qaani visited Bamiyan as the deputy ambassador of Iran to Kabul. On 11 July 2018, Bamiyan governor Tahir Zuhair posted photographs of Qaani on his Facebook account, writing that the latter had visited a hospital in the Bamiyan Province.[131] The Bamiyan governor confirmed Qaani's visit to Bamiyan, commenting 'It was said that the Iranian deputy ambassador is visiting the construction of a hospital (in Bamiyan) and then he will have a meeting with the governor, and he will return after that. They exactly implemented this plan.'[132] Soon after the Taliban's takeover, Qaani held a meeting with some parliamentarians in Iran. He used this occasion to provide details of the IRGC's policies in Afghanistan and claimed that the Taliban's takeover was not a surprise to the Quds Force.[133] Deeply concerned about the presence of the ISKP in Afghanistan and its attacks on Shi'as, Iran continues its collaboration with the Taliban. The Islamic Emirate of Afghanistan is also keen to cooperate with Iran and this was reflected through exchanges that happened during the visit of Amir Khan Muttaqi, Taliban's foreign minister to Tehran, in January 2022.[134] As the Taliban lack capacity to fully counter groups like the ISKP, it is likely that the IRGC's role will increase in Afghanistan.

Conclusion

Since the Islamic Revolution of Iran in 1979, Tehran has initiated several activities to gain and expand its political influence in Afghanistan and Pakistan. However, these efforts have achieved mixed results because of the differing dynamics of each of the targeted countries. While Iran's political influence in Pakistan was largely

[128] Alfoneh, 'Esmail Qaani'.
[129] Ibid.
[130] 'Ismail Qaani was Appointed as the Quds Forces Commander'.
[131] Ibid.
[132] Ibid.
[133] Fatemeh Aman, 'Will Iran turn to al-Qaeda to combat Islamic State?' *Middle East Institute*, 23 September 2022, https://www.mei.edu/publications/will-iran-turn-al-qaeda-combat-islamic-state.
[134] 'Taliban Foreign Minister Visits Iran for Talks Focused on Refugees, Economic Issues', *Radio Free Europe*, 8 January 2022, https://www.rferl.org/a/taliban-foreign-minister-iran-visit/31645303.html.

limited to Shi'a groups, Tehran's political influence in Afghanistan is more visible, especially before the Taliban's takeover in August 2021. Indeed, while Iran managed to exercise influence on official politics in Afghanistan especially under the Karzai government, it has not achieved such a success in Pakistan. As examined in this chapter, Iran has attempted to gain greater influence in Afghanistan through direct connections with policymakers and government officials. In Pakistan, however, Iran's influence has remained limited to Shi'a groups and has not expanded to most political parties in the parliament, despite the participation of some Shi'a groups.

7
Economic Relations and Influence

To be able to assess a state's influence on another country, it is important to look at a variety of factors that contribute to its soft and hard power. In this sense, it is crucial to examine a state's economic influence on another state to see if it has used its leverage in this area to achieve its political goals. In previous chapters we have discussed a variety of soft power resources and instruments that Iran employs to enhance its goodwill in Afghanistan and Pakistan. This chapter focuses on Iran's economic ties with Afghanistan and Pakistan to examine the degree to which economic relations have helped Iran to achieve its national interests. At times, the focus will be on coercive diplomacy, whereby economic sanctions are enacted to achieve political goals. This chapter also explores the ways in which Iran's economic influence and related strategies are viewed in the target countries.

Iran–Afghanistan economic relationship

A key Iranian interest in Afghanistan lies within the economic realm. After the fall of the Taliban regime in 2001, Iran was one of Afghanistan's largest international donors. Iran was the fifth largest contributor to Afghanistan's reconstruction project in the post-Taliban period – after the United States, the European Union, Japan and India.[1] From 2002 onwards, Iran invested heavily in a variety of projects in Afghanistan, including schools, infrastructure and social services. Iran's aid to Afghanistan was particularly channelled into projects in Afghanistan's western provinces, particularly those that border Iran. As Stephen Carter argues, Iran views 'western Afghanistan as an extension of its traditional sphere of economic and political influence . . . [and as] an integral buffer zone for its national security'.[2] Many cities in the western provinces of Afghanistan eventually became dependent on Iran's aid for fuel and electricity and, in general, for their economic well-being.[3] As of 2006, according to the Afghanistan Chamber of Commerce and Industry (ACCI), roughly 2,000 Iranian private firms were active in Afghanistan.[4] In addition, Iranian businessmen invested heavily in Afghan industries. According to a report released

---

[1] Saikal, *Iran Rising*, 162.
[2] Carter, 'Iran's Interests in Afghanistan and Their Implications for NATO', 980.
[3] Saikal, *Iran Rising*, 17–18.
[4] Henner Fürtig, 'Afghanistan in the Foreign Policies of Middle Eastern Countries', *Asian Perspective* 38(4) (2014): 548.

in 2009, 'Iranian businessmen are operating pretty freely in Afghanistan, and more consumer goods are being exported into the country from Iran.'[5] Trade with Iran reportedly represents half of Afghanistan's total international trade.[6]

Iran's initial response to the reconstruction of Afghanistan after the fall of the Taliban was very positive. Iran pledged US$570 million for the reconstruction of Afghanistan at the 2002 Tokyo International Conference on Reconstruction Assistance to Afghanistan, and continued to contribute approximately US$50 million annually.[7] Iran accounted for approximately 12 per cent of the international total of US$4.5 billion pledged towards the reconstruction of Afghanistan.[8] Afghan president Hamid Karzai publicly thanked Iran for its 'boundless assistance in helping bring peace and stability to Afghanistan'.[9] After 2002, Iran's priorities in terms of economic aid in Afghanistan were centred on energy, health care, customs and trade, road construction, agriculture and water supply.[10] During 2002–2003, of the international total of US$1.5 billion of exports flowing into Afghanistan, Iranian exports accounted for US$120 million; trade has significantly increased since 2003, and the annual value of Iranian exports increased to US$250 million in 2005.[11] At a December 2005 meeting in Kabul, Karzai told Iran's foreign minister Manouchehr Mottaki that the assistance granted by Iran had greatly helped the reconstruction of Afghanistan. In this meeting both leaders further emphasised the importance of bilateral trade between the two countries.[12]

During the London Conference on Afghanistan Reconstruction in 2006, Iran pledged an additional US$100 million aid to Afghanistan, and declared that the last instalment of its original US$560 million commitment would be delivered before the end of the year.[13] Iran's economic influence in Afghanistan has not been limited to projects such as bridge construction, agriculture and power generation, but has also extended to Afghanistan's radio and television infrastructure, through which Iran sought to increase its own Dari-language radio and television broadcasting.[14] Iran's reconstruction investment also included the funding of a number of infrastructure projects, such as road and bridge construction in Herat Province. Notable among these projects was the construction of a 176-km railway from Iran to the city of Herat.[15]

---

[5] Anand Gopal, 'US–Iran Thaw Could Bolster Afghanistan Rebuilding Efforts', *Christian Science Monitor*, 3 April 2009, http://www.csmonitor.com/World/Asia-South-Central/2009/0403/p06s01-wosc.html.
[6] Akbarzadeh, 'Iran's Policy towards Afghanistan', 67.
[7] Koepke, *Iran's Policy on Afghanistan*, 1.
[8] Milani, 'Iran's Policy Towards Afghanistan', 251.
[9] Cited in Akbarzadeh, 'Iran's Policy towards Afghanistan', 67.
[10] Koepke, *Iran's Policy on Afghanistan*, 12.
[11] Milani, 'Iran's Policy towards Afghanistan', 251–2.
[12] 'Karzai: Iran's Help Has Contributed to Afghanistan Development', *Payvand*, 27 December 2005, http://payvand.com/news/05/dec/1216.html.
[13] Milani, 'Iran's Policy towards Afghanistan', 251.
[14] Ibid. For further discussion of Iran's influence on the Afghan media, see Chapter 5.
[15] Mohsen Milani, 'Iran and Afghanistan', *The Iran Primer*, 5 October 2010, https://iranprimer.usip.org/resource/iran-and-afghanistan.

Between 2002 and 2007, Iran committed US$560 million to Afghanistan.[16] According to Danesh Yazdi, former Iranian representative to the United Nations, as of March 2007, Iran had spent more than US$270 million on 'mutually agreed projects in the areas of infrastructure, technical and educational services and financial and in-kind assistance'.[17] Iran donated an additional US$50 million in addition to its previous commitment to Afghanistan, and also offered Karzai's government a US$300 million loan in 2008.[18] Since 2008, Iran increased its investment in Afghanistan's infrastructure, industry and mining, and doubled the value of its exports to the country. Iran's exports to Afghanistan increased from US$800 million in 2008 to more than US$2 billion in 2011, while more than 2,000 private Iranian firms were operating across Afghanistan.[19] After 2008, Iran also extended the scope of its Afghanistan funding projects to the education sector. One notable project was Iran's US$100 million donation to the University in Kabul in 2009.[20] While the newly built Khatam al-Nabyeen Islamic University in Kabul does not acknowledge receiving funding from Tehran,[21] it is important to mention that this university is operated by Grand Ayatollah Muhammad Asif Mohseni, who is one of the prominent Shi'a figures in Afghanistan and is closely linked to Tehran, as examined in Chapter 5.[22] Iranian businessmen also began to increase private investment in local industries and mining projects. In January 2012, a delegation of fifty-five Iranian businessmen interested in investing in Afghan industry visited Kabul and signed a series of trade agreements with ACCI.[23] To increase the volume of trade between the two countries, Iran also offered Afghan merchants a 30 per cent discount in customs tariffs and permitted them to unload up to 50,000 tons of goods at Chabahar Port.[24]

As explained in the last chapter, Iran also granted an substantial amount of money to President Karzai annually until 2014 for the expenses of his office.[25] Karzai openly admitted in 2010 that Iran gave between €500,000 and €700,000 to his office 'once or twice a year', and that Afghanistan 'will continue to ask for cash from Iran'.[26] Although Western media considered this to be a corrupt practice, Afghan officials have often argued that cash donations to the Karzai government were necessary for the daily running of the administration of the country, including

[16] Koepke, *Iran's Policy on Afghanistan*, 11.
[17] Cited in Nader and Laha, *Iran's Balancing Act in Afghanistan*, 7.
[18] Saikal, *Iran Rising*, 178.
[19] Fredrick W. Kagan, Ahmad K. Majidyar, Danielle Pletka and Marisa Cochrane Sullivan, *Iranian Influence in the Levant, Egypt, Iraq and Afghanistan* (Washington: American Enterprise Institute and Institute for the Study of War, 2012), 79.
[20] Gopal, 'US–Iran Thaw Could Bolster Afghanistan Rebuilding Efforts'.
[21] Nazar and Recknagel, 'Controversial Madrasah Builds Iran's Influence in Kabul'.
[22] Nader et al., 'Iran and Afghanistan: A Complicated Relationship'.
[23] Kagan et al., *Iranian Influence in the Levant, Egypt, Iraq, and Afghanistan*, 79.
[24] Ibid., 80.
[25] Saikal, *Iran Rising*, 162–3.
[26] Fürtig, 'Afghanistan in the Foreign Policies of Middle Eastern Countries', 549.

establishing good relations with tribal elders in Afghanistan, which, in turn, contributed to the stabilisation of the country.[27]

It was widely acknowledged by our Afghan interviewees that Iran exercises significant economic influence in Afghanistan. One of our respondents from the Women's Activities and Social Services Association (WASSA) stated that Afghanistan's 'economic market is under the control of Iran'.[28] Further, it was highlighted that Iranian investment increased to US$500 million during Karzai's presidency.[29] Another participant explained that Afghanistan has become 'an import market for Iranian products'.[30] Various Iranian products are found in Afghan markets and, as some participants argued, this level of economic cooperation is beneficial to Iran as well because it results in a significant foreign exchange for Tehran.[31] In 2021, Iranian exports to Afghanistan were valued at US$1.8 billion.[32] A former member of the Afghanistan parliament categorised economic relations between Iran and Afghanistan as 'the main reason for Iran and Afghanistan's relationship'.[33] According to her, Afghanistan has become a corridor for Iranian trade with Central and South Asia.[34] Another participant noted that Iran's projects that sought to 'connect Herat and Nimruz with the Bandar Abbas railway project' were also aimed at facilitating trade with and access to the Central and South Asian markets.[35]

It was noted in the interviews that the Afghan government is financially dependent on neighbouring countries especially Iran, and that Iran has used the economic problems of Afghanistan to enhance its influence there by exporting goods and services. Participants generally attributed Iran's economic influence in Afghanistan to two main causes: (1) Iran's economic interest in Afghanistan; and (2) Afghanistan's weak economy which makes it dependent on Iran. Some respondents acknowledged that Iran provided significant financial assistance to the Karzai government. According to a participant from the Afghanistan Analysts Network, Karzai received 'a box of money' during one of his trips to Iran.[36] Two other participants confirmed that Karzai had received cash from Iran and that this created controversy in Afghanistan.[37]

The bilateral trade balance between Iran and Afghanistan increased from US$150 million in 2002 to US$1.5 billion in 2010,[38] and reached US$2 billion in

---

[27] Akbarzadeh, 'Iran's Policy towards Afghanistan', 68.
[28] A25, interviewed on 29 June 2019, Kabul.
[29] A7, interviewed on 29 June 2019, Kabul.
[30] A22, interviewed on 29 May 2019, Kabul.
[31] Ibid.; also, A14, interviewed on 12 June 2019, Kabul
[32] 'Iran's Annual Exports to Afghanistan Exceed $1.8b', *Tehran Times*, 5 April 2022, https://www.tehrantimes.com/news/471372/Iran-s-annual-exports-to-Afghanistan-exceed-1-8b.
[33] A15, interviewed on 12 June 2019, Kabul.
[34] Ibid.
[35] A8, interviewed on 28 May 2019, Kabul.
[36] A7, interviewed on 29 June 2019, Kabul.
[37] A22, interviewed on 29 May 2019, Kabul; A24, interviewed on 27 June 2019, Kabul.
[38] Ali Sheikholeslami, 'Iran–Afghanistan Trade is More than $1.5 Billion, President Karzai Says', *Bloomberg*, 5 August 2010, http://www.bloomberg.com/news/2010-08-05; iran-afghanistan-trade-is-more-than-1-5-billion-president-karzai-says.html.

late 2012.[39] In the period between 2002 and 2012, Afghanistan's exports to Iran also increased from US$500,000 to over US$1.1 million.[40] The economic relationship between Iran and Afghanistan also reflected Iran's 'look east' policy, through which Iran sought to build stronger relations with South and Central Asia. As Barzegar notes, 'because of pipeline geopolitics and regional integration, Afghanistan could serve as the main economic and developmental link between [Iran and] Southern and Central Asia'.[41] For Iran, Afghanistan has traditionally been the transit route facilitating the transportation of various goods from Iran to countries in East Asia, including China. According to Mohsen Milani, one of the objectives of Iran's economic influence in Afghanistan has been to become 'the hub for the transit of goods and services between the Persian Gulf, Afghanistan, Central Asia, China and India'.[42] As explained in Chapter 4, India has been assisting Iran in developing Chabahar Port to facilitate its trade with Afghanistan.[43] India's contribution to this project is a reflection of its desire to bypass Pakistan – which offers the shortest route to Central Asia – because of conflictual India–Pakistan relations.[44] To give a sense of the historical importance of Chabahar Port, a trade agreement was signed in January 2003, aiming for Chabahar to replace Karachi Port as Afghanistan's key trade outlet. In this agreement, Iran committed giving a 90 per cent discount on tariffs for all goods exported via the Chabahar Free Trade Industrial Zone. The Chabahar project played a significant role in increasing Iran–Afghan trade.[45] In particular, through the Chabahar project, Iran funded and constructed other infrastructure projects, including a bridge and a major road directly linking Chabahar to Afghanistan. Therefore, through the Chabahar project Iran has managed to increase its economic influence in Afghanistan, and also to increase its trade with India. In addition, this project has helped India to achieve greater connectivity with Afghanistan, with an associated road constructed between Zaranj and Delaram.[46]

The Chabahar project has played some role in increasing trade relations between Iran and Afghanistan as well. There are, however, other factors at work here; Pakistan has repeatedly closed its borders with Afghanistan for security reasons and had conflictual relations with the Ghani government. One study argued that 'regular border closures are also a reflection of the strained trade relations [between Afghanistan and Pakistan], often used as a strategy to pressurise Afghanistan to accept Pakistan's dominance as a coastal state'.[47] Hence, in recent years, Iran's trade with Afghanistan has increased. The total volume of trade between Iran and

---

[39] Barzegar, 'Iran's Foreign Policy in post-Taliban Afghanistan', 121.
[40] Koepke, *Iran's Policy on Afghanistan*, 13.
[41] Barzegar, 'Iran's Foreign Policy in post-Taliban Afghanistan', 122.
[42] Milani, 'Iran's Policy towards Afghanistan', 251.
[43] Nader et al., 'Iran and Afghanistan: A Complicated Relationship', 11.
[44] Saikal, *Iran Rising*, 178.
[45] Fürtig, 'Afghanistan in the Foreign Policies of Middle Eastern Countries', 548.
[46] Saikal, *Iran Rising*, 178.
[47] Stuti Bhatnagar and Zahid Shahab Ahmed, 'Geopolitics of Landlocked States in South Asia: A Comparative Analysis of Afghanistan and Nepal', *Australian Journal of International Affairs* 75(1) (2021): 72.

Afghanistan reached US$2.4 billion in 2015, of which US$2.3 billion comprised Iranian exports. In general, the balance of trade between Iran and Afghanistan is overwhelmingly in Iran's favour. Afghan exports to Iran accounted for only US$10 million and consisted of mostly plants and seeds.[48] In 2017, Afghanistan's envoy to Iran, Nasir Ahmad Noor, stated that Iranian goods imported by Afghanistan were valued at a total of US$2.8 billion.[49] Iran has been one of the main energy suppliers to Afghanistan. An agreement was signed between Iran and Afghanistan on 26 December 2011, according to which Iran promised to export roughly 1 billion kg of various oil products to Afghanistan annually, including diesel, gasoline and jet fuel.[50] Iran has shown interest in expanding its energy cooperation with Afghanistan in various areas of this industry, such as electricity contracts, power plant maintenance and energy waste reduction. Iranian energy minister Reza Ardakanian visited Afghanistan in 2019 and signed an MoU on the expansion of cooperation in these areas. In this agreement, the two sides committed to collaboration in several areas, including the reconstruction of Afghanistan's transmission equipment, construction of the Zaranj electricity transmission line and synchronisation of the two countries' networks.[51]

As previously stated, one of the areas in Afghanistan in which we can see significant investment by Iran is in Herat Province – an important market for Iran. Some of our interviewees explained the economic significance of Herat for Iran. It was highlighted that many small residential cities in Herat are dependent on Iranian financial support.[52] Iran also reportedly uses Herat to smuggle foreign currencies, especially US$, into Iran.[53] Connecting Herat and Nimruz with Bandar Abbas was considered by some interviewees to be a crucial part of Iran's economic influence in Afghanistan. Indeed, Herat is viewed by Iran as a gateway to further its economic influence not only throughout Afghanistan, but also as an access point to the Central and South Asian markets.

Herat holds historical as well as geographical significance for Tehran, which can be considered factors in receiving considerable funding from Iran. According to former Iranian president Hashemi Rafsanjani, Herat was once an 'integral part' of Iran.[54] Iran's investment in Herat was significant in the post-Taliban era. Gopal writes, 'Unlike most of the country, the city [Herat] boasts 24-hour electricity, dozens of industrial zones, paved roads, and more. Iran is responsible for much of this.'[55] Iran funded the development of the Herat transportation system

---

[48] Ibid.
[49] 'Afghanistan, Iran Trade at $2.8 Billion', *Tolo News*, 27 February 2017, https://tolonews.com/afghanistan/afghanistan-iran-trade-28-billion.
[50] Barzegar, 'Iran's Foreign Policy in post-Taliban Afghanistan', 121.
[51] 'Iran Capable of Boosting Electricity Exports to Afghanistan', *Tehran Times*, 19 October 2019, https://www.tehrantimes.com/news/441270/Iran-capable-of-boosting-electricity-exports-to-Afghanistan.
[52] A23, interviewed on 25 June 2019, Kabul.
[53] A25, interviewed on 29 June 2019, Kabul.
[54] Cited in Milani, 'Iran's Policy Towards Afghanistan', 252.
[55] Gopal, 'US–Iran Thaw Could Bolster Afghanistan Rebuilding Efforts'.

and energy infrastructure during the 2000s. One significant transportation project funded by Iran in Herat Province was the construction of a 123-km paved road from the Iranian border at Dogharoun to Herat city, which was inaugurated on 27 January 2007.[56] In addition, Iran has begun the construction of a railway from Herat to the northeastern city of Mashhad – a project that facilitates commerce and provides revenue to the Afghan central government through import duties.[57] In 2012, Iran significantly increased its investment in Herat, constructing Herat's electrical grid. Also, in February 2012, Rahim Muhammad Yakta, head of Iran's consulate in Herat, said that Iran was interested in building a gas pipeline to Herat. In the same year, President Karzai approved an Iranian company's proposal to build a cement factory in Herat and gave permission for Iran to extract coal from the Pahlawanan coal mine in the region.[58] In 2012, Iran invested US$150 million in Herat and pledged to build a school, a mosque, residential apartments and a 7-mile (11.2 km) road connecting the cement factory to the main road.[59]

It is important to note that at times Iran has used its economic advantage in Afghanistan for certain political objectives. As noted by Nazir Ahmad Haidar, the head of Herat's provincial council, 'Iran has influence in every sphere: economic, social, political and daily life [of Afghans in Herat] . . . When someone gives so much money, people fall into their way of thinking. It's not just a matter of being neighborly.'[60] One instance in which Iran used its economic influence and advantage for political purposes was the halting of Iranian fuel exports to Afghanistan during the winter of 2010–2011 in order to negatively impact the operations of international troops in Afghanistan.[61] Iranian officials claimed that they had stopped the supply of fuel since they suspected it was being used by the United States and NATO. This, however, had an adverse effect on fuel prices across Afghanistan; in Kabul, for instance, fuel prices increased by 35 per cent and in Herat by 60 per cent.[62] Some scholars believe that hindering the oil supply to Afghanistan was part of Iran's plan to ultimately influence the result of the September 2010 Afghanistan parliamentary elections and pave the way for pro-Iranian candidates.[63] At times, some Afghan officials have accused Iran of using its economic influence 'to help drive a wedge between the Afghans and their American and NATO benefactors'.[64] The *New York Times* journalist Dexter Filkins, who assured his interviewees of anonymity, revealed that Afghan officials told him that Iran sought to poison the relationship between the Karzai government

---

[56] 'Iran to Herat Railway', n.d., http://www.andrewgrantham.co.uk/afghanistan/railways/iran-to-herat.
[57] Nader and Laha, 'Iran's Balancing Act in Afghanistan', 8.
[58] Kagan et al., *Iranian Influence in the Levant, Egypt, Iraq, and Afghanistan*, 79.
[59] Ibid., 80.
[60] Ibid.
[61] Nader et al., 'Iran and Afghanistan: A Complicated Relationship', 11.
[62] Kagan et al., *Iranian Influence in the Levant, Egypt, Iraq, and Afghanistan*, 80.
[63] Ibid., 80–1.
[64] Filkins, 'Iran is Said to Give Top Karzai Aide Cash by the Bagful'.

and the United States by providing significant financial assistance to Karzai.[65] The provision of significant financial assistance to Karzai by Tehran took the form of a lever by which Iran could achieve certain political objectives and fulfil certain interests in Afghanistan. While Karzai thanked Iran on several occasions for its generous financial support to Afghanistan's reconstruction, he was at other times critical of Iran's strategy, stating that Iran was 'trying to sabotage Afghanistan's development to prevent it from becoming an important regional transit hub, and to protect its natural gas exports to India and Pakistan from central Asian competition'.[66]

As examined above, Iran's economic influence in Afghanistan increased significantly between 2001 and 2021. This increase cannot be attributed solely to Tehran's policy towards Afghanistan as there are other factors, including India's investment in Chabahar Port. Nonetheless, Iran used its economic influence to gain political influence in Afghanistan, which was criticised by some of our Afghan research participants. While there is evidence of Iran funding Kabul and certain Afghan elites, there is no evidence to suggest that Tehran achieved all its political objectives through economic coercion. Since the Taliban's takeover the dynamics have changed for various reasons. While Iran wishes to avoid international sanctions, it is not in a position to openly support the Islamic Emirate of Afghanistan as the new Taliban regime is not recognised by any country. Even the Emirate's erstwhile supporters, namely, Pakistan, Saudi Arabia and the UAE, have not recognised the new Taliban regime. Unlike the case between 1996 and 2001, Iran is keen to cooperate with the Taliban and therefore has kept its diplomatic missions open in Afghanistan since the Taliban's takeover. Moreover, it has reacted positively to the Taliban's requests by continuing to provide gasoline and gasoil since August 2021.[67] In the first year of the Taliban's new government, Iranian exports to Afghanistan dropped by 40 per cent to US$1.2 billion.[68] If this trend continues, Afghanistan will have to look towards other economic partners, for example, its erstwhile leading trading partner, that is, Pakistan. This ultimately has a potential to significantly reduce Iran's economic influence.

Focusing on Iranian exports to Afghanistan, it is important to look at the China factor because both Afghanistan and Iran have joined the BRI. China and Iran have signed an agreement under which Beijing plan to invest approximately US$400 billion in Iran, especially in Chabahar.[69] Similar to the case of Gwadar Port under

---

[65] Ibid.
[66] Cited in Koepke, *Iran's Policy on Afghanistan*, 13.
[67] Bozorgnehr Sharafedin and Julia Payne, 'Iran Resumes Fuel Exports to Neighbouring Afghanistan', *Reuters*, 24 August 2021, https://www.reuters.com/world/middle-east/iran-resumes-fuel-exports-afghanistan-after-taliban-request-union-says-2021-08-23.
[68] Amina Hakimi, 'Afghanistan–Iran Trade has Dropped: ACCI', *Tolo News*, 25 August 2022, https://tolonews.com/business-179543.
[69] Farnaz Fassihi and Steven Lee Myers, 'China, with $400 billion Iran Deal, Could Deepen Influence in Mideast', *New York Times*, 27 March 2021, https://www.nytimes.com/2021/03/27/world/middleeast/china-iran-deal.html.

the CPEC in Pakistan, China views Chabahar as an alternative route to connect with Afghanistan and the Central Asian republics. Like Iran, China has kept its embassy open in Kabul and continues to expand its economic cooperation with the Islamic Emirate of Afghanistan. Beijing has, however, been cautious since the Taliban's takeover but, as Hussain argues, both Iran and China might find common ground in Afghanistan because of the BRI.[70] The Taliban has welcomed the opportunity to join the BRI, which offers Afghanistan with not just much-needed investment but greater connectivity with Iran and Pakistan.[71] China's investment in Afghanistan and Iran will likely increase its influence in both countries and their bilateral relations. This could play a positive role in terms of increasing trade and connectivity between Afghanistan and Iran.

Iran–Pakistan economic relationship

Since Pakistan's independence from the British Empire in 1947, its relationship with Iran has transformed significantly. Iran was the first country to recognise Pakistani independence in 1947 and it established diplomatic relations with Pakistan in the following year. Pakistan found a natural partner in Iran after India chose to support Jamal Abdel Nasser of Egypt who subscribed to a pan-Arab ideology rather than the pan-Islamism promoted by Pakistan and Iran.[72] Throughout the 1950s, relations between Iran and Pakistan grew, and the two countries signed a cultural agreement in March 1956, an air travel agreement in 1957 and a border agreement in February 1958.[73] Iran mediated to normalise Afghanistan–Pakistan relations after they were disrupted in 1961–1963 due to Pakistani allegations that Kabul was supporting armed separatists in Pakistan.[74] In May 1963, Mohammad Reza Shah brought Afghan and Pakistani delegates to Tehran and proudly announced that diplomatic and economic relations between Afghanistan and Pakistan had been restored.[75] Further, Iran provided material support to Pakistan in its 1965 and 1971 wars with India.[76] Despite the fluctuations in political and strategic relations between Iran and Pakistan, matters related to economic cooperation continued to play a significant role in their bilateral relations. Pakistan, Iran and Turkey signed the Regional Cooperation for Development (RCD) agreement in July 1964 with the aim of

---

[70] Agha Hussain, 'How China and Iran Could Find More Common Ground – in Afghanistan', *South China Morning Post*, 7 August 2022, https://www.scmp.com/comment/opinion/article/3187824/how-china-and-iran-could-find-more-common-ground-afghanistan.

[71] Adnan Aamir, 'Taliban Rolls Out Red Carpet to China's Belt and Road Initiative', *Nikkei Asia*, 12 September 2021, https://asia.nikkei.com/Politics/International-relations/Afghanistan-turmoil/Taliban-rolls-out-red-carpet-to-China-s-Belt-and-Road-Initiative.

[72] Pant, 'Pakistan and Iran's Dysfunctional Relationship', 43–50.

[73] Rafique, 'Prospects of Pakistan–Iran Relations', 6.

[74] Barnett R. Rubin and Abubakar Siddique, 'Resolving the Pakistan–Afghanistan Stalemate', United States Institute of Peace, October 2006, https://www.usip.org/sites/default/files/SRoct06.pdf.

[75] Vatanka, *Iran and Pakistan*, 34.

[76] Ahmed and Akbarzadeh, 'Understanding Pakistan's Relationship with Iran', 86.

strengthening their economic relations – an agreement that was later replaced by the Economic Cooperation Organisation (ECO) in January 1985.[77] The economic relationship between Iran and Pakistan strengthened during the 1980s with significant growth in Pakistan's exports to Iran in 1979–1980 and 1983–1984, although the value of two-way trade reduced in 1984–1985.[78] Tehran was chosen to host the ECO headquarters. One of the main reasons for Iran's involvement in the ECO at that time was that it was attempting to find ways out of its international isolation. According to Shamshad Ahmad, former Pakistani ambassador to Tehran, 'The Iranians revived the ECO in 1985 because they were by then six years after the revolution tasting the costs of regional and international isolation.'[79]

During President Khamenei's visit to Pakistan in January 1986, then president of Pakistan Zia-ul-Haq stated that his government would strive for greater economic cooperation at the bilateral level. In particular, the Pakistani president referred to the ECO as a milestone 'in the efforts to promote economic collaboration among the member states', including Iran and Pakistan.[80] The ECO, Zia-ul-Haq insisted, would strengthen ties of Islamic brotherhood, culture and history among the Muslim countries of Iran, Pakistan and Turkey.[81] During Khamenei's visit to Pakistan in 1986, the two countries agreed on a number of areas in which bilateral cooperation could be strengthened: (1) oil and trade; (2) agricultural and rural development; and (3) telecommunication and the development of roads and the railways between Iran and Pakistan.[82]

However, the relationship between Iran and Pakistan gradually declined owing to certain issues including the mobilisation of Pakistani Shi'as against the government's Zakat and Ushr Ordinance in 1980,[83] by virtue of supporting opposing factions in Afghanistan, and Iran's support for Shi'a activism in Pakistan, including supporting the group Tehrik-i-Nifaz-i-Fiqah-i-Jafaria, as explained in Chapter 6. As Pakistan suffered the worst era of sectarian violence due to a 'brutal wave of violence in Punjab and Karachi in the 1990s',[84] Iran's relationship with Pakistan became conflictual. In December 2001, Iran's foreign minister, Kamal Kharazi, visited Pakistan to restore bilateral relations. Kharazi stated, 'Relations between Pakistan and Iran are back to normal and the two sides now share absolute unanimity on all issues including Afghanistan.'[85] In December 2002, Iranian president Mohammad Khatami visited Pakistan. While Khatami had already visited Pakistan in December 1999, his

---

[77] Rafique, 'Prospects of Pakistan–Iran Relations', 6.
[78] Sabiha Hasan, 'Pakistan Foreign Policy', *Pakistan Horizon* 39(1) (1986): 15.
[79] Vatanka, *Iran and Pakistan*, 182.
[80] Hasan, 'Pakistan Foreign Policy', 15.
[81] Ibid.
[82] Ibid., 15–16.
[83] Nasir Iqbal, 'Marching on the Capital: A History', *Dawn*, 17 August 2014, https://www.dawn.com/news/1125851.
[84] Arif Rafiq, 'Pakistan's Resurgent Sectarian War', United States Institute of Peace, November 2014, https://www.usip.org/sites/default/files/PB180-Pakistan-Resurgent-Sectarian-War.pdf.
[85] Vatanka, *Iran and Pakistan*, 226.

2002 visit was a sign of the improvement in political and economic relations between the two countries after the fall of the Taliban regime in Afghanistan. Pakistani foreign minister Khurshid Kasuri stated that 'we have spent 50 years on photo opportunit[ies] and we should take concrete steps to promote economic ties'.[86] Indeed, the rise of the Taliban regime in Afghanistan in 1996 and the relationship between Pakistan and the Taliban had strained relations between Tehran and Islamabad. During Khatami's visit in 2002, Iran and Pakistan signed a Bilateral Trade Agreement and a Bilateral Agreement on Cooperation in Plant Protection and Quarantine.[87] These were crucial agreements seeking to realise the true potential of bilateral trade, which until that time was very low – US$200 million in 2002.[88]

Pakistan and Iran signed a Preferential Trade Agreement (PTA) in Islamabad in March 2004 – which was converted into a Free Trade Agreement (FTA). The purpose of this agreement was to strengthen economic relations between the two countries and to promote bilateral trade by exploring new areas of cooperation. Under this agreement, both countries agreed to reduce customs duties on tradable items, and Pakistan committed to give a duty concession on 338 items to Iran. In return, Tehran committed to give a duty concession on 309 items to Islamabad.[89] The two countries also pledged to remove all non-tariff barriers and adopt other equivalent measures on the movement of goods. They also agreed not to increase their respective preferential tariff rates without mutual consent. According to this agreement, Pakistan also committed to providing technical assistance to Iran to achieve accession to the World Trade Organization (WTO).[90] To enhance their economic cooperation and bilateral trade, the countries identified 'twin provinces' in their 2004 agreement. The governor of Iran's Sistan and Baluchestan Province, Hussein Amini, and his Pakistani counterpart from Balochistan Province, Owais Ghani, signed the agreement linking their provinces. The latter commented that 'The declaration of two Baluchistans as twin [regions] will further improve the trade, economic and cultural ties between the two countries.'[91] Through this project, both countries aimed to address their security concerns as well as issues related to trade.

These agreements played some role in improving economic cooperation between Iran and Pakistan. Compared with the late 1990s, Iran's trade with Pakistan improved during the 2000s, although the volume of trade between the two countries remained low. Iran exported US$265 million worth of goods to Pakistan and imported US$92 million worth of goods from Pakistan during the financial year 2003–2004.[92] The principal items of trade between the two countries included textiles, agricultural

---

[86] Ibid., 228.
[87] Shah Alam, 'Iran–Pakistan Relations', 538.
[88] Vatanka, *Iran and Pakistan*, 228.
[89] Shah Alam, 'Iran–Pakistan Relations', 539.
[90] 'Pakistan, Iran to Cut Duty on 647 Items: Preferential Trade', *Dawn*, 22 August 2004, https://www.dawn.com/news/396250.
[91] Shah Alam, 'Iran–Pakistan Relations', 539.
[92] Ibid., 538.

products, fruits and iron ore. Pakistan was the first country to begin importing iron ore from Iran. Iran assured Pakistan of the provision of technical assistance in the form of experts in the exploration, expansion and modernisation of steel production plants in Karachi.[93] Iran also committed to investment in economic, industrial and mining sectors. Pakistani prime minister Shaukat Aziz visited Tehran in February 2005 for bilateral discussions focusing on the development of further economic and trade relations.[94] One of the major ECO projects was concluded in 2008 when Iran, Pakistan and Turkey established the Istanbul–Islamabad–Tehran railway network. This 6,500-km long rail network aimed to connect Central Asia with Europe. As a result of this project, Pakistan Railways started to operate between Zahedan in Iran and Quetta in Pakistan.[95] Under the ECO, Pakistan, Iran and Turkey also established a number of initiatives, including the ECO Trade and Development Bank headquartered in Turkey and its representative office in Karachi, although these initiatives have yet to achieve their goal of increasing trade between Iran and Pakistan.[96]

While the overall trade between Iran and Pakistan significantly increased in the late 2000s, from 2012 onwards the trade between the two countries decreased as a result of Iran facing international sanctions. In 2014, the overall trade between Iran and Pakistan was valued at US$217 million, including US$53 million of Pakistani exports.[97] This shows that the volume of trade between the two countries dipped even lower than during the early 2000s. The key export items from Iran to Pakistan in this period were iron ore, iron scrap, dates, detergents, transformers, chemicals, bitumen, polyethylene and propylene, whereas items exported by Pakistan to Iran included rice, fresh fruits, meat, textiles and mechanical machinery.[98]

The export of electricity from Iran to Pakistan has been an important factor in trade between the two countries. In 2002, Iran and Pakistan signed an agreement for the export of 74 MW of electricity from Iran. The project was later postponed because of international sanctions on banking transactions with Iran. Later in 2012, Pakistan signed an MoU pledging to import 1,000 MW of electricity from Iran and, according to the National Electricity and Power Regulatory Authority (NEPRA) of Pakistan, the country imported 31.3 GWh of electricity from Iran in December 2014.[99] In March 2015, the Iranian company Tavanir and the National Transmission and Dispatch Company (NTDC) approved an 1,000-MW electricity supply from Iran to Pakistan, and in August 2015, Iran offered to export 3000 MW of electricity to Pakistan.[100]

---

[93] Ibid.
[94] Rafique, 'Prospects of Pakistan–Iran Relations', 8.
[95] Ibid., 12.
[96] Ibid.
[97] Ibid., 10.
[98] Ibid.
[99] Ibid.
[100] Ibid.

Pakistan and Iran also signed five MoUs to increase their trade cooperation during a ceremony in Islamabad hosted by Pakistani prime minister Nawaz Sharif in December 2014. The MoUs included the pledge to create a Joint Investment Committee to identify potential areas of bilateral investment. Another significant aspect of these agreements was that the two countries committed to opening branches of their banks in the other's country. In addition, the agreements identified trading centres and markets on the Iran–Pakistan border, which the two countries agreed that these centres could be used to facilitate trade among local communities residing in the border provinces and offered concessional tariff rates in order to control illegal trading.[101] In April 2015, Iran and Pakistan also agreed on a five-year trade facilitation plan to increase the volume of bilateral trade to US$5 billion. Both countries called for the early elimination of all non-tariff barriers under the PTA of 2006. They also emphasised the need for joint investment in other areas such as agro-food processing and infrastructure, particularly in the field of establishing rail, air, road and sea links, as well as opening new border trade posts at Mand-Pishin and Gabd-Reemdan.[102] In a visit to Pakistan in 2015, Iranian foreign minister Zarif asserted that there was potential for greater economic cooperation between Iran and Pakistan and stated that, 'Ties with Pakistan were among the fundamentals of his country's external relations.'[103] During this visit, Iran and Pakistan agreed to enhance their cooperation on a number of issues, including the expansion of economic linkages, enhancing bilateral collaboration in the energy sector and progress on the Iran–Pakistan gas pipeline.[104] Zarif also stressed the importance of the Iran–Pakistan gas pipeline project, saying that his country was 'interested and determined' to complete it. Zarif hoped that Pakistan could identify investors who would finance the pipeline project in its territory.[105]

Pakistan welcomed Iran's nuclear deal with the P5+1 in 2015, hoping that it would deliver increased opportunities for Iran and Pakistan to enhance their economic relations.[106] Tehran and Islamabad moved forward to reach an agreement on two major energy projects: a natural gas pipeline and an electricity transmission line. These projects have the potential to help alleviate Pakistan's electricity and vehicle fuel shortages. In February 2016, Islamabad decided to revive economic and commercial relations with Tehran in the areas of trade, investment, banking, finance and energy.[107] In 2016, Tehran also made additional investments in Balochistan. Iran and Pakistan finalised a 1,000-MW electricity transmission deal that would supply

---

[101] 'Pakistan, Iran Sign 5 MoUs to Enhance Bilateral Cooperation', *Pakistan Today*, 9 December 2014, https://www.pakistantoday.com.pk/2014/12/09/pakistan-iran-sign-5-mous-to-enhance-bilateral-cooperation.

[102] 'Pakistan, Iran Eye Trade at $5 billion', *Dawn*, 23 April 2015, https://www.dawn.com/news/1177635.

[103] Syed, 'Iran Wanted Expanded Relations with Pakistan'.

[104] Ibid.

[105] Ibid.

[106] Rafique, 'Prospects of Pakistan–Iran Relations', 1.

[107] Syed, 'Iran Wanted Expanded Relations with Pakistan'.

Pakistan's Balochistan Province.[108] Further, in July 2019, in a meeting with Iran's minister of industries, mining and trade Reza Rahmani, Pakistani prime minister Imran Khan stressed Pakistan's commitment to strengthen relations with Iran, ensuring the creation of more business opportunities for the people residing along the border. Khan emphasised the need 'to enhance mutual trade and economic cooperation for the benefit of the two countries'.[109] In return, Rahmani expressed his great satisfaction at the removal of obstacles to mutual trade and development. In this meeting, Iran and Pakistan came to an agreement 'to create a committee to identify goods for promoting barter trade'.[110] Pakistan promised to enhance the export of goods such as wheat, sugar, rice and fruit to Iran. Iran showed an interest in importing 500,000 tons of rice from Pakistan and creating a mechanism for the shipment of rice. To further enhance bilateral trade and curtail possibilities for illegal trade, Iran asked the Pakistani government to create more border checkpoints, and to remove taxation measures such as road taxes on vehicles and trucks crossing the borders.[111] Overall, this meeting between Khan and Rahmani called for the promotion of trade between the two countries, stressing that Pakistan had greater potential in agriculture exports, including fruit and vegetables, while Iran had the potential to export crude oil and petroleum products to Pakistan. Finally, in a meeting between Iranian president Ebrahim Raisi and the Pakistani foreign minister in June 2022, both sides emphasised the importance of extending their relationship in the economic arena, including through energy, gas and trade cooperation, as well as border sustenance marketplaces.[112]

Gas pipeline

The Iran–Pakistan pipeline project has been the subject of discussion between the two countries since 1994. Iran signed an agreement with Pakistan in 1994 (in the era of Benazir Bhutto's premiership) to build a 2,700-km pipeline to supply Iranian natural gas from a field in the Persian Gulf to Pakistan.[113] Iran then proposed the extension of the pipeline into India and signed a preliminary agreement with India in February 1999, with India joining the project in 2005. The project was called the Iran–Pakistan–India Gas Pipeline, and aimed to create an atmosphere of peace and to facilitate the promotion of trade between these countries.[114] The project was

---

[108] Rafique, 'Prospects of Pakistan–Iran Relations', 3.
[109] 'Iran, Pakistan Keen on Promoting Trade Ties', *Financial Tribute*, 6 July 2019, https://financialtribune.com/articles/domestic-economy/98793/iran-pakistan-keen-on-promoting-trade-ties.
[110] Ibid.
[111] Ibid.
[112] 'As Much As I am a Child Of Pakistan, I am Also a Child of Iran: Bilawal Tells Ebrahim Raisi', *News International*, 15 June 2022, https://www.thenews.com.pk/latest/966357-in-meeting-with-iranian-president-bilawal-reiterates-pakistans-desire-to-strengthen-bilateral-ties.
[113] Vatanka, *Iran and Pakistan*, 213.
[114] Muhammad Saleem Mazhar and Naheed S Goraya, 'Challenges in Iran–Pakistan Gas Pipeline', *NDU Journal* 28 (2013): 164.

indeed regional in its scope at this stage because it was designed to deliver Iranian natural gas to the Indian market through Pakistan. It was also envisaged to benefit India which has a growing energy need.

In 2009, however, India withdrew from the project, claiming that it created security issues and committed the country to spending more money than it had initially expected.[115] Another factor prompting India's withdrawal from the project was that the India–US Civil–Nuclear Agreement in 2009 included the condition that India would not accept gas from Iran, but nuclear energy from the United States instead.[116] In January 2010, the United States also put pressure on Pakistan to withdraw from the project, promising Pakistan that it would receive assistance from the United States for the 'construction of a liquefied natural gas terminal and importing electricity from Tajikistan through Afghanistan's Wakhan Corridor'.[117] However, Iran and Pakistan signed a final agreement on 16 March 2010, according to which each country committed to laying its section of the pipeline by the end of 2014.[118] While Iran announced that it had finalised its section of the pipeline in July 2011 and reportedly offered Pakistan US$500 million to help with its part of the construction, Pakistan declared in March 2012 that private investors did not show enough interest and thus the government was forced either to impose a tax on consumers or to seek other agreements with Iran, China and Russia to build the pipeline.[119] Despite these difficulties, then Pakistan president Zardari and his Iranian counterpart Ahmadinejad officially inaugurated the construction of the 780-km pipeline from Iran to Pakistan in the Iranian city of Chabahar in March 2013.[120]

However, no real progress was made by Pakistan in terms of the gas pipeline project with Iran, and it began to explore other options to secure its growing energy needs. Since 2014, Pakistan has increased its imports of liquefied natural gas (LNG) from Qatar and has also been importing LNG from the United States since 2017.[121] Further, in April 2015, Pakistan signed an agreement with China to build an LNG pipeline between Gwadar and Nawabshah in addition to an LNG terminal. The contractor for this project was China National Petroleum Corporation (CNPC), which provided 85 per cent of the financing for the project.[122] During a February 2019 visit to Pakistan, King Salman of Saudi Arabia offered several energy project proposals

---

[115] Muhammad Munir, Muhammad Ahsan and Saman Zulfqar, 'Iran–Pakistan Gas Pipeline: Cost–Benefit Analysis', *Journal of Political Studies* 20(2) (2013): 162.
[116] Mazhar and Goraya, 'Challenges in Iran–Pakistan Gas Pipeline', 166.
[117] Munir, Ahsan and Zulfqar, 'Iran–Pakistan Gas Pipeline', 162.
[118] Ibid.
[119] Ibid.
[120] Safdar Sial, *An Analysis of Emerging Pakistani–Iranian Ties* (Oslo: Norwegian Peacebuilding Resource Centre, 2015), https://www.files.ethz.ch/isn/190006/d7f90a473ca2847f0ccf74f31d02fb8e.pdf.
[121] Haroon Janjua, 'Iran Gas Pipeline Deal with Pakistan Hampered by US Sanctions', *DW*, 20 May 2019, https://www.dw.com/en/iran-gas-pipeline-deal-with-pakistan-hampered-by-us-sanctions/a-48802450.
[122] Zafar Iqbal, 'Pakistan's Hope for Energy Pipeline with Iran Evaporate', *Asia Times*, 1 July 2019, https://asiatimes.com/2019/07/pakistans-hopes-for-an-energy-pipeline-with-iran-evaporate.

to Pakistan, suggesting Saudi Arabia as a replacement of Iran in terms of Pakistan's energy security. As will be explained in the next section, Pakistan finally withdrew from the pipeline project with Iran in 2019. It should be noted that the gas pipeline could play an important role in Pakistan's energy requirements by minimising its natural gas shortage of 1,000–1,500 Mcf and compensate for the shortage of 5,000–6,000 MW electricity in the country.[123] As such, from a geoeconomic perspective, the project is important for Pakistan as it would also allow Pakistan to reduce its oil imports by US$5.3 billion.[124]

The US factor

The level of economic cooperation between Iran and Pakistan is generally low. According to the International Monetary Fund, Pakistan is Iran's eleventh largest trading partner.[125] The volume of trade between the two countries has remained much lower than its potential.[126] There is, however, a high volume of trade between Iran and Pakistan through third-country channels and illegal financial transactions, owing primarily to Western sanctions on Iran.[127] These indirect modes of business transactions between Iran and Pakistan are mostly undertaken through the UAE.[128]

The level of economic cooperation between Iran and Pakistan is less than expected even though there is huge potential for expanding trade between them. Factors which explain the marginal trade between Pakistan and Iran are American pressure and international sanctions on Iran, as well as Pakistan's relations with Arab states especially Saudi Arabia. As Vatanka states, 'Since Iran's revolution of 1979, Islamabad has without doubt prioritized its ties to the US and the oil rich Arab countries of the Persian Gulf region over Tehran.'[129] America has repeatedly attempted to dissuade Pakistan from engaging in negotiations on the Iran–Pakistan–India pipeline. The United States believed that this project would nullify its efforts to isolate Iran economically and would instead allow Iran to improve its economic conditions. US president George W. Bush's energy secretary Samuel Bodman visited Pakistan in 2005 and publicly expressed the US dissatisfaction over the pipeline project.[130] In the same year, US secretary of state Condoleezza Rice reiterated the US position on the project, stressing that it was against US laws.[131] In April 2007, the US embassy's deputy chief of mission in Pakistan, Peter Bodde,

---

[123] Munir, Ahsan and Zulfqar, 'Iran–Pakistan Gas Pipeline', 167.
[124] Ibid.
[125] Sial, *An Analysis of Emerging Pakistani–Iranian Ties*, 2.
[126] Ibid.
[127] Rafique, 'Prospects of Pakistan–Iran Relations', 4.
[128] Sial, *An Analysis of Emerging Pakistani–Iranian Ties*, 2.
[129] Vatanka, *Iran and Pakistan*, 256.
[130] Sumita Kumar, 'Pakistan–Iran Relations: The US Factor', *Strategic Analysis* 35 (2008): 779.
[131] Ibid.

stated that 'we will continue our opposition [to the pipeline]. At the same time, Pakistan should put more focus on finding means for alternate energy resources, such as coal or wind or solar energy.'[132] The United States remained opposed to the pipeline project and tried to persuade Pakistan to withdraw from it during the Obama presidency before the JCPOA agreement. Further, under the Obama administration, the United States offered an alternative project to Pakistan in 2010 – namely, the Turkmenistan, Afghanistan, Pakistan and India (TAPI) project. In addition, the United States helped Pakistan to construct a joint LNG terminal through facilitating the provision of electricity from Tajikistan, on the condition that Pakistan withdrew from the project involving Iran.[133]

Islamabad, for its part, has attempted to persuade the United States that trade with Iran is critical for Pakistan. In 2013, Pakistani officials emphasised that the scale of US aid was insufficient to resolve the energy crisis facing the nation. Pakistan told then US secretary of state John Kerry that the planned US$7.5 billion gas pipeline from Iran was important for Pakistan.[134] Despite this, Pakistan told Iran in 2013 that it could not complete its part of the pipeline by the deadline of December 2014 due to international sanctions on Iran, stating further that despite the country's best efforts, international contractors and equipment suppliers were unwilling to involve themselves in the project. As noted by Sial, Pakistan did not even allocate any funds for the pipeline project in its 2013–2014 federal budget.[135] At that time, Pakistan was under significant pressure from the United States to abandon the project. The US factor in hindering better relations between Iran and Pakistan has been pointed out by Iranian leaders. For example, during Sharif's visit to Iran in May 2014, Iranian supreme leader Ayatollah Khamenei asked the Pakistani prime minister not to wait for 'permission' from other countries to improve relations between Iran and Pakistan, an implicit reference to the pipeline project.[136]

Despite efforts by both Pakistan and Iran to remain in the pipeline project, in 2019 Pakistan withdrew from it because of the threat of US sanctions. The United States warned Pakistan that it would face a heavy financial penalty if it remained in a bilateral agreement with Iran. In May 2019, Pakistan informed Iran that it could not complete the pipeline project as long as Iran was under the US sanctions. The Pakistani managing director of Inter State Gas, Mobin Saulat, stated that 'Under present US sanctions on Iran, it is impossible to execute the IP [Iran–Pakistan] gas pipeline project and we have conveyed it to them [Iran] in writing recently.'[137] Saulat

---

[132] Ibid., 780.
[133] Munir, Ahsan and Zulfqar, 'Iran–Pakistan Gas Pipeline', 166.
[134] Vatanka, *Iran and Pakistan*, 254.
[135] Sial, *An Analysis of Emerging Pakistani–Iranian Ties*, 2.
[136] Ibid.
[137] 'US Sanctions: Pakistan Refuses to Work on Gas Pipeline Project with Iran', *The News*, 12 May 2019, https://www.thenews.com.pk/print/470290-us-sanctions-pakistan-refuses-to-work-on-gas-pipeline-project-with-iran.

continued, 'We cannot risk US sanctions by going ahead with the project as America has clearly said that anybody who will work with Iran will also be sanctioned.'[138] According to Fatemeh Aman, the failure of the pipeline project in part reflects the lack of funds from Pakistan in addition to its lack of will to complete the project. According to Aman, 'Pakistan's economic situation is much worse than when the project started.' Aman also considers the United States and regional tensions between Iran and Arab states as factors that contributed to the failure of the project.[139]

In addition to the US factor, it is important to note that the low volume of trade between Iran and Pakistan is partly due to the latter's lack of political will and its other strategic priorities. According to Sial, 'Pakistan could prepare a strong case to convince the US that the Gas Purchase Agreement for the project was signed before the latest sanctions on Iran came into force.'[140] The failure of the pipeline project is also partly due to regional tensions between Saudi Arabia and Iran. A close ally of Pakistan, Saudi Arabia exerted pressure on Pakistan in April 2012 to withdraw from the project and offered Pakistan oil, gas and cash in compensation.[141] In May 2013, Riyadh agreed to provide Pakistan with US$12–15 billion in oil supplies over three years via a deferred payment plan, on the condition that Pakistan reconsidered pushing ahead with the pipeline project with Iran.[142]

The economic relationship between Iran and Pakistan was viewed in a range of ways by our interviewees in Pakistan. The majority of interviewees believed that there is no strong economic relationship between Iran and Pakistan. One interviewee from al-Mustafa University in Islamabad stated that 'there is no common economic interest with Iran, however there is a potential for these interests'[143] and that 'Pakistan has not been able to benefit out of Iran economically'.[144] Only one of our interviewees, who was a former ambassador and lieutenant general in the Pakistan army, acknowledged some forms of economic cooperation between Iran and Shia's in Pakistan, particularly Hazaras in Quetta and Shi'as in Karachi.[145] Iran's economic influence in Balochistan was also acknowledged by some participants, who considered that the province was a source of trade between Iran and Pakistan and described it as a region 'dependent on Iran'.[146] Even though Balochistan is a mainly Sunni-populated province, Iran's significant influence there, especially in Makran, was highlighted by some of our research participants.[147] For several participants, Pakistan's alliances with the United States and Saudi Arabia explained the lack of economic cooperation between Iran

---

[138] Ibid.
[139] Aman, 'Water Dispute Escalating between Iran and Afghanistan'.
[140] Sial, *An Analysis of Emerging Pakistani–Iranian Ties*, 2.
[141] Mazhar and Goraya, 'Challenges in Iran–Pakistan Gas Pipeline', 168.
[142] Vatanka, *Iran and Pakistan*, 256.
[143] P13, interviewed on 17 May 2019, Islamabad.
[144] Ibid.
[145] P18, interviewed on 30 May 2019, Islamabad.
[146] P6, interviewed on 24 May 2019, Islamabad.
[147] Ibid.

and Pakistan.[148] It was argued that US sanctions on Iran leave 'very little space for Pakistan to cooperate economically [with Iran]'.[149]

Conclusion

As demonstrated in this chapter, the fall of the first Taliban regime in 2001 assisted Iran in terms of its economic influence in Afghanistan. This initially happened through Iran's gradual involvement in internationally backed reconstruction projects in Afghanistan. Many Afghan cities, especially in the west of the country, gradually became dependent on Iranian-funded projects for their economic wellbeing. The volume of trade between Iran and Afghanistan increased, and with that Iran's economic influence, due to Afghanistan's dependence on Iranian goods. Iran's economic influence, however, is more visible in some Afghan regions, such as Herat. As explained, Iran at times used its economic influence in Afghanistan to achieve certain political goals. Since the Taliban's takeover, Iranian exports to Afghanistan have significantly declined but it is hard to predict its trajectory as Afghanistan and Iran are eager to benefit from China's BRI – something with huge potential for investment not just in both countries, but also for economic cooperation between Afghanistan and Iran.

As examined in this chapter, Iran's economic cooperation with Pakistan has not been smooth. In the early years after the establishment of the Islamic Republic of Iran, economic relations between the two countries grew significantly, but declined again during the 1990s. In the early 2000s, Iran tried to increase its trade with Pakistan and although the economic relations between the two countries improved, the bilateral trade remained low. The overall trade between Iran and Pakistan decreased from the early 2010s mainly because of US sanctions on Tehran. Although officials from Iran and Pakistan have met several times to discuss their trade relationship, Iran has not yet been able to increase its trade with Pakistan. Pakistan–Saudi relations were also identified as a significant element and source of contention between Iran and Pakistan as Islamabad has a tilt towards Riyadh. Unlike the case of Afghanistan, Iran's economic ties with Pakistan are not so significant that they could help Tehran use them as a lever to achieve certain political goals.

Moving from soft power influence to hard power capabilities, Chapter 8 explores Iran's recruitment policy and addresses the extent to which Iran has managed to recruit Shi'a fighters from Afghanistan and Pakistan to fight in Syria against anti-Assad forces and fighters associated with radical Sunni Islamists there. As soft and hard power strategies are part of Iran's 'Twenty-year Vision Document' to achieve regional supremacy, we will focus on the degree to which Iran's soft power helped the country to achieve hard power goals through the recruitment of Afghan and Pakistani Shi'as for geopolitical gain in Syria.

---

[148] P12, interviewed on 27 May 2019, Islamabad.
[149] P17, interviewed on 29 May 2019, Islamabad.

8
Recruitment: Shi'a Brigades in Syria

Syria is one of Iran's key allies in the Middle East. After the beginning of the Arab Spring uprisings in Syria and since the outbreak of civil war in the country, Syrian rebels have been supported and equipped by some countries in the region, such as Saudi Arabia and Turkey, as well as by the United States and its Western allies. In response, Iran supported the Bashar al-Assad regime. The reason for Iranian involvement in the Syrian conflict is that Assad's government protects Iranian interests, preserves Tehran's influence in the Levant and, most importantly, facilitates Iran's access to Hezbollah. Indeed, Syria has often functioned as the main transit route for Iranian weapons and equipment to Hezbollah.[1] In addition, Hezbollah has been a significant strategic asset for Iran, providing Tehran with deterrent capacity against Israel – Tehran's most significant regional enemy. Considering this, from the early days of the Syrian civil war, many Iranian strategists and military figures have seen it as necessary to take active measures to support Assad's forces. Those active measures included direct military support in which the IRGC has been instrumental in terms of supplying tactical and military support as well as combatants (e.g., Shi'as from Afghanistan and Pakistan). In this chapter we explore the extent to which Iran's soft power in Afghanistan and Pakistan has played a role in its ability to recruit Shi'as from both countries towards the Fatemiyoun and the Zainabiyoun Brigades, respectively, to support the Assad regime against the rebels and ISIS in the Syrian civil war. Like previous chapters, we refer to our interview data to understand how some prominent opinion-makers from Afghanistan and Pakistan view Iranian recruitment of Shi'as from their countries.

Afghan Shi'a fighters in Syria

Since the start of the Syrian conflict in 2011, Tehran has been playing an active role in keeping Bashar al-Assad in power. Iran has funded, armed, trained and sent commanders to Syria to help Assad's army. Iran's close ally Hezbollah also sent commanders and soldiers to support the Syrian government. Even though Iran often denied the military presence of its commanders in Syria, Iranian IRGC leaders at times confirmed the presence of their own soldiers and commanders in different cities of Syria. For example, senior IRGC commander General

---

[1] W. Andrew Terrill, 'Iran's Strategy for Saving Asad', *Middle East Journal* 69(2) (2015): 226.

Hussein Hamadani, who was killed in Syria in 2015, confirmed in 2014 that Iran had trained some soldiers for Syria.[2] Iran is also reported to have recruited and trained fighters from established organisations in Syria, such as Asaib Ahl al-Haqq (AAH) and Kataib Hezbollah. As will be discussed, the IRGC recruited and trained Shi'as from other countries, especially Pakistan and Afghanistan, to fight in Syria to help the Assad regime. Iran appears to have taken advantage of its cultural and religious links with Afghan and Pakistani Shi'as in its recruitment strategy.

Liwa Fatemiyoun, or the Fatemiyoun Brigade, is one of the proxy forces deployed by Iran to Syria. It comprises Afghan fighters who counter rebels and opposition groups. According to a report published by the Iranian *Kayhan* newspaper in 2015, the name 'Fatemiyoun', literally meaning 'the followers of Fatima' (Fatima was the daughter of the Prophet Muhammad and the wife of the fourth Muslim caliph and the first Shi'a imam, Ali ibn Abi Talib), was chosen because the group was formed during the annual period of mourning for Fatima, although the report does not mention during which year's commemorations the brigade was established.[3] Iran has repeatedly denied any role in the formation of the Fatemiyoun Brigade, stressing that it has a solely advisory role in Syria. *Kayhan* reported that the Fatemiyoun Brigade operates independently from Iranian forces in Syria.[4] Iranian officials often describe Afghan fighters in Syria as religious volunteers who want to defend holy Shi'a shrines from ISIS.[5] As early as 2018, it was estimated that as many as 841 Afghan fighters have been killed in Syria.[6] Some survivors recount hard-fought battles around Damascus and Aleppo. It is estimated that between 5,000 and 12,000 Afghans have participated in the Fatemiyoun Brigade.[7] According to a Carnegie Endowment for International Peace survey of funerals for Shi'a foreign fighters who fought in Syria, the Fatemiyoun Brigade has suffered the second largest number of losses in Syria after Hezbollah among Tehran's Shi'a foreign legions.[8]

Afghan recruits, like Hezbollah and most Iranians, are Shi'as and support the Assad regime in Syria. Afghan recruits were either chosen from Afghan refugees living in Iran or were recruited directly from Afghanistan. According to Hashemi, 'Iran wants to play a command and control role in Syria and with the Afghan

---

[2] Farnaz Fassihi, 'Iran Pays Afghans to Fight for Assad', *Wall Street Journal*, 22 May 2014, https://www.wsj.com/articles/iran-recruiting-afghan-refugees-to-fight-for-regime-in-syria-1400197482?tesla=y.

[3] 'How Was the Fatemiyoun Brigade Formed?' *Kayhan*, 22 May 2015, http://kayhan.ir/fa/news/46030/لشکر-فاطمیون-چگونه-شکل-گرفت

[4] Ibid.

[5] Pamela Constable, 'Recruited by Iran to Fight for Syrian Regime, Young Afghans Bring Home Cash and Scares', *Washington Post*, 30 July 2018, https://www.washingtonpost.com/world/asia_pacific/recruited-by-iran-to-fight-for-syrian-regime-young-afghans-bring-home-cash-and-scars/2018/07/29/ecf9e34c-64e0-11e8-81ca-bb14593acaa6_story.html.

[6] Ali Alfoneh, 'Tehran's Shia Foreign Legions', Carnegie Endowment for International Peace, 30 January 2018, https://carnegieendowment.org/2018/01/30/tehran-s-shia-foreign-legions-pub-75387.

[7] Constable, 'Recruited by Iran to Fight for Syrian Regime'.

[8] Alfoneh, 'Tehran's Shia Foreign Legions'.

refugees, they are purchasing mercenaries to do the fighting for them.'[9] Given the significant population of Afghan refugees in Iran as we explained in Chapter 3, Iran may have viewed them as a tool to extend its influence in Syria. As argued by Smyth, Afghan Shi'a refugees could appear good candidates for Tehran to fight rebels in Syria because some of them have formative experiences fighting the Taliban in Afghanistan.[10] In addition, it is often claimed that Iran used the legal and socioeconomic vulnerability of the large population of Afghan refugees on its soil to recruit them for the war in Syria. Indeed, as discussed Chapter 3, Afghan refugees are among the most vulnerable and poor groups in Iran. Many of the Afghans living in Iran are unregistered migrants and they do not have official permission to work in Iran, or even register births or marriages. Many Afghan refugees experience high unemployment and uncertain residency status; therefore, it is not surprising that they have been easy targets for militia recruitment drives. Some Afghans might have also travelled to Syria to defend sacred Shi'a shrines and mosques as a religious obligation, but, as will be discussed below, other factors including their socioeconomic situation could have also contributed to their choice to fight in Syria.

It was argued by the vast majority of Afghan participants in our research that Afghans joined the Fatemiyoun Brigade for ideological and economic reasons. Interviewees thought that 'by giving them [Afghans] money, a place to live and citizenship' Iran attracted people to join Fatemiyoun.[11] As one of our participants noted, recruited Afghans 'consented to fight in Syria just to support their families'.[12] Economic and religious factors were acknowledged among the main reasons for Afghan fighters being recruited by Tehran.[13] Participants emphasised economic factors very strongly in motivating Afghans to fight in Syria. It was highlighted by one interviewee that 'Iran gives between US$500 and US$700 [per month] to Afghan refugees to fight in Syria.' Afghans therefore 'didn't go [to Syria] for religion [alone], but for the money they were promised'.[14]

Other reasons highlighted by interviewees for the involvement of Afghan fighters in the Syrian conflict included the defencelessness of Afghan refugees in Iran. It was argued that Afghan refugees who are recruited and sent to Syria receive no support from the Afghan government and are therefore the best targets for Tehran's recruitment drives.[15] It was also noted that Iran recruits Afghans in exchange for an offer of Iranian citizenship. Another response we received from our Afghan participants was that Iran used many illegal Afghan residents in Iran, meaning those without valid visas, to fight in Syria. Such Afghan nationals are often arrested and

---

[9] Fassihi, 'Iran Pays Afghans to Fight for Assad'.
[10] Philip Smyth, 'Iran's Afghan Shiite Fighters in Syria', *Washington Institute*, 3 June 2014, https://www.washingtoninstitute.org/policy-analysis/view/irans-afghan-shiite-fighters-in-syria.
[11] A6, interviewed 22 May 2019, Kabul; A23, interviewed on 25 June 2019, Kabul.
[12] Ibid.
[13] A2, interviewed on 12 May 2019, Kabul.
[14] A23, interviewed on 25 June 2019, Kabul.
[15] A1, interviewed on 8 May 2019, Kabul.

imprisoned in Iran because they do not have proper documentation to stay in Iran and that is where many were offered a deal to gain a permanent residency in Iran in exchange of fighting in Syria. Several respondents noted that Iran also uses various TV programmes and social media campaigns to convince Afghans to fight in Syria.[16]

Iran's recruitment of Afghan Shi'as to join the Fatemiyoun Brigade has been occurring since the beginning of Iran's involvement in the Syrian civil war. While it was highlighted by most research participants that Afghan Hazaras have been recruited by Iran, some stated that Shi'as from other ethnic groups, like Uzbeks and Tajiks, have also been targeted. Participants noted that various methods have been adopted for the recruitment of Afghan fighters, including through travel agencies that facilitate Shi'a pilgrims' travel from Afghanistan to pilgrimage sites via Afghan refugee camps in Iran.[17] An Afghan political analyst revealed that 'these travel agencies take people to holy places and on the way, during the visit, incite them against ISIS and convince them to go [to Syria] and fight [ISIS]'.[18] Participants asserted that some travel agencies engaging in such recruitment processes were located in west Kabul and Herat. Another participant stated that the recruitment process is reportedly undertaken in two ways: '[Either] Iran recruited Afghan refugees from refugee camps inside Iran by pressuring them, especially those who have gone there for work . . . [or] they [Iranians] created a network through which they could hire Afghans from inside Afghanistan.'[19] The Iranian cities from which Iran recruited Afghans include Mashhad, Tehran, Shiraz and Qom. It was highlighted that the IRGC was directly involved in recruiting Afghans and had established centres in cities including Esfahan, Mashhad, Tehran and Shiraz to facilitate the recruitment process.[20] Afghan refugees without a military background were trained at certain IRGC military bases.[21] Interviewees noted that recruitment for the Fatemiyoun Brigade also took place in Afghan cities such as Kabul, Ghazni, Bamyan, Daikondi and Orozgan.[22]

In terms of the operational presence of Afghan fighters in Syria, there are some reports demonstrating that Iran had begun to deploy them by late 2012. In October 2012, some members of the main Syrian opposition group, the Free Syrian Army, claimed to have captured an Afghan Shi'a fighter and after interrogating him found that he had received a payment from Iran to fight in Syria.[23] The presence of Afghan Shi'a fighters in Syria became more prominent in 2013 as opposition groups circulated images of Afghan fighters holding weapons on their social media pages. In addition, some social media posts appeared on pro-Shi'a militia Facebook pages

---

[16] A18, interviewed on 16 June 2019, Kabul.
[17] A6, interviewed 22 May 2019, Kabul.
[18] A11, interviewed on 9 June 2019, Kabul.
[19] A7, interviewed on 29 June 2019, Kabul.
[20] A21, interviewed on 22 June 2019, Kabul.
[21] A23, interviewed on 25 June 2019, Kabul.
[22] Ibid.
[23] Smyth, 'Iran's Afghan Shiite Fighters in Syria'.

suggesting that there were some Afghan Shi'a Hazaras fighting alongside Bashar al-Assad's forces against rebels and opposition groups including radical Sunni militant groups. Some photos and videos were released showing Afghan Shi'a militias. Some of these fighters who were killed in Syria were called martyrs, and their faces were shown, although their names were never mentioned.[24] According to Ostovar, in December 2013, an official Iranian outlet *Fars News* declared the formation of a Fatemiyoun Brigade in Kabul to defend the Sayyida Zaynab shrine in Syria.[25]

Public funerals held in Iran during November and December 2013 indicated that Afghan Shi'a fighters had resided in different cities of Iran, including Isfahan, Mashhad, Tehran and Qom. According to a report published in the *Wall Street Journal* in 2014, based on an account published in December 2013 by the *Fars News* agency, one person killed in Syria in 2013 was Reza Ismail, a 19-year-old Afghan refugee from the northeastern Iranian city of Mashhad, relatively close to the Afghan border. He was recruited by the IRGC to fight in Syria and received promotions in quick succession to become a leader of the Fatemiyoun Brigade.[26] In May 2014, a large funeral was held in Mashhad for four Afghan refugees killed in Syria.[27] In the same month, Kabul asked Tehran to stop the recruitment of Afghan citizens for the war in Syria. Without any concrete evidence, the Afghan government threatened Iran that it would file a complaint with the UN High Commissioner for Refugees if the recruitment of its citizens by Iran did not cease.[28] Members of the Afghan parliament, including Shokriye Peykan, openly accused Iran of using the poor conditions of Afghan refugees in Iran to entice them to fight in Syria.[29] It should be noted that at the same time as the funerals, Iranian officials like Hamid Babaei, a spokesman for Iran's mission to the United Nations in New York, denied all allegations that Iran had sent Afghan refugees to Syria. He stated that the 'Iranian presence in the country is solely advisory in nature in order to help counter the extremist . . . al-Qaeda groups from committing more massacre and bloodshed.'[30]

There are various reasons for the presence of Afghan fighters in Syria. Some reports show that the IRGC recruited Afghan refugees by promising them a remuneration of US$500–US$600 per month in addition to Iranian residency documents.[31] An Afghan fighter captured by rebels in Syria near Aleppo in 2013

---

[24] Philip Smyth, 'Hizballah Cavalcade: The Lion of Damascus, and Afghans, and Africans', *Jihadology*, 30 July 2013, https://jihadology.net/2013/07/30/hizballah-cavalcade-the-lion-of-damascus-and-afghans-and-africans-oh-my-fighters-from-exotic-locales-in-syrias-shia-militias/#_ftn2.

[25] Afson Ostovar, *Vanguard of the Imam: Religion, Politics and Iran's Revolutionary Guards* (Oxford: Oxford University Press, 2016), 219.

[26] Fassihi, 'Iran Pays Afghans to Fight for Assad'.

[27] Ibid.

[28] Smyth, 'Iran's Afghan Shiite Fighters in Syria'.

[29] 'Iran is Forcing Poor Afghans to Fight and Die in Syria', *Medium*, 22 October 2014, https://medium.com/war-is-boring/iran-is-forcing-poor-afghans-to-fight-and-die-in-syria-4e58fc839be2.

[30] Fassihi, 'Iran Pays Afghans to Fight for Assad'.

[31] Smyth, 'Iran's Afghan Shiite Fighters in Syria'.

claimed that he was an illegal immigrant from Varamin, an impoverished town near Tehran, and Iranian authorities had offered him a monthly payment of US$600 to fight in Syria.[32] Another captured Afghan fighter stated that he was offered release from an Iranian prison and a monthly payment of US$600 to fight in Syria.[33] The office of Ayatollah Mohaghagh Kaboli, a senior Afghan cleric in Qom, once described the recruitment process: '[the IRGC] find a connection to the refugee community and work on convincing our youth to go and fight in Syria ... They give them everything from salary to residency.'[34] According to a US Institute of Peace report, the marginalisation of Shi'as in Afghanistan, particularly Hazaras, had a significant role in Iran's success in recruiting them for the war in Syria.[35] One fighter named Naeem said that he decided to sign up to fight against ISIS in Syria in 2015 when he was visiting Iran in search of work to support his family in Herat. Naeem said, 'Afghans are dying for $30 a day. My cousin died in front of my eyes ... But there is no work for us anywhere. There is nothing to do but fight. I know I am gambling with my life, but it is a matter of necessity.' He also said that the main reason why he kept fighting in Syria was to save enough money to marry his fiancée.[36] Some fighters seem to be family breadwinners, and thus fight in Syria to provide adequate financial assistance to their families in Afghanistan. The mother of one fighter from Herat said that her son was sent to Iran and then to Syria in order to earn money to send to his family.[37] Besides other benefits, it has also been reported that Iranian authorities also offered education for Afghan children as a reward for their fathers fighting in Syria.[38]

There is also other evidence to suggest that the recruitment of Afghans has the official backing of Tehran. Hussain, an Afghan Shi'a Hazara who has served four times in Syria since 2014, stated in an interview that, 'Nobody forced us to go fight, but it gives you a kind of pride.'[39] He further revealed that he was trained by Iranian instructors and in return was promised medical treatment and the necessary documents to move freely inside Iran.[40] During the early years of the Syrian civil war, when the presence of Sunni militant groups especially ISIS was very strong, the pace and intensity of the recruitment of Afghan fighters by Iran was high. According to Hussain, at first, the authorities 'would take anyone, young or old, Shiite or Sunni. We would register in the morning, and they would send us for training in the afternoon'.[41]

[32] 'Iran is Forcing Poor Afghans to Fight and Die in Syria'.
[33] Ibid.
[34] See at: https://www.memri.org/reports/afghan-mps-slam-iran-forcibly-sending-afghan-refugees-fight-syria-alongside-bashar-al-assads.
[35] Alfoneh, 'Four Decades in the Making'.
[36] Constable, 'Recruited by Iran to Fight for Syrian Regime'.
[37] Ibid.
[38] Alfoneh, 'Four Decades in the Making'.
[39] Constable, 'Recruited by Iran to Fight for Syrian Regime'.
[40] Ibid.
[41] Ibid.

Tehran's role in recruiting Afghan refugees for the war in Syria was widely criticised by our Afghan research participants. The Fatemiyoun Brigade was described as part of 'a war machine of Iran in the Middle East against its rivals' by one interviewee.[42] By recruiting Afghans for the war in Syria, Iran was also argued to be openly interfering 'in Afghanistan without considering any law or principle'.[43] The impact of the Fatemiyoun within Afghanistan was also a matter of concern for one participant who stated that 'if the situation continues like this, religious wars will start in this country'.[44] It was also suggested that the recruitment process may increase the degree of 'racism against Hazaras or Shi'a Afghans and threaten Afghan Hazaras' security inside the country'.[45]

Despite these criticisms, some respondents had a less negative view about the Fatemiyoun Brigade, suggesting that Afghan Shi'as were not forcibly sent to Syria to fight.[46] Noting that 'forceful actions cannot last for long', one participant concluded, 'people of Afghanistan completely consent to go to the Syrian war'.[47] Another interviewee from Afghanistan's PTRO noted that 'our Shi'a countrymen are fighting in the [Syrian] war . . . not forcefully [recruited] but via agreement'.[48] Reflecting scepticism of the Fatemiyoun Brigade altogether, one respondent noted, 'I do not believe that Fatemiyoun even exists . . . [the concept of] Fatemiyoun is propaganda against Iran by Europe and the USA . . . I have not seen any evidence proving that Iran has created a group named Fatemiyoun.'[49]

As we explored in our data, Iran's recruitment of Afghan Shi'as has had a negative impact on its goodwill. This was clearly reflected in the views of numerous participants. Some participants stated that many Afghans, even Hazaras, are critical of Iran's policy towards Afghanistan, in particular the recruitment of the country's Shi'as for the war in Syria. A political analyst acknowledged, 'our non-partisan people [in Afghanistan] are thinking, why are our innocent young people going to Iran, and how can Iran be recruiting them openly? This is not favourable for the Afghan people.'[50] Similarly, a representative of the State Ministry for Parliamentary Affairs stated that people in Afghanistan follow news related to the Fatemiyoun Brigade, and 'feel sorry' for their brothers killed in Syria.[51] A general viewpoint was that Iran has been exploiting Afghan refugees to achieve its geopolitical objectives in Syria. Some respondents stated that Iran's involvement in Afghanistan and the recruitment of Afghans could be dangerous for Afghanistan's security in both the

---

[42] A11, interviewed on 9 June 2019, Kabul.
[43] A6, interviewed 22 May 2019, Kabul.
[44] A24, interviewed on 27 June 2019, Kabul.
[45] A8, interviewed on 8 May 2019, Kabul.
[46] A2, interviewed on 12 May 2019, Kabul.
[47] Ibid.
[48] A24, interviewed on 27 June 2019, Kabul.
[49] A2, interviewed on 12 May 2019, Kabul.
[50] A6, interviewed 22 May 2019, Kabul.
[51] A17, interviewed on 16 June 2019, Kabul.

short and long term, potentially transforming Afghanistan into a 'backyard for proxy wars'.[52] From this perspective, they criticised the recruitment process. According to one participant, an academic at Khatam Al-Nabieen University and a former member of parliament, 'the recruitment process can indeed transform Afghanistan into a "competition between Iran and Saudi Arabia" which is very dangerous for the country'.[53] When condemning Iran's recruitment efforts, some participants also criticised its unacceptable treatment of Afghan refugees and labelled this exploitation of Afghan citizens as a human rights violation.[54]

Some participants were highly critical of the role of local Afghan religious leaders, stressing that many Shi'a leaders in Afghanistan do not consider Afghanistan's national interest. One respondent asserted, 'They [Afghan Shi'a leaders] are [merely] preaching for the Fatemiyoun division and they are not acting based on the national interest.'[55] The argument was also made that those Shi'a religious leaders in Afghanistan who are supported by Tehran are the ones not objecting to the recruitment process.[56] Some participants added that other Afghan religious scholars have occasionally criticised the recruitment process. For instance, some Shi'a leaders in Afghanistan, including Ayatollah Wahid Behsoodi, have denounced Iran's actions in recruiting Afghans.[57] Yet Iran's support of Shi'a religious leaders in Afghanistan, such as Mohammad Mohaqiq, is noteworthy as well. This support has arguably led to Shi'a leaders either supporting or ignoring the Iranian recruitment of Afghan Shi'as.[58] When he was a parliamentarian in 2017, Mohaqiq participated in a Fatemiyoun gathering in Iran.[59]

In our data, we noticed that the Afghan participants talked about two groups of religious leaders in Afghanistan. One group that 'followed Iranian political Shi'a jurisprudence and issued decrees that saw fighting with the Fatemiyoun as a privilege', and the other that did not support this, viewing the Syrian war as purely a domestic problem in Syria.[60] According to the latter group, it is only when ISIS fights directly against Shi'as in Afghanistan that it is incumbent upon Afghan Shi'as to engage.[61] Most of the participants thought that Shi'a religious leaders in Afghanistan should raise their voices more and should react more seriously against the recruitment process. An official of Afghan High Peace Council stated that, 'our religious leaders must prevent this [recruitment process] by giving speeches

[52] A11, interviewed on 9 June 2019, Kabul.
[53] A19, interviewed on 17 June 2019, Kabul.
[54] A13, interview on 11 June 2019, Kabul.
[55] A11, interviewed on 9 June 2019, Kabul.
[56] A10, interviewed on 2 June 2019, Kabul; A11, interviewed on 9 June 2019, Kabul.
[57] A7, interviewed on 29 June 2019, Kabul.
[58] A21, interviewed on 22 June 2019, Kabul.
[59] 'Afghan Govt Leader Spotted in Fatemiyoun Brigade Gathering Sparks Concerns', *Khaama*, 26 November 2017, https://www.khaama.com/afghan-govt-leader-spotted-in-fatemiyoun-brigade-gathering-sparks-concerns-03919.
[60] A23, interviewed on 25 June 2019, Kabul.
[61] Ibid.

about this matter'.⁶² Others stated that Afghan Shi'a leaders have no role in the recruitment and cannot do anything when the government lacks the capacity to react effectively.⁶³

Respondents also noted that many Afghan political groups are themselves connected to foreign countries and receive funds from them, and thus do not consider the Afghan national interest when it comes to issues such as the recruitment of Afghan Shi'as. Others considered that there are some political parties in Afghanistan that disagree with the recruitment process, but have not expressed their objections publicly. For instance, while some political parties associated with the Hazaras disagree with Iran's recruitment of Afghans to fight in Syria, they have no power to put pressure on Iran.⁶⁴ In general, there is a widespread perception that political parties in Afghanistan have not expressed concern over the recruitment of Afghan Shi'as by Iran. There have, however, been sporadic criticisms made of the recruitment process. For example, one of our research participants reported that Dr Abdullah Abdullah (former chief executive officer of Afghanistan) criticised Iran's recruitment of Afghan Shi'as in a press conference.⁶⁵ The head of the Ministry of Foreign Affairs of Afghanistan also reportedly summoned the Iranian ambassador in Kabul to express Afghanistan's objection to Iran's recruitment of Afghan Shi'as.⁶⁶ While we cannot confirm all these reports, some could be validated. For example, we found evidence that Dr Abdullah had expressed his government's opposition to the participation of Afghan citizens in any foreign war in very strong terms. Other reports have also recorded strong reactions of several former Afghan parliamentarians, including Rauf Ibrahimi, to the recruitment drive.⁶⁷ Despite this opposition, there was also some agreement with Afghans fighting in Syria. For example, the former deputy chief executive of Afghanistan and a Hazara Shi'a, Mohammad Mohaqiq, spoke in favour of Afghans fighting in Syria, stating that:

> I thank all the warriors who co-operated in these wars from Iraq, Syria, Afghanistan and Pakistan and other parts of the world who attended the wars . . . In fact, it was the war of Islam against infidelity and against the conspiracies of the world's arrogance.⁶⁸

Most participants highlighted that Afghanistan lacked the instruments to counter Iranian influence and did not take any effective action to prevent Afghans from fighting in Syria. An Afghan participant shared that the 'Afghan government's

---

⁶² A4, interviewed on 20 May 2019, Kabul.
⁶³ A24, interviewed on 27 June 2019, Kabul.
⁶⁴ A26, interviewed on 29 June 2019, Kabul; A11, interviewed on 9 June 2019, Kabul.
⁶⁵ A25, interviewed on 29 June 2019, Kabul.
⁶⁶ A21, interviewed on 22 June 2019, Kabul.
⁶⁷ Ahmad Majidyar, 'Afghan Official in Deep Water after Praising Role of Soleimani and Shiite Militias in Syria', *Middle East Institute*, 29 November 2017, https://www.mei.edu/publications/afghan-official-deep-water-after-praising-role-soleimani-and-shiite-militias-syria.
⁶⁸ 'Mohaqiq Draws Fire for Praising Iran's Recruitment of Afghans in Syrian War', *Salaam Times*, 1 December 2017, https://afghanistan.asia-news.com/en; GB/articles/cnmi_st/features/2017/12/01/feature-04.

reaction [to the recruitment process] has been really weak'.[69] Many participants noted that the Afghan government is incapable of undertaking any effective measures, either diplomatically or in terms of border control, to stop the recruitment process.[70] Indeed, participants highlighted the weakness of Afghanistan – at both the individual and the state level – to resist Iranian influence in Afghanistan. This factor, as already noted, is one of the reasons explaining why Afghans are appropriate candidates for recruitment. It was also suggested by some participants that the Afghan government should convince Iran to stop recruiting Afghan fighters and that negotiations should be initiated with Tehran regarding this issue. Participants also pointed to a few other factors which have led to the failure of the Afghan government to respond to the recruitment of Afghan Shi'as by Iran. For example, an official from the Office of the President of the Islamic Republic of Afghanistan stated, 'continuous wars, the existence of millions of refugees, security and economic dependency, have tied our hands behind our backs. To some extent, the lack of a fair governmental system is also responsible, but the main cause is the lack of economic opportunities.'[71] An academic from Avicenna University suggested that the Afghan government has many other priorities and does not consider dealing with Fatemiyoun recruitment to be urgent.[72] According to a civil society activist from WASSA, the Afghan government does not have the sovereignty to respond or react to the recruitment process.[73]

In general, respondents were critical of the Afghan government and criticised it for not taking any action to stop Tehran's recruitment process. A civil society activist mentioned, 'I believe that Afghan political groups are not leaders that work for the masses or for public benefit ... They work just for themselves. For the benefit of themselves, they may knock on one door today, and knock on another tomorrow.'[74] Similarly, another participant noted that the Afghan government's limited capacity caused its failure to engage in diplomatic negotiations with Iran to stop the process of recruitment, stating that the Afghan government 'has been really weak to show any objection to this matter'.[75] Another participant, a political analyst, argued that it is the responsibility of the government to 'protect Afghan citizens' values, maintaining their citizenship and human rights ... Those who are sent to fight in Syria, their human and citizenship rights are violated ... We don't have a strong, united and independent government to protect its citizens' rights and values.'[76] Another

[69] A15, interviewed on 12 June 2019, Kabul, a parliamentarian,.
[70] A9, interviewed on 30 May 2019, Kabul, an official of Afghan civil society; A20, interviewed on 18 June 2019, Kabul; A19, interviewed on 17 June 2019, Kabul, a representative of Khatam Al-Nabieen University.
[71] A14, interviewed on 12 June 2019, Kabul.
[72] A8, interviewed on 8 May 2019, Kabul.
[73] A25, interviewed on 12 May 2019, Kabul.
[74] Ibid.
[75] A7, interviewed on 29 June 2019, Kabul.
[76] A11, interviewed on 9 June 2019, Kabul.

participant, an independent expert, criticised the Afghan government, stating that 'it does not care if our young people are being killed in Syria'.[77]

Therefore, most participants highlighted the weakness of Afghanistan in resisting or criticising the Iranian influence on the country (including its recruitment of Afghans to fight in Syria). Noting that the Afghan government has insufficient capacity to oppose Iran and that the government is unwilling to allow its relations with Tehran to deteriorate, another participant stressed that the Afghan government's reaction to the recruitment process is often limited to issuing condemning declarations.[78] An expert on Afghanistan's political and economic development was of the view that only a strong and independent Afghan government could have reacted strongly to the recruitment of Afghan citizens. He said Kabul has limited options due to Afghanistan's economic dependence on Iran and 'if the Afghan government reacts severely to Iran, Iran can close its Chabahar Port or stop trading with Afghanistan', which in turn could lead to the further deterioration of Afghanistan's economy.[79]

It was also argued by some of our research participants that if the Afghan government creates employment opportunities for Afghans, the likelihood of them being recruited would significantly decrease. According to one participant, the government should also develop infrastructure projects in the areas populated by Hazara groups, which would create job opportunities and in turn prevent them from fleeing the country or being recruited.[80] Most of the respondents noted that in the long term, the only solution to stopping problems such as the recruitment issue would be the emergence of a powerful and capable government in Kabul. Our Afghan participant did not focus on internal and external factors responsible for forcing millions of Afghans to take refuge in other countries. Besides ongoing wars and state fragility, Afghanistan has largely been dependent on foreign aid unless some industries are created in the country.

Pakistani Shi'a fighters in Syria

Iran used its strong cultural influence in Pakistan to recruit Shi'a fighters from Pakistan into the Zainabiyoun Brigade in Syria. The brigade was named after the Prophet Muhammad's granddaughter and Imam Hussain's sister, Zaynab bint Ali. Unlike the Fatemiyoun Brigade, little is known about the Zainabiyoun Brigade except that it largely comprises Pakistani Shi'as defending Assad in Syria and fighting against ISIS. Its Pakistani fighters were recruited from different places, for example, there were some who were already in Iran as pilgrims and travelled to Syria from there. A large number, however, came directly from Pakistan especially from areas with sizeable Shi'a populations like Parachinar and Quetta.[81]

---

[77] A10, interviewed on 2 June 2019, Kabul.
[78] Ibid.
[79] A22, interviewed on 29 May 2019, Kabul.
[80] A26, interviewed on 29 June 2019, Kabul.
[81] Dehghanpisheh, 'Iran Recruits Pakistani Shi'ites for Combat in Syria'.

In November 2015, a Facebook page bearing the name of Zainabiyoun showed pictures of what was described as a funeral in Iran, with members of the IRGC standing next to men wearing the long tunics and trousers (*shalwar kameez*) commonly worn in Pakistan.[82] There is some evidence to suggest that the IRGC used social media for its recruitment from Pakistan. For example, a Facebook post targeting 18–35-year-old Pakistanis, quoted details such as a forty-five-day military training course in Syria, a monthly salary of US$1,100 and fifteen days leave after three months. Another offer made to fighters was that if they were killed, their children's education would be paid for and their family would be taken on pilgrimages to Iran, Iraq and Syria.[83] Seyed Abbas Mousavi, a prominent member of the Zainabiyoun Brigade, claimed in an interview in March 2016 that Pakistani Shi'a fighters had been in touch with the IRGC for many years.[84] According to him, some Pakistani Shi'as had written a letter to Iranian Supreme Leader Khamenei asking for his opinion about their involvement in the Syrian civil war, to which Khamenei responded: 'Whoever is capable of performing duty, should do it to the best of his ability.'[85]

Our Pakistani research participants who acknowledged the recruitment of Shi'as by Iran often considered ideological and economic factors as the key drivers. It was noted that some people from Balochistan were recruited 'due to ideological affiliation or because of [a lack of] employment opportunities'.[86] Shi'a fighters who were recruited in Quetta were reportedly paid between US$500 and US$1,000 per month.[87] Among various ideological/religious motivations, most participants agreed that the perceived threat to Shi'a holy sites and mosques in Syria was the main factor inspiring Pakistani Shi'as to fight. One participant noted that 'religious affiliation persuaded people to go to Syria'.[88] Other factors identified in the recruitment success included lack of education, humanitarian reasons and anti-Western sentiments. It was highlighted by some participants that several pro-Iran Shi'a clerics in Pakistan used Friday sermons to encourage the local Shi'as to fight against ISIS in Syria. According to a research participant, Shi'a fighters recruited by Tehran were offered free pilgrimages to Iran and Iraq for their families and parents, health care, education for their kids and Iranian citizenship.[89]

While there is no precise estimate of the number of Pakistani Shi'as recruited by Iran, according to some reports, the brigade consisted of 1,000 fighters in 2015.[90] The number of Zainabiyoun combatants was much lower than that of

---

[82] Ibid.
[83] Ibid.
[84] Alfoneh, 'Tehran's Shia Foreign Legions'.
[85] Ibid.
[86] P11, interviewed on 16 May 2019, Kabul.
[87] A26, interviewed on 29 June 2019, Kabul.
[88] P16, interviewed on 27 May 2019, Islamabad.
[89] Ibid.
[90] Farhan Zahid, 'The Zainabiyoun Brigade: A Pakistani Shiite Militia Amid the Syrian Conflict', 27 May 2016, *Terrorism Monitor*, https://www.refworld.org/docid/57567e114.html.

the Fatemiyoun Brigade. According to Dehghanpisheh, Zainabiyoun fighters have been active around Aleppo as well as at the shrine of Sayyida Zainab near Damascus. The Zainabiyoun Brigade has also fought alongside Syrian forces in the southern Darra region.[91] On 9 April 2015, seven fighters from the Zainabiyoun Brigade were killed defending the Imam Hasan mosque in Damascus.[92] A further six fighters from the Zainabiyoun Brigade died in March 2016 and were buried in Qom.[93] By early 2018, it was reported that the Zainabiyoun Brigade fighters had suffered 153 fatalities.[94] Some reports have indicated that the government and security agencies in Pakistan have taken the recruitment issue seriously and launched a security crackdown against suspected members of the Zainabiyoun Brigade, and this was blamed for missing Shi'as in the country. It is estimated that 140 Pakistani Shi'as disappeared between 2016 and 2018, and local Shi'a leaders believe that they were kidnapped by the state's intelligence agencies for their alleged participation in the war in Syria. The families of the missing people have been protesting in Pakistan to demand the release of their family members.[95]

Our research participants expressed various views about the recruitment of Pakistani Shi'as by Iran. Almost half of the participants were aware of the recruitment of Pakistani Shi'as by Tehran, and explicitly acknowledged the existence of the Zaynabiyoun Brigade. It was highlighted by a former ambassador and lieutenant general of the Pakistan army that many Shi'a fighters recruited by Iran died in Syria and on many occasions their bodies were returned to Pakistan.[96] Another participant stated that the recruitment of Pakistani Shi'as by Iran is grounded in Iran's desire 'to dominate the Middle East'.[97] Most of the participants who confirmed the recruitment of Pakistani Shi'as by Iran stated that they became aware of this matter through foreign media reports. This could be because official Pakistani sources have remained silent on this issue. However, some participants questioned Iran's direct involvement in the recruitment process. A common view was represented by one interviewee's statement that 'Some organisations might have emotionally motivated people and these organisations possibly may have indirect links with the state agenda of Iran but as a state, Iran has not been involved in any recruitment ... Iran has not actively sponsored the recruitment of Pakistanis at a state level.'[98] Therefore, compared with the viewpoints expressed by Afghan participants, the vast majority of whom showed awareness of the recruitment of Afghan fighters by Iran, several Pakistani participants did not agree that Iran has officially recruited Pakistani Shi'as to fight in Syria, at least on a large scale. It was also highlighted

---

[91] Dehghanpisheh, 'Iran Recruits Pakistani Shi'ites for Combat in Syria'.
[92] Zahid, 'The Zainabiyoun Brigade'.
[93] Ibid.
[94] Alfoneh, 'Tehran's Shia Foreign Legions'.
[95] Kermani, 'The Story of Pakistan's "Disappeared" Shias'.
[96] P11, interviewed on 15 May 2019, Islamabad.
[97] P10, interviewed on 18 May 2019, Islamabad.
[98] P16, interviewed on 27 May 2019, Islamabad; P4, interviewed on 9 May 2019, Islamabad.

that non-Shi'a communities in Pakistan were unhappy about the recruitment of Pakistani Shi'as by Iran.[99]

The possible security implications of the recruitment process on Pakistan were also explored, particularly regarding Pakistan's facing 'poverty and illiteracy'.[100] Participants did not extensively comment on how Pakistani Shi'as were recruited. One participant stated that, 'There are media reports that few recruits from Kurram Agency went to Iraq and Syria to fight ... Iran has been recruiting youth from Pakistan and they go through a proper work visa. [However] a few recruits traverse the border without a visa as well.'[101] In terms of the areas in Pakistan from which the recruitment process took place, some participants pointed to central Punjab and the Hazara community in Balochistan. Others revealed that recruitment took place from places such as Kurram Agency, Hangu, Parachinar, Gilgit-Baltistan and Quetta. These estimates are based on the idea that Iran's influence in Pakistan is greater in these areas and that there are significant Shi'a communities there. Several academics and security experts in the study provided further details of how Pakistani recruits were motivated by the IRGC. One participant, an academic based in Bahawalpur, who visits Iran three to four times a year, stated:

> In 2016, during my visit to Tajrish (in Tehran), I met a Syrian army soldier. I was surprised when he spoke Urdu. He told me that he is from Parachinar and, along with other 99 students, visited Iran as a pilgrim. Their Shi'a teacher motivated them to participate in the war in Syria. In Iran, the Revolutionary Guards near Koh-e-Namak trained them.[102]

These students then reportedly travelled to Damascus via an Iran Air flight with the support of the IRCG. It was stated that Qom is one of the Iranian cities where Pakistani recruits receive military training. Therefore, in terms of Pakistani fighters, it can be stated that they are either (1) recruited inside Pakistan and travel directly from Pakistan to Syria, or (2) receive military training inside Iran and then travel to Syria.

Most of our research participants stated that Shi'a religious scholars in Pakistan remained silent on the recruitment process and did not take any action against it. Some participants asserted that Shi'a religious figures and scholars have either avoided talking about the recruitment of Pakistani Shi'as by Iran or denied any Iranian involvement in their recruitment.[103] This inaction was not limited to Shi'a scholars; our research participants said that even Sunni religious figures, including from the Jamaat-e-Islami and Jamiat Ulema-e-Islam, have remained silent and

---

[99] P29, interviewed on 20 May 2019, Islamabad.
[100] P22, interviewed on 12 June 2019, Islamabad.
[101] P2, interviewed on 2 May 2019, Islamabad.
[102] P31, interviewed on 30 May 2019, a college lecturer in Rawalpindi and expert on Iran.
[103] P8, interviewed on 20 May 2019, Islamabad; P20, interviewed on 23 May 2019, Islamabad; P2, interviewed on 2 May 2019, Islamabad.

have not reacted to the recruitment process.¹⁰⁴ It was argued that religious scholars intentionally remain silent because they do not want to stop their followers from defending Shi'a holy shrines and mosques in Syria. It was also observed that some Shi'a scholars in Pakistan covertly support the recruitment of Pakistani Shi'as and that 'Shi'a religious scholars are definitely covertly involved in supporting, propagating and instigating such recruitment'.¹⁰⁵

Participants also suggested that political parties in Pakistan were silent about Iran's recruitment efforts.¹⁰⁶ While it was predominantly argued that mainstream political parties in Pakistan have taken little interest in Iranian recruitment from Pakistan, an alternative viewpoint was that 'there is no response on this at official level, but at unofficial level, several comments were from different political groups in Pakistan'.¹⁰⁷ Some 'informal discussions on this subject' were also argued to have taken place in some Pakistani political parties.¹⁰⁸

In outlining the causes of this silence by political parties in Pakistan, it was pointed out that discussing the issue too publicly could potentially strengthen sectarianism in the country.¹⁰⁹ Political parties in Pakistan were therefore 'quiet' mainly 'because of the sensitivity of the issue and to save their vote count'.¹¹⁰ This reason for silence is thus very different from the silence of Afghan politicians on the recruitment issue. The latter, as explained earlier, has more to do with the weakness of the central government in Afghanistan.

A few participants expressed other views concerning the reaction of political parties to the recruitment of Pakistani Shi'as by Tehran. An academic in defence studies mentioned that Sunni political parties have spoken about the recruitment of Shi'as by Iran and have warned the government of Pakistan to undertake appropriate measures.¹¹¹ Many participants stated that the Pakistan government remained silent and did not react to Iran's recruitment of Shi'a fighters from Pakistan. For example, a journalist with *Hum News* was of the view that the 'government has not responded to the recruitment of Shiites from Pakistan by Iran'.¹¹² Similarly another journalist stated, 'I cannot see a discussion on any level by the government of Pakistan regarding the rehabilitation of the recruits who come back to Pakistan.'¹¹³ Along similar lines, an official of the Council of Islamic Ideology said,

---

¹⁰⁴ P24, interviewed on 2 June 2019, Islamabad, a former ambassador of Pakistan; P2, interviewed on 2 May 2019, Islamabad, a peace-building expert from Islamabad.
¹⁰⁵ P21, interviewed on 24 May 2019, Islamabad.
¹⁰⁶ P8, interviewed on 20 May 2019, Islamabad; P16, interviewed on 27 May 2019, Islamabad; P5, interviewed on 14 May 2019, Islamabad.
¹⁰⁷ P6, interviewed on 24 May 2019, Islamabad.
¹⁰⁸ P21, interviewed on 24 May 2019, Islamabad.
¹⁰⁹ P16, interviewed on 27 May 2019, Islamabad.
¹¹⁰ P27, interviewed on 4 May 2019, Islamabad.
¹¹¹ P17, interviewed on 29 May 2019, Islamabad; P7, interviewed on 10 May 2019, Islamabad.
¹¹² P22, interviewed on 12 June 2019, Islamabad.
¹¹³ P16, interviewed on 27 May 2019, Islamabad.

'the Government of Pakistan has not publicly said anything about the recruitment of Shiites from Pakistan'.[114] Participants often noted that the recruitment problem is not one of the 'government's priorities'. A former brigadier and now academic in Islamabad considered the possibility that the prime minister of Pakistan may have talked about the recruitment issue with Iranian officials, but released no official statement about it.[115]

The government of Pakistan has reportedly been monitoring the activities of Shi'a groups, especially those connected to Iran. One of our participants noted, 'The government has never been oblivious of the activity of Shi'a groups working under the shadow of Iran. While the Pakistan government would not want to irk Iran, Islamabad has moderately tamed the activity of Shi'a groups that could escalate into domestic or regional conflict.'[116] Several participants believed that more could have been done to challenge Iran's political influence in Pakistan, especially when it comes to the recruitment of Pakistani Shi'as to fight in countries such as Iraq and Syria. Some suggested that the Pakistani government should engage in a series of official negotiations with the Iranian government, persuading the Iranians to stop the recruitment process. Another suggestion was that the areas where the recruitment takes place should be more strongly monitored. Stronger border security control measures were also suggested. It was also recommended that as part of its 'National Action Plan' to counter violent extremism, the government should devote resources to establishing a counter-narrative against ideologies that could potentially lead to the recruitment of its citizens to fight in other countries.[117] Another viewpoint was that the government of Pakistan should create more job opportunities in the areas in which the recruitment mostly takes place, since many potential recruits go to Syria due to financial problems.

Most viewpoints expressed during fieldwork in Pakistan reflected that either the participants were not aware of the Iranian recruitment of Pakistani Shi'as or were hesitant to share that information. Many did mention that the Pakistani army has been involved in security operations against combatants returning from Iran or Syria.[118] This is because the army is deeply concerned about the implications of this phenomenon for Pakistan's own security.[119] Another participant believed that the army's reaction could be linked to its or Pakistan's partnership with Iran's arch-rival, Saudi Arabia, in the Islamic Military Alliance to Fight Terrorism (IMAFT).[120] Despite its initial hesitation in relation to joining the IMAFT due to the sensitive sectarian dynamics at home, Pakistan ultimately joined under pressure from Saudi

---

[114] P14, interviewed on 14 June 2019, Islamabad.
[115] P10, interviewed on 18 May 2019, Islamabad.
[116] P16, interviewed on 27 May 2019, Islamabad, a journalist with *Dawn*.
[117] P7, interviewed on 10 May 2019, Islamabad.
[118] P13, interviewed on 17 May 2019, Islamabad; P4, interviewed on 9 May 2019, Islamabad; P14, interviewed on 14 June 2019, Islamabad.
[119] Ibid.
[120] P17, interviewed on 29 May 2019, Islamabad.

Arabia and its other Gulf allies like the UAE.[121] A former army general and current defence analyst noted that the Pakistan army has increased border surveillance along the Iranian border and has been interrogating those who went to Iran.[122] Perhaps some Pakistani participants did not know about the issue because the local authorities were secretly dealing with this matter at the time of our fieldwork, that is, in 2019. As we have explored, there is a strong collaboration between various security and intelligence agencies and a 'red book' has been prepared with the names of the most wanted terrorists, including members of the Zainabiyoun Brigade. At the beginning of 2021, a police operation in Balochistan led to the arrest of Abbas Jafri, and a spokesperson from the local police force's counter-terrorism department said, 'Jafri had received training from a neighbouring country in 2014, where he was taught medical and intelligence services'.[123] An official from Pakistan's Defence Ministry shared with the media that the arrested Zainabiyoun members have 'confessed in interrogations that they had been receiving training and Iranian funding in Parachinar, Karachi, Kurram Agency, Khushab Punjab, and other parts of the country'.[124] Due to these incidents and reports, anti-Iranian sentiment is widely expressed in the media by Pakistani defence and foreign policy analysts, who believe that Islamabad needs to do more to neutralise Iran's subversive activities in Pakistan.[125] This clearly shows that the Iranian recruitment of Pakistani Shi'as has dented its image in Pakistan.

Conclusion

In terms of hard power dynamics, Iran's recruitment of Shi'as from Afghanistan and Pakistan does not fit the standard definition of hard power that focuses on, for example, the use of military power to influence the behaviour of other political bodies or countries. This is because the IRCG has mainly been involved in recruiting Afghan and Pakistani Shi'as from inside Iran, for example, Shi'a pilgrims of both countries and Afghan refugees. Also, Iran has not used these trained combatants for political gains in either Afghanistan or Pakistan. As neither Kabul nor Islamabad have any role in the recruitment managed by Iran's IRCG, we cannot label this as hard power. Iran's ability to recruit Shi'as from both countries, however, provides enough evidence to suggest that it has benefited from its soft power in Afghanistan and Pakistan for military and geopolitical gains elsewhere, that is, in the wider

---

[121] Zahid Shahab Ahmed, 'Understanding Saudi Arabia's Influence on Pakistan: The Case of the Islamic Military Alliance to Fight Terrorism', *The Muslim World* 109(3) (2019): 308–26.
[122] P27, interviewed on 4 May 2019, Islamabad.
[123] 'Zainabiyoun Militant Held in Surjani', *Dawn*, 28 January 2021, https://www.dawn.com/news/1604005.
[124] Abdul Ghani Kakar, 'Arrest of Zainabiyoun Recruiter Highlights Iran's Posture toward Pakistan', *Pakistan Forward*, 2 August 2021, https://pakistan.asia-news.com/en_GB/articles/cnmi_pf/features/2021/02/08/feature-01.
[125] Ibid.

Middle East. While most Afghan combatants, mainly Hazara refugees, were lured through promises of permanent residency and financial benefits, most of the Pakistani combatants joined to protect sacred Shi'a shrines in Syria, that is, Pakistani fighters were inspired by religious factors more than Afghan fighters. Despite Iran's influence on Shi'a groups in both countries, we found no evidence to suggest that local religious groups were involved in the recruitment process. However, there was evidence to suggest that most Shi'a religious figures were hesitant to talk about the Iranian recruitment of Shi'as. In Pakistan, there was no Shi'a religious group or scholar who criticised the recruitment process, and in Afghanistan one prominent Hazara Shi'a politician supported the involvement of Afghans in regional wars. This reflects Iran's influence on Shi'a groups and individuals in both countries.

Our interview data revealed that while the Pakistani government has remained silent on this issue, there was evidence to suggest that some Afghan government officials have been critical of Iranian recruitment of Afghan Shi'as. There was, however, no serious action taken by Kabul to protect its citizens at home and abroad, for example, Afghan refugees in Iran, from fighting in Syria. Many Afghan participants said that this is because the state of Afghanistan is incapable of handling the challenge due to its own fragility and continuous struggle with decades of war. In comparison, Pakistan's security forces have taken serious action by interrogating Shi'a returnees from Iran, Iraq and Syria. This has already caused upheaval among some Shi'a communities in Pakistan who have not heard from their loved ones allegedly picked up by Pakistan's security forces. They are called the missing Shi'as of Pakistan as no one really knows if they died in Syria or returned and are now imprisoned in Pakistan. Islamabad's policy of avoiding any crisis in terms of its relationship with Iran has been consistent since the 1980s. This policy is driven by Pakistan's inherent security dilemma vis-à-vis India due to which it is not willing to open another front. This is reflected through Pakistan's choice to refrain from directly blaming Iran for sectarian violence at home and the IRCG's recruitment of its Shi'a citizens for the war in Syria.

9
Conclusion

By focusing on Iran's cultural, religious, social, ideological, political and economic influences in Afghanistan and Pakistan, this book has examined Iran's soft power in both countries. It explored the effectiveness of various soft power tools and strategies that Tehran has employed to increase its soft power across its eastern borders. In addition, relying on primary data collected through in-person interviews in Afghanistan and Pakistan, this study explored the reception of Iran's soft power in both countries.

The book has presented a few interconnected arguments. It argued that Iran's national interests in Afghanistan and Pakistan, driven by geostrategic concerns, have prompted Tehran to enhance its influence in both countries. In addition to its interest in exporting natural gas to energy-deficient Pakistan and India via a pipeline going through Pakistan, as this study argued, Iran was also concerned about the US military presence at bases in Pakistan. Iran's policies in Afghanistan have been strongly influenced by Tehran's security concerns, in particular the significant threat of US troops across its eastern border. Indeed, Tehran's increasing influence in Afghanistan and Pakistan, as we argued, was connected to these concerns. However, these concerns have now been resolved as US troops withdrew from Afghanistan in August 2021 and Pakistan has refused to allow the United States to use any military bases for continued operations in Afghanistan. Since the Taliban's takeover of Afghanistan, Iran is more concerned about how the Taliban-led government will serve its interests in terms of its cultural, ideological and economic influence in Afghanistan. While the Taliban has included ethnic and sectarian minorities, such as Hazaras, in the interim government, its mistreatment of Shi'as will remain a cause of concern for Tehran.

Iran has certain advantages in terms of influencing its eastern neighbours due to the Persian colonial legacy. Iran has benefited from the imperial legacy of the Persian Empire, as well as its strong historical ties with both Afghanistan and Pakistan, to promote its goodwill in the two South Asian countries. From a historical perspective, the city of Herat was a centre of Persian culture, and witnessed the development of Persian literature, poetry, arts and architecture during the medieval period. Regarding Pakistan, many areas of the Indian subcontinent, including Punjab and Sindh in today's Pakistan, came under Persian influence during the medieval era. The Persian language is a significant measure that Iran uses today to increase its soft power in both countries. From a historical perspective, Persian was reinforced throughout centuries in Afghanistan, and is prevalent today in the central, southern and northern parts of Afghanistan as well as in Kabul. The Persian language was also the language of administration in the western parts of the Indian subcontinent during some periods of history.

In this context, the instruments used by Iran to enhance its soft power in both countries include the promotion of the Persian language and some of its key cultural features like the celebration of Persian New Year (*Nowruz*). The strategies that Iran uses to promote its language and culture include investment in education, cultural centres and the media in Afghanistan and Pakistan. In Pakistan, Iran has established *Khana-e-Farhang* in several cities such as Karachi, Peshawar, Lahore and Quetta, where Persian-language classes as well as lectures and seminars about Persian history and culture are often held. While in Pakistan, Iran does not exercise any significant influence via official media outlets, Iran's influence in the Afghan media is substantial, and pro-Iranian media outlets in Afghanistan were receiving significant funding from Tehran until the return of the Taliban to power in August 2021. Further, as this study argued, Shiism and certain political messages, such as Iran's anti-American discourse, are promoted by Tehran in both countries, mainly through the abovementioned strategies.

Although Iran has used its leverage to influence domestic politics in Afghanistan, and such attempts were especially successful during Hamid Karzai's presidency, this has not been so successful in Pakistan. With regard to Iran's influence in Afghanistan in the political sphere, our interviewees confirmed that Tehran played an important role in Afghanistan's domestic politics, with some pointing to Tehran's strong connection with the Karzai government, and others noting that at times, Iran even established strong connections with Sunni political groups in Afghanistan. General Ismail Qaani, the head of the IRGC, has been in contact with Afghan leaders – another sign of Iranian political influence in Afghanistan. The book argues that rather than wielding its influence in formal Pakistani politics or political parties in the parliament, Iran has played an important role in establishing relations with Shi'a political groups, such as the MWM and Tehrik-e-Jafaria Pakistan. The formation and development of these groups, as many of our interviewees also confirmed, are inspired by Tehran. Such inspiration was evident after many local Shi'a groups in Pakistan organised protests in various cities following General Qasem Soleimani's assassination by the United States in Iraq. Therefore, from a comparative perspective, Iran has exercised much less influence on formal politics in Pakistan compared with Afghanistan. This is also because Iran's economic influence in Pakistan is negligible, except for certain parts of Balochistan. Also, Afghanistan's fragility and troubled relations with Pakistan offered Iran an ideal opportunity to expand its economic relations after 2001. By virtue of this economic contribution, Tehran gradually began to influence domestic politics in Afghanistan. Despite its formal linkages with the Taliban, Iran now faces a dilemma in terms of maintaining the same level of influence in Afghanistan. For now, it seems, the Taliban needs Iran like other regional players in terms of not just international recognition of its government but also for day-to-day economic activities in the country. Tehran has also listened to the Taliban and provided an uninterrupted supply of goods and oil to Afghanistan since the Taliban's takeover.

In the economic sphere, Iran's economic influence in Afghanistan significantly increased between 2001 and 2021 as it overtook Pakistan to become Afghanistan's top trading partner. Iran, however, has not been able to establish strong economic cooperation with Pakistan. Although Pakistan has been interested in expanding trade with Iran, international sanctions on Iran and Pakistan's tilt towards Saudi Arabia have been continuous hindrances. Iran's concern in exercising economic influence in Afghanistan stems from Tehran's interest in extending its economic relations with the Central Asian republics. One key reason explaining the success of Iran's economic influence in Afghanistan, as acknowledged by most of our interviewees, is Afghanistan's economic dependence on Iran. After the fall of the Taliban regime in 2001, many cities in Afghanistan, especially in the western parts of the country, gradually became dependent on Iranian investment. Since 2017, Iran has become Afghanistan's leading trading partner – a position which was previously held by Pakistan. While the new Islamic Emirate of Afghanistan is interested in more trade with Iran, Iranian exports to Afghanistan declined significantly between August 2021 and August 2022. The Islamic Emirate realises that Iran is Afghanistan's key trading partner and most of its oil imports come from Iran. Hence, the Taliban's relationship with Iran will very likely be a positive one, paving the way for more economic cooperation. Here China's role will also be crucial as both Afghanistan and Iran have joined the BRI through which Beijing plans to invest in better trade and connectivity between Iran and Afghanistan. Based on this assessment, Iran's economic influence might recover to the level it was during the Ghani administration in Afghanistan. In contrast, Iran is not among Pakistan's key trading partners and might not be as Pakistan trades more with the Persian Gulf states, Europe and North America.

Drawing on our interview data, this book captured a diversity of opinions as well as discernible trends concerning the reception of Iranian soft power in Afghanistan and Pakistan. Indeed, two distinct but comparable pictures emerge in Afghanistan and Pakistan. In Afghanistan, many of our interviewees were very critical of Tehran's attitude towards Afghan refugees living in Iran. They were also critical of Iran's use of the refugee card to gain political leverage in Afghanistan. Iran has often threatened to repatriate Afghan refugees in the context of its water-sharing dispute with Kabul. In addition, many participants pointed to Tehran's ambiguous role in Afghanistan, stating that Iran supported Kabul, on the one hand, but also supported the Taliban, on the other. Further, there was widespread concern expressed by Afghan participants about Iran's cultural influence in the Afghan media. In addition, Kabul's incapacity to resist pressure from Iran was a strong theme in the interviews, with many participants criticising the Afghan government for not being able to address this matter. Our interviewees were also critical of Iran's efforts to recruit Shi'a Afghans to pursue its foreign policy objectives in the wider Middle East. Many participants believed that

Tehran used the vulnerability of Afghan migrants and refugees in Iran to recruit them to fight in Syria and Iraq.

Among our Pakistani interviewees, opinions on Iran also varied. While many were somewhat positive towards Iran, there was a clear concern expressed about Iran's influence in Pakistan. This concern was predicated on the belief that Iran pursues a sectarian agenda to advance its interests in the country. In recent years, this concern has centred on the recruitment of Pakistani Shi'as for Iran's proxy wars in the Middle East. The fear of being drawn into a sectarian quagmire, with domestic and regional implications, has undermined some of the positive aspects of Iran's Persian cultural assets in Pakistan. As we found in the interviews, despite Iran's influence on Shi'a groups in both Afghanistan and Pakistan, there is no evidence to suggest that local religious groups were involved in the recruitment of Shi'a fighters for the war in Syria. Our research participants, however, were critical of local religious leaders given their failure to strongly condemn the recruitment process. In addition, many participants in both countries criticised their governments for being indifferent towards the issue of Shi'a recruitment, stating that they (and the army in the case of Pakistan) should have taken a stronger stand and implemented stricter enforcement measures to stop the recruitment process. As the analysis of this research showed, security authorities in Pakistan have taken serious action on the issue and have arrested many Shi'as returnees from Syria. The issue of 'missing Shi'as' is ongoing in Pakistan as detainees' families are unaware of the whereabouts of their family members. Still, Islamabad has not directly communicated any of its concerns to Tehran.

With regard to the recruitment process, there were some differences between the views of the Afghan and Pakistani participants. For example, while the vast majority of the Afghan participants showed awareness of the recruitment of Afghan fighters by Iran, some Pakistani participants did not believe that Iran recruited Pakistani Shi'as to fight in Syria, at least on a large scale. In addition, although many Afghan and Pakistani participants believed that their governments or dominant political parties had remained silent on the issue of recruitment, they attributed such inaction to different reasons. While Afghan participants mentioned the weakness of the central government in Afghanistan as the main reason for such silence, Pakistani participants pointed to reasons such as the sensitivity of the issue and its potential to strengthen sectarianism in the country.

The last point that should be emphasised is that Tehran's policy to exert influence across its eastern border seems likely to continue in the coming years because of its geopolitical objectives in South and Central Asia that are tied to both Afghanistan and Pakistan. With regard to Afghanistan, Iran's cultural influence is likely to continue, but Tehran may face challenges in continuing its activities through *Khana-e-Farhang*s as well as exercising influence on the local media. The Taliban might not allow Iranian cultural centres to continue their ideological engagement in Afghanistan. Similarly, Iran's economic influence on Afghanistan may not be as strong as it was between 2001 and 2021. Considering how Iran's recruitment of Shi'as from both countries has led not just to anti-Iran sentiment but also to strong action against Shi'as in Pakistan, Tehran needs to re-evaluate its soft power strategy to revive its goodwill in Afghanistan and Pakistan. Having said this, as the Assad government has won the war in Syria and the Iranian recruitment of foreign combatants has also stopped, Iran could increase its goodwill in Afghanistan and Pakistan.

Among the most viable options for Iran's soft power strategy going into the future, Iran of course will continue to enjoy its ideological influence because of its sacred status for millions of Shi'as in Afghanistan and Pakistan. Therefore, *Khana-e-Farhang*s are likely to remain important tools of Iranian soft power. Looking ahead, it seems that Iran will be compelled to invest more in promoting Persian heritage and culture rather than Shi'a ideological influence through its cultural centres in Afghanistan and Pakistan.

Annexure 1
Afghan Participants

No.	Profession/Affiliation
A1	Academic/Ahle Bait University
A2	Academic/Afghanistan University
A3	Former member of parliament in Afghanistan
A4	Official/Afghan High Peace Council and adviser to Afghan CEO
A5	Civil society activist/independent
A6	Political analyst/independent
A7	Researcher/Afghanistan Analyst Network
A8	Official/Avicenna University
A9	Official/Afghan civil society
A10	Regional analyst/independent
A11	Political analyst/independent
A12	Political analyst/independent
A13	Academic/Kabul University
A14	Senior official/Office of the President of Islamic Republic of Afghanistan
A15	Member parliament in Afghanistan
A16	Former member parliament in Afghanistan
A17	Adviser, State Ministry for Parliamentary Affairs in Afghanistan
A18	Researcher/Afghanistan Analyst Network
A19	Former member of the Afghanistan parliament and academic/Khatam Al-Nabieen University
A20	Regional expert/independent
A21	Academic/Kabul University
A22	Economic and political expert/independent
A23	Academic/Herat University
A24	Executive/Peace Training and Research Organisation (PTRO)
A25	Executive/Women Activities and Social Services Association (WASSA)
A26	Independent analyst/independent

Annexure 2
Pakistani Participants

No.	Profession/Affiliation
P1	Academic/Iqbal International Institute for Research and Dialogue (IRD), International Islamic University
P2	Educationist/Peace and Education Foundation
P3	Administrator/Al-Basirah Trust
P4	Religious scholar/Jamat ul Kausr
P5	Academic/Quaid-i-Azam University, Islamabad
P6	Executive/Pak Institute for Peace Studies
P7	Journalist/*Dawn*
P8	Journalist/*GEO News*
P9	Defence analyst/independent
P10	Academic/Department of Peace and Conflict Studies, National University of Sciences and Technology, Islamabad
P11	Executive/Centre for Research and Security Studies
P12	Writer/researcher/International Islamic University, Islamabad
P13	Religious scholar/Al Mustafa University-Madrassah-Islamabad
P14	Official/Council of Islamic Ideology
P15	Academic/Quaid-i-Azam University
P16	Journalist/*Dawn*
P17	Academic/Quaid-i-Azam University
P18	Former ambassador and lieutenant general in the Pakistan army
P19	Academic/International Islamic University, Islamabad
P20	Research associate/Institute of Strategic Studies, Islamabad
P21	Journalist/independent
P22	Journalist/*Hum News*
P23	Academic/International Islamic University, Islamabad
P24	Former ambassador of Pakistan
P25	Former senator of Pakistan

P26 Senior journalist/*The News*
P27 Journalist/*Washington Post*
P28 Academic/University of Peshawar
P29 Journalist/*The Express Tribune*
P30 Academic/University of Peshawar

Bibliography

Aamir, Adnan, 'Taliban Rolls Out Red Carpet to China's Belt and Road Initiative', *Nikkei Asia*, 12 September 2021, https://asia.nikkei.com/Politics/International-relations/Afghanistan-turmoil/Taliban-rolls-out-red-carpet-to-China-s-Belt-and-Road-Initiative.

Abbas, Hassan, 'Shiism and Sectarian Conflict in Pakistan: Identity Politics, Iranian Influence, and Tit-for-Tat Violence', *Combating Terrorism Center*, 22 September 2010, https://ctc.usma.edu/wp-content/uploads/2011/05/CTC-OP-Abbas-21-September.pdf.

Afkhami, Amir Arsalan, 'From Punishment to Harm Reduction: Resecularization of Addiction in Contemporary Iran', in Ali Gheissari (ed.), *Contemporary Iran: Economy, Society, Politics* (New York: Oxford University Press, 2009), 194–210.

Ahmad, Jehanzeb, Iftikhar Ahmad and Sohail Shehzad, 'Regional and International Interest in Oil & Gas Pipelines to Gwadar', *The Dialogue* 2(2) (2014).

Ahmed, Zahid Shahab, 'Political Islam, the Jamaat-e-Islami, and Pakistan's Role in the Afghan–Soviet War, 1979–1988', in Philip E. Muehlenbeck (ed.), *Religion and the Cold War: A Global Perspective* (Nashville, TN: Vanderbilt University Press, 2012), 275–96.

Ahmed, Zahid Shahab, 'Understanding Saudi Arabia's Influence on Pakistan: The Case of the Islamic Military Alliance to Fight Terrorism', *Muslim World* 109(3) (2019): 308–26.

Ahmed, Zahid Shahab and Shahram Akbarzadeh, 'Understanding Pakistan's Relationship with Iran', *Middle East Policy* 25(4) (2018): 86–100.

Ahmed, Zahid Shahab and Stuti Bhatnagar, 'The India–Iran–Pakistan Triad: Comprehending the Correlation of Geo-economics and Geopolitics', *Asian Studies Review* 42(3) (2018): 517–36.

Ahmed, Zahid Shahab, Abbas Farasoo and Shahram Akbarzadeh, 'The Taliban Develops Regional Relationships as It Makes Territorial Gains in Afghanistan', *Melbourne Asia Review*, 10 September 2020, https://melbourneasiareview.edu.au/the-taliban-is-actively-developing-relationships-with-regional-powers-as-it-makes-territorial-gains-in-afghanistan.

Akbar, Ali, 'Iran's Soft Power in Syria after the Syrian Civil War', *Mediterranean Politics* 28(2) (2023): 227–49.

Akbar, Ali, 'Iran's Regional Influence in Light of Its Security Concerns', *Middle East Policy* 28(3/4) (2021): 186–202.

Akbarzadeh, Shahram, 'Iran's Policy towards Afghanistan: In the Shadow of the United States', *Journal of Asian Security and International Affairs* 1(1) (2014): 63–78.

Akbarzadeh, Shahram and James Barry, 'State Identity in Iranian Foreign Policy', *British Journal of Middle Eastern Studies* 43(4) (2016): 617.

Akbarzadeh, Shahram and Niamatullah Ibrahimi, 'The Taliban: A New Proxy for Iran in Afghanistan?' *Third World Quarterly* 41(5) (2020): 764–82.

Alam, Muzaffar, 'The Culture and Politics of Persian in Precolonial Hindustan', in Sheldon Pollock (ed.), *Literary Cultures in History: Reconstructions from South Asia* (Berkeley: University of California Press, 2003), 131–98.

Alam, Shah, 'Iran–Pakistan Relations: Political and Strategic Dimensions', *Strategic Analysis* 28(4) (2004): 526–45.

Alfoneh, Ali, 'Esmail Qaani: The Next Revolutionary Guards Quds Force Commander?' American Enterprise Institute, 11 January 2012, https://www.aei.org/research-products/report/esmail-qaani-the-next-revolutionary-guards-quds-force-commander.

Alfoneh, Ali, 'Four Decades in the Making: Shia Afghan Fatemiyoun Division of the Revolutionary Guard', Arab Gulf Studies Institute, 25 July 2018, https://agsiw.org/four-decades-in-the-making-shia-afghan-fatemiyoun-division-of-the-revolutionary-guards.

Alfoneh, Ali, 'Tehran's Shia Foreign Legions', Carnegie Endowment for International Peace, 30 January 2018, https://carnegieendowment.org/2018/01/30/tehran-s-shia-foreign-legions-pub-75387

Ali, Imtiaz, '4 "Missing Persons" Return after More than Two Years: Committee', *Dawn*, 10 May 2019, https://www.dawn.com/news/1481436.

Ali, Mukhtar Ahmad, *Sectarian Conflict in Pakistan: A Case Study of Jhang* (Colombo: Regional Centre for Strategic Studies, 2000).

Aman, Fatemeh, 'Afghan Water Infrastructure Threatens Iran, Regional Stability', *Al-Monitor*, 5 January 2013, https://www.al-monitor.com/pulse/originals/2013/01/afghanwatershortageiranpakistan.html.

Aman, Fatemeh, 'Iran–Afghanistan Differences over Helmand River Threaten Both Countries', *Atlantic Council*, Washington, 17 March 2016, https://www.atlanticcouncil.org/blogs/iransource/iran-afghan-differences-over-helmand-river-threaten-both-countries.

Aman, Fatemeh, 'Water Dispute Escalating between Iran and Afghanistan', *Atlantic Council*, Washington, August 2016, https://www.atlanticcouncil.org/wp-content/uploads/2016/09/Water_Dispute_Escalating_between_Iran_and_Afghanistan_web_0830.pdf.

Aman, Fatemeh, 'Will Iran turn to al-Qaeda to Combat Islamic State?' *Middle East Institute*, 23 September 2022, https://www.mei.edu/publications/will-iran-turn-al-qaeda-combat-islamic-state.

Amirthan, Shawn, 'What are India, Iran and Afghanistan's Benefits from the Chabahar Port Agreement?' *Strategic Analysis* 41(1) (2017): 87–93.

Arbabzadeh, Nishin, 'Women and Religious Patronage in the Timurid Empire', in Nile Green (ed.), *Afghanistan's Islam: From Conversion to the Taliban* (Berkeley: University of California Press, 2017), 56–70.

Ashraf, Malik Muhammad, 'Pak–Iran Relations', *The News*, 5 April 2016, https://www.thenews.com.pk/print/110365-Pak-Iran-relations.

Atkinson, Carol, 'Does Soft Power Matter? A Comparative of Student Exchange Programs 1980–2006', *Foreign Policy Analysis* 6(1) (2010): 1–22.

Azad, Arezou, 'The Beginning of Islam in Afghanistan: Conquest, Acculturation and Islamization', in Nile Green (ed.), *Afghanistan's Islam: From Conversion to the Taliban* (Berkeley: University of California Press, 2017), 41–55.

Azami, Dawood, 'Afghanistan: How Does the Taliban Make Money?' *BBC News*, 22 December 2018, https://www.bbc.com/news/world-46554097.

Bakhtiari, Faranak, 'World Youth Day: Can Iran Meet Growing Youth Population's Needs?' *Tehran Times*, 12 August 2020, https://www.tehrantimes.com/news/451175/World-Youth-Day-can-Iran-meet-growing-youth-population-s-needs.

Balland, D., 'Afghanistan x. Political History', *Encyclopaedia Iranica*, 1983, http://www.iranicaonline.org/articles/afghanistan-x-political-history.

Barzegar, Kayhan, 'Iran and the Shiite Crescent: Myths and Realities', *Brown Journal of World Affairs* 15(1) (2008): 87–99

Barzegar, Kayhan, 'Iran's Foreign Policy in post-Taliban Afghanistan', *Washington Quarterly* 37(2) (2014): 119–37.

Basit, Saira, 'Explaining the Impact of Militancy on Iran–Pakistan relations', *Small Wars & Insurgencies* 29(5/6) (2018): 1040–64.

Bateman, Kate and Asfandyar Mir, 'Taliban Seek Recognition, but Offer Few Concessions to International Concerns', *United States Institute of Peace*, 28 September 2021, https://www.usip.org/publications/2021/09/taliban-seek-recognition-offer-few-concessions-international-concerns.

Bezhan, Frud, 'Afghan Migrant Boy's Rough Treatment in Iran Sparks Outrage', *Radio Liberty*, 26 July 2019, https://www.rferl.org/a/afghan-migrant-boy-s-rough-treatment-in-iran-sparks-anger/30077657.html.

Bhatnagar, Stuti and Zahid Shahab Ahmed, 'Geopolitics of Landlocked States in South Asia: A Comparative Analysis of Afghanistan and Nepal', *Australian Journal of International Affairs* 75(1) (2021): 60–79.

Bivar, Adrian, 'Introduction', in Peter J. Chelkowski (ed.), *The Gift of Persian Culture: Its Continuity and Influence in History* (Salt Lake City, UT: University of Utah Press, 2011).

Blanchard, Jean-Marc F. and Fujia Lu, 'Thinking Hard About Soft Power: A Review and Critique of the Literature on China and Soft Power', *Asian Perspective* 36(4) (2012): 565–89.

Bosworth, Clifford Edmund, *Sistan under the Arabs from the Islamic Conquest to the Rise of the Saffarids (30–250/651–864)* (Rome: IsMEO, 1968).

Bosworth, Clifford Edmund, 'The Kūfichīs or Qufṣ in Persian History', *Iran* 14 (1976): 9–17.

Bosworth, Clifford Edmund, 'Ghaznavids', *Encyclopaedia Iranica*, 2001, http://www.iranicaonline.org/articles/ghaznavids.

Bosworth, Clifford Edmund, 'India v. Relations: Medieval Period to the 13th Century', *Encyclopaedia Iranica*, 2004, http://www.iranicaonline.org/articles/india-v-relations-medieval-period-to-the-13th-century.

Bosworth, Clifford Edmund, 'Iran and Afghanistan in Contact and Interaction through the Ages', in Peter J. Chelkowski (ed.), *The Gift of Persian Culture: Its Continuity and Influence in History* (Salt Lake City, UT: University of Utah Press, 2011).

Callieri, Pierfrancesco, 'India iv. Relations: Seleucid, Parthian, Sasanian Period', *Encyclopaedia Iranica*, 2004, http://www.iranicaonline.org/articles/india-iv-relations.

Carter, Stephen, 'Iran's Interests in Afghanistan and Their Implications for NATO', *International Journal* 65(4) (2010): 977–94.

Çevik, Senem B., 'Turkish Historical Television Series: Public Broadcasting of neo-Ottoman Illusions', *Southeast European and Black Sea Studies* 19(2) (2019): 227–42.

Chatin, Mathilde and Giulio M. Gallarotti, 'The BRICS and Soft Power: An Introduction', *Journal of Political Power* 9(3) (2016): 335–52.

Chellaney, Brahma, 'Chabahar: Gateway to Afghanistan and Central Asia', *Hindustan Times*, 26 April 2018, https://chellaney.net/2018/04/26/chabahar-gateway-to-afghanistan-and-central-asia.

Chong, Alan, 'Smart Power and Military Force: An Introduction', *Journal of Strategic Studies* 38(3) (2015): 233–44.

Cohen, Stephen P., *The Idea of Pakistan* (Washington, DC: Brookings Institution Press, 2004).

Cole, Juan R. I., *Roots of North Indian Shiism in Iran and Iraq* (Berkeley: University of California Press, 1989).

Cole, Juan R. I., 'Iranian Culture and South Asia: 1500–1900', in Nikki R. Keddie and Rudi Matthee (eds), *Iran and the Surrounding World: Interactions in Culture and Cultural Politics* (Washington: University of Washington Press, 2002), 15–35.

Constable, Pamela, 'Recruited by Iran to Fight for Syrian Regime, Young Afghans Bring Home Cash and Scares', *Washington Post*, 30 July 2018, https://www.washingtonpost.com/world/asia_pacific/recruited-by-iran-to-fight-for-syrian-regime-young-afghans-bring-home-cash-and-scars/2018/07/29/ecf9e34c-64e0-11e8-81ca-bb14593acaa6_story.html.

Daniels, Rorry, 'Strategic Competition in South Asia: Gwadar, Chabahar, and the Risks of Infrastructure Development', *American Foreign Policy Interests* 35(2) (2013): 93–100.

Dashti, Naseer, *The Baloch Conflict with Iran and Pakistan: Aspects of a National Liberation Struggle* (Bloomington, IN: Trafford Publishing, 2017).

Dawn, 'Pakistan, Iran to Cut Duty on 647 Items: Preferential Trade', 22 August 2004, https://www.dawn.com/news/396250.

Dawn, 'Iran Blames US and Pakistan for Attack', 20 October 2009, https://www.dawn.com/news/497566/iran-blames-us-and-pakistan-for-attack.

Dawn, 'Pakistan, Iran Eye Trade at $5 billion', 23 April 2015, https://www.dawn.com/news/1177635.

Dawn, 'Rouhani Denies Discussing "RAW's involvement in Balochistan" with Pakistani Leadership', 27 March 2016, https://www.dawn.com/news/1248078.

Dawn, 'Al-Quds Rally Rejects "Deal of the Century"', 1 June 2019, https://www.dawn.com/news/1485881.

Dehghanpisheh, Babak, 'Iran Recruits Pakistani Shi'ites for Combat in Syria', *Reuters*, 11 December 2015, https://www.reuters.com/article/us-mideast-crisis-syria-pakistan-iran/iran-recruits-pakistani-shiites-for-combat-in-syria-idUSKBN0TT22S20151210.

Elfenbein, J., 'Baluchistan, iii. Baluchi Language and Literature', *Encyclopaedia Iranica*, 1998, http://www.iranicaonline.org/articles/baluchistan-iii.

Farmer, Ben, 'Taliban Opens Office in Iran', *The Telegraph*, 1 August 2012, https://www.telegraph.co.; uk/news/worldnews/middleeast/iran/9444402/Taliban-opens-office-in-Iran.html.

Farrar-Wellman, Ariel, 'Pakistan–Iran Foreign Relations', *Critical Threats*, 5 July 2010, https://www.criticalthreats.org/analysis/pakistan-iran-foreign-relations#_ftn1.

Fassihi, Farnaz, 'Iran Pays Afghans to Fight for Assad', *Wall Street Journal*, 22 May 2014, https://www.wsj.com/articles/iran-recruiting-afghan-refugees-to-fight-for-regime-in-syria-1400197482?tesla=y.

Fassihi, Farnaz and Steven Lee Myers, 'Defying U.S., China and Iran Near Trade and Military Partnership', *New York Times*, 11 July 2020, https://www.nytimes.com/2020/07/11/world/asia/china-iran-trade-military-deal.html.

Fassihi, Farnaz and Steven Lee Myers, 'China, with $400 billion Iran Deal, Could Deepen Influence in Mideast', *New York Times*, 27 March 2021, https://www.nytimes.com/2021/03/27/world/middleeast/china-iran-deal.html.

Fattahi, Mehdi and Isabel DeBre, 'As Iran–Taliban Tensions Rise, Afghan Migrants in Tinderbox', *The Diplomat*, 2 May 2022, https://thediplomat.com/2022/05/as-iran-taliban-tensions-rise-afghan-migrants-in-tinderbox.

Fazl-e-Haider, Syed, 'Shifting Alliances in the Gulf a Boon to China', *The Interpreter*, 18 November 2019, https://www.lowyinstitute.org/the-interpreter/shifting-alliances-gulf-boon-china.

Feizi, Hiva, 'Discourse, Affinity and Attraction: A Case Study of Iran's Soft Power Strategy in Afghanistan', Graduate thesis, University of South Florida, 2018, https://core.ac.uk/download/pdf/213968957.pdf.

Ferris-Rotman, Amie, 'Insight: Iran's "Great Game" in Afghanistan', *Reuters*, 24 May 2012, https://www.reuters.com/article/us-afghanistan-iran-media-idUSBRE84N0CB20120524.

Filkins, Dexter, 'Iran is Said to Give Top Karzai Aide Cash by the Bagful', *New York Times*, 23 October 2010, https://www.nytimes.com/2010/10/24/world/asia/24afghan.html.

Financial Times, 'Iran, Pakistan Keen on Promoting Trade Ties', 6 July 2019, https://financialtribune.com/articles/domestic-economy/98793/iran-pakistan-keen-on-promoting-trade-ties.

Freeman, Colin, 'Iran Poised to Strike in Wealthy Gulf States', *The Telegraph*, 4 March 2007, https://www.telegraph.co.uk/news/worldnews/1544535/Iran-poised-to-strike-in-wealthy-Gulf-states.html.
Frye, Richard N., 'The Persepolis Middle Persian Inscriptions from the Time of Shapur II', *Acta Orientalia* 30 (1966): 83–94.
Fürtig, Henner, 'Afghanistan in the Foreign Policies of Middle Eastern Countries', *Asian Perspective* 38(4) (2014): 541–64.
Ghani, Ashraf, 'Work of Construction of 21 Water Dams to Start in Near Future', *Khaama Press*, 20 February 2016, https://www.khaama.com/ghani-work-on-construction-of-21-water-dams-to-start-in-near-future-0120.
Ghiabi, Maziyar, 'The Paradox of Iran's War on Drugs and its Progressive Treatment of Addiction', *The Conversation*, 3 July 2014, https://theconversation.com/the-paradox-of-irans-war-on-drugs-and-its-progressive-treatment-of-addiction-28701.
Ghobadzadeh, Naser, *The Religious Secularity: A Theological Challenge to the Islamic State* (New York: Oxford University Press, 2015).
Gishkori, Zahid, 'Flights to Iran being Considered for Shia Pilgrims', *Express Tribune*, 26 September 2011, https://tribune.com.pk/story/260458/flights-to-iran-being-considered-for-shia-pilgrims.
Gohel Sajjan M., 'Iran's Ambiguous Role in Afghanistan', *CTC Sentinel* 3(3) (2010): 13–16.
Gopal, Anand, 'US–Iran Thaw Could Bolster Afghanistan Rebuilding Efforts', *Christian Science Monitor*, 3 April 2009, http://www.csmonitor.com/World/Asia-South-Central/2009/0403/p06s01-wosc.html.
Green, Nile, 'Introduction', in Nile Green (ed.), *Afghanistan's Islam: From Conversion to the Taliban* (Berkeley: University of California Press, 2017), 1–40.
Guardian, The, 'Suicide Bomber Kills 30 on Shia Procession in Karachi', 20 December 2009, https://www.theguardian.com/world/2009/dec/28/pakistan-suicide-attack-kills-30.
Gul, Ayaz, 'Indian Wheat Makes History, Arriving in Afghanistan via Iran', *Voice of America*, 11 November 2017, https://www.voanews.com/a/indian-wheat-makes-history-arriving-in-afghanistan-via-iran/4110774.html.
Gul, Ayaz, 'Afghan Leader Demands Iranian Oil in Exchange for River Water', *Voice of America*, 24 March 2021, https://www.voanews.com/south-central-asia/afghan-leader-demands-iranian-oil-exchange-river-water.
Habibi, Nader and Hans Yue Zhu, 'What CPEC Means for China's Middle East Relations', *The Diplomat*, 22 January 2020, https://thediplomat.com/2020/01/what-cpec-means-for-chinas-middle-east-relations.
Hagström, Linus and Chengxin Pan, 'Traversing the Soft/Hard Power Binary: The Case of the Sino-Japanese Territorial Dispute', *Review of International Studies* 46(1) (2020): 37–55.
Haider, Mateen and Mahnoor Bari, 'Chabahar Not a Rival to Gwadar, Iranian Envoy Tells Pakistan', *Dawn*, 27 May 2016, https://www.dawn.com/news/1261006.

Hakimi, Amina, 'Afghanistan–Iran Trade has Dropped: ACCI', *Tolo News*, 25 August 2022, https://tolonews.com/business-179543.
Haji-Yousefi, Amir M., 'Iran Foreign Policy in Afghanistan: The Current Situation and Future Prospects', *South Asian Studies* 27(1) (2012): 63–75.
Hanasz, Paula, 'The Politics of Water Security between Afghanistan and Iran', Strategic Analysis Paper, 1 March 2012, https://www.futuredirections.org.au/publication/the-politics-of-water-security-between-afghanistan-and-iran.
Haqqani, Husain, 'Weeding Out the Heretics: Sectarianism in Pakistan', *Hudson Institute*, 1 November 2006, https://www.hudson.org/research/9769-weeding-out-the-heretics-sectarianism-in-pakistan.
Hasan, Sabiha, 'Pakistan Foreign Policy', *Pakistan Horizon* 39(1) (1986): 3–18.
Hastert, Paul, 'Al-Qaeda and Iran: Friends or Foes, or Somewhere in Between?' *Studies in Conflict & Terrorism* 30(4) (2007): 327–36.
Hawza News, '30 Million Pilgrims Visit the Holy Shrine of Imam Reza Annually' (in Persian), 12 March 2022, https://www.hawzahnews.com/news/1013400.
Hindustan Times, 'India, Iran Talk Chabahar Funding', 5 May 2013, https://www.hindustantimes.com/world/india-iran-talk-chabahar-port-funding/story-wThJi-3190IRnZdoQUG7o1N.html.
Hiro, Dilip, *Cold War in the Islamic World: Saudi Arabia, Iran and the Struggle for Supremacy* (New York: Oxford University Press, 2018).
Houk, Andrew, 'Iran's Response to Drugs from Afghanistan', Stimson Center, 29 January 2011, https://www.stimson.org/2011/irans-response-to-drugs-from-afghanistan.
Hugo, Graeme, Mohammad Jalal Abbasi-Shavazi and Rasoul Sadeghi, 'Refugee Movement and Development: Afghan Refugees in Iran', *Migration and Development* 1(2) (2012): 261–79.
Human Rights Watch, 'Unwelcome Guests: Iran's Violation of Afghan Refugees and Migrant Rights', 20 November 2013, https://www.hrw.org/report/2013/11/20/unwelcome-guests/irans-violation-afghan-refugee-and-migrant-rights.
Huntington, Susan L., *The Art of Ancient India: Buddhist, Hindu, Jain* (New York: Weatherhill, 1985).
Hussain, Agha, 'How China and Iran Could Find More Common Ground – in Afghanistan', *South China Morning Post*, 7 August 2022, https://www.scmp.com/comment/opinion/article/3187824/how-china-and-iran-could-find-more-common-ground-afghanistan.
Iqbal, Nasir, 'Marching on the Capital: A History', *Dawn*, 17 August 2014, https://www.dawn.com/news/1125851.
Iqbal, Zafar, 'Pakistan's Hope for Energy Pipeline with Iran Evaporate', *Asia Times*, 1 July 2019, https://asiatimes.com/2019/07/pakistans-hopes-for-an-energy-pipeline-with-iran-evaporate; iran-afghanistan-trade-is-more-than-1-5-billion-president-karzai-says.html.
Islam Times, 'Imam Khomeini Aroused Oppressed People of the World: Raja Nasir Jafari', 12 February 2014, https://www.islamtimes.org/en/news/350753/imam-khomeini-aroused-oppressed-people-of-the-world-raja-nasir-jafari.

Islamic Republic News Agency, 'Protests Held in Pakistan to Condemn Assassination of General Suleimani', 3 January 2020, https://en.irna.ir/news/83618950/Protests-held-in-Pakistan-to-condemn-assassination-of-General.

Janjua, Haroon, 'Iran Gas Pipeline Deal with Pakistan Hampered by US Sanctions', *DW*, 20 May 2019, https://www.dw.com/en/iran-gas-pipeline-deal-with-pakistan-hampered-by-us-sanctions/a-48802450.

Jenkins, William Bullock, 'Bonyads as Agents and Vehicles of the Islamic Republic's Soft Power', in Shahram Akbarzadeh and Dara Conduit (eds), *Iran in the World: President Rouhani's Foreign Policy* (New York: Palgrave Macmillan, 2016), 155–75.

Jödicke, Ansgar, 'Religious Soft Power in the South Caucasus: The Influence of Iran and Turkey', Brookings Institution, 2018, https://www.brookings.edu/blog/order-from-chaos/2018/12/13/religious-soft-power-in-the-south-caucasus-the-influence-of-iran-and-turkey.

Jones, Seth G. and Danika Newlee, 'The United States' Soft War with Iran', *CSIS Briefing*, 11 June 2019, https://www.csis.org/analysis/united-states-soft-war-iran.

Kagan, Frederick W., Kimberly Kagan and Danielle Pletka, *Iranian Influence in the Levant, Iraq, and Afghanistan* (Washington, DC: American Enterprise Institute, 2008).

Kagan, Fredrick W., Ahmad K. Majidyar, Danielle Pletka and Marisa Cochrane Sullivan, *Iranian Influence in the Levant, Egypt, Iraq and Afghanistan* (Washington, DC: American Enterprise Institute and Institute for the Study of War, 2012).

Kakar, Abdul Ghani, 'Arrest of Zainabiyoun Recruiter Highlights Iran's Posture toward Pakistan', *Pakistan Forward*, 2 August 2021, https://pakistan.asia-news.com/en_GB/articles/cnmi_pf/features/2021/02/08/feature-01.

Kakar, Hasan M., *The Pacification of the Hazaras of Afghanistan* (New York: Afghanistan Council of the Asia Society, 1973).

Kamal, Abdol Moghset Bani and Wahabuddin Ra'ees, 'Iran's Aid Diplomacy in Afghanistan: The Role of Imam Khomeini Relief Committee', *Contemporary Review of the Middle East* 5(4) (2018): 308–26.

Karim, Umer, 'Death of Qassem Soleimani: What to Expect in Afghanistan and Pakistan', *RUSI*, 24 January 2020, https://rusi.org/commentary/death-qassem-soleimani-what-expect-afghanistan-and-pakistan.

Kaura, Vinay, 'India's Aims in Central Asia and India–Afghanistan–Iran Triangular Relationship', *Journal of Central Asian Studies* 24(1) (2017): 23–41.

Kayhan, 'How was the Fatemiyoun Brigade formed?' 30 May 2015, http://kayhan.ir/fa/news/46030/لشکر-فاطمیون-چگونه-شکل-گرفت

Kermani, Secunder, 'The Story of Pakistan's "Disappeared" Shias', *BBC News*, 31 May 2018, https://www.bbc.com/news/world-asia-44280552.

Khan, Iftikhar A., 'Iran Responds to Letter about Indian Spy', *Dawn*, 16 June 2016, https://www.dawn.com/news/1265187.

Khan, Raja Muhammad, 'Towards Harmonization of Pak–Iran Relationship', *Margalla Papers* (2010): 88–111.

Khan, Zahid Ali, 'Balochistan Factor in Pak–Iran Relations: Opportunities and Constraints', *South Asian Studies* 27(1) (2012): 121–40.

Khan, Zahid Ali, 'China's Gwadar and India's Chahbahar: An Analysis of Sino-India Geostrategic and Economic Competition', *Strategic Studies* 32/33(4) (2012): 79–101.

Khetran, Mir Sherbaz, 'Gwadar and Chabahar', *Strategic Studies* 38(2) (2018): 43–55.

Koepke, Bruce, 'The Situation of Afghans in the Islamic Republic of Iran Nine Years after the Overthrow of the Taliban Regime in Afghanistan', in John Calabrese and Jean-Luc Marret (eds), *Transatlantic Cooperation on Protracted Displacement: Urgent Need and Unique Opportunity* (Washington, DC: Middle East Institute Press, 2012), 57–69.

Koepke, Bruce, *Iran's Policy on Afghanistan: The Evolution of Strategic Pragmatism* (Stockholm: Stockholm International Peace Research Institute, 2013).

Korybko, Andrew, 'Iran's Interest in CPEC Strengthens Regional Integration', *The Diplomat*, 16 September 2019. https://thediplomat.com/2020/01/what-cpec-means-for-chinas-middle-east-relations.

Kumar, Sumita, 'Pakistan–Iran Relations: The US Factor', *Strategic Analysis* 35(5) (2008): 773–89.

Latifi, Ali M., 'How Iran Recruited Afghan Refugees to Fight Assad's War', *New York Times*, 30 June 2017, https://www.nytimes.com/2017/06/30/opinion/sunday/iran-afghanistan-refugees-assad-syria.html.

Li, Eric, 'The Rise and Fall of Soft Power', *Foreign Policy*, 20 August 2018, https://foreignpolicy.com/2018/08/20/the-rise-and-fall-of-soft-power.

Lodhi, Maleeha, 'Pakistan's Shia Movement: An Interview with Arif Hussaini', *Third World Quarterly* 10(2) (1988): 806–17.

Logan, Lara, 'Cooperation Rises between Iran and Taliban', *CBS News*, 7 October 2009, https://www.cbsnews.com/news/cooperation-rises-between-iran-and-taliban.

Majidyar, Ahmad K., 'The Shiites of Pakistan? A Minority Under Siege', *American Enterprise Institute*, 11 June 2014, https://www.aei.org/research-products/report/the-shiites-of-pakistan-a-minority-under-siege.

Majidyar, Ahmad, 'Afghan Official in Deep Water after Praising Role of Soleimani and Shitte Militias in Syria', *Middle East Institute* 29 November 2017, https://www.mei.edu/publications/afghan-official-deep-water-after-praising-role-soleimani-and-shiite-militias-syria.

Majidyar, Ahmad and Ali Alfoneh, 'Iranian Influence in Afghanistan: Imam Khomeini Relief Committee', *Middle Eastern Outlook*, 27 July 2010, https://www.aei.org/research-products/report/iranian-influence-in-afghanistan.

Malik, Hasan Yaser, 'Strategic Importance of Gwadar Port', *Journal of Political Studies* 19(2) (2012): 57–69.

Mandaville, Peter and Shadi Hamid, 'Islam as Statecraft: How Governments Use Religion in Foreign Policy', in *The New Geopolitics Middle East* (Washington, DC: Brookings Institution, 2018).

Martin, Venessa, *Creating an Islamic State: Khomeini and the Making of a New Iran* (London: I. B. Tauris, 2000).

Mazhar, Muhammad Saleem and Naheed S. Goraya, 'Challenges in Iran–Pakistan Gas Pipeline', *NDU Journal* 28 (2013): 163–78.

McKernan, Bethan, 'Iran's "Exemplary" Refugee Hosting Efforts Praised by UN', *Independent*, 16 March 2017, http://www.independent.co.uk.

Medium, 'Iran is Forcing Poor Afghans to Fight and Die in Syria', 22 October 2014, https://medium.com/war-is-boring/iran-is-forcing-poor-afghans-to-fight-and-die-in-syria-4e58fc839be2.

Milani, Mohsen, 'Iran's Policy Towards Afghanistan', *Middle East Journal* 60(2) (2006): 235–56.

Milani, Mohsen, 'Iran and Afghanistan', *The Iran Primer*, 5 October 2010, https://iranprimer.usip.org/resource/iran-and-afghanistan.

Mitra, Ryan, 'India's Persian Desire: Analyzing India's Maritime Trade Strategy vis-à-vis the Port of Chabahar', *Maritime Affairs: Journal of the National Maritime Foundation of India* 15(1) (2019): 41–50.

Mohaddessin, Mohammad, *Islamic Fundamentalism: The New Global Threat* (Washington: Seven Locks Press, 2001).

Motamedi, Maziar, 'US "Defeat" in Afghanistan a Chance for Peace: Iran President', *Al-Jazeera*, 16 August 2021, https://www.aljazeera.com/news/2021/8/16/raisi-us-defeat-in-afghanistan-should-become-chance-for-peace.

Motamedi, Maziar, 'Iran Insists on "Inclusive" Government in Afghanistan', *Al-Jazeera*, 9 September 2021, https://www.aljazeera.com/news/2021/9/9/iran-insists-on-inclusive-afghan-government.

Munir, Muhammad, Muhammad Ahsan and Saman Zulfqar, 'Iran–Pakistan Gas Pipeline: Cost–Benefit Analysis', *Journal of Political Studies* 20(2) (2013): 161–77.

Nader, Alireza and Joya Laha, *Iran's Balancing Act in Afghanistan* (Washington: RAND Corporation, 2011).

Nader, Alireza, Ali G. Scotten, Ahmad Idrees Rahmani, Robert Stewart and Leila Mahnad, 'Iran and Afghanistan: A Complicated Relationship', in Alireza Nader (ed.), *Iran's Influence in Afghanistan: Implications for the US Drawdown* (Washington: RAND Corporation, 2014), 5–22.

Naseh, Mitra, Miriam Potocky, Paul H. Stuart and Sara Pezeshk, 'Repatriation of Afghan Refugees from Iran: A Shelter Profile Study', *Journal of International Humanitarian Action* 3(1) (2018), https://jhumanitarianaction.springeropen.com/articles/10.1186/s41018-018-0041-8.

Nasr, Vali, *The Shia Revival: How Conflicts within Islam Will Shape the Future* (New York: W. W. Norton, 2007).

National University of Sciences and Technology, *Challenges and Opportunities in the Iran–Pakistan Relationship*, NUST Research Team, Monthly Background Report (Islamabad: National University of Sciences and Technology, 2015), p. 5.

Nazar, Zarif and Charles Recknagel, 'Controversial Madrasah Builds Iran's Influence in Kabul', *Radio Free Europe*, 6 November 2010, https://www.rferl.org/a/Controversial_Madrasah_Builds_Irans_Influence_In_Kabul/2212566.html.

Neto, Rabêlo Alexandre, José Milton de Sousa-Filho, Áurio Lúcio Leocádio and João Carlos Hipolito Bernardes do Nascimento, 'Internationalization of Cultural Products: The Influence of Soft Power', *International Journal of Market Research* 62(3) (2020): 335–49.

News Day 24, 'Top Pakistani Religious Leader calls for Stronger Regional Ties with Iran', 29 August 2020, https://www.newsday24.com/iran/top-pakistani-religious-leader-calls-for-stronger-regional-ties-with-iran.

Nikpour, Golnar, 'Drugs and Drug Policy in the Islamic Republic of Iran', *Middle East Brief*, 2018, https://www.brandeis.edu/crown/publications/middle-east-briefs/pdfs/101-200/meb119.pdf.

Nye, Joseph S., *Bound to Lead: The Changing Nature of American Power* (New York: Basic Books, 1990).

Nye, Joseph S., 'Soft Power', *Foreign Policy* 80 (1990): 153–71.

Nye, Joseph S., *Soft Power: The Means to Success in World Politics* (New York: Public Affairs, 2004).

Nye, Joseph S., 'Soft Power and Higher Education', *Forum*, 2005, http://forum.mit.edu/articles/soft-power-and-higher-education.

Nye, Joseph S., 'Public Diplomacy and Soft Power', *Annals of the American Academy of Political and Social Science* 616(1) (2008): 94–109.

Nye, Joseph S., *Understanding International Conflicts* (New York: Pearson, 2009).

Nye, Joseph S., *The Future of Power* (New York: Public Affairs, 2011).

Nye, Joseph S., 'Soft Power: The Evolution of a Concept', *Journal of Political Power* 14(1) (2021): 196–208.

Ohnesorge, Hendrik W., *Soft Power: The Forces of Attraction in International Relations* (Cham: Springer, 2020).

Olesen, Asta, *Islam and Politics in Afghanistan* (London: Curzon, 1995).

Ostovar, Afson, *Vanguard of the Imam: Religion, Politics and Iran's Revolutionary Guards* (Oxford: Oxford University Press, 2016).

Pahlavi, Pierre and Eric Ouellet, 'Iran: Asymmetric Strategy and Mass Diplomacy', *Journal of Strategic Security* 13(2) (2020): 94–106.

Pakistan Today, 'Pakistan, Iran Sign 5MoUs to Enhance Bilateral Cooperation', 9 December 2014, https://www.pakistantoday.com.pk/2014/12/09/pakistan-iran-sign-5-mous-to-enhance-bilateral-cooperation.

Pakistan Today, 'Iran Ready to Connect Gwadar Port with Chabahar', 25 May 2019, https://www.pakistantoday.com.pk/2019/05/24/iranian-fm-zarif-calls-on-pm-qureshi-amid-rising-tensions-with-us.

Pamment, James, *British Public Diplomacy and Soft Power: Diplomatic Influence and the Digital Revolution* (Cham: Palgrave Macmillan, 2016).

Pant, Harsh V., 'Pakistan and Iran's Dysfunctional Relationship', *Middle East Quarterly* 16(2) (2009): 43–50.

Pant, Harsh V. and Ketan Mehta, 'India in Chabahar: A Regional Imperative', *Asian Survey* 58(4) (2018): 660–78.

Payvand, 'Karzai: Iran's Help Has Contributed to Afghanistan Development', 27 December 2005, http://payvand.com/news/05/dec/1216.html.

Quraishi, Ahmad, 'Iranian University Launches Pashtu Faculty', *Pajhwok Afghan News*, 3 March 2017, https://www.pajhwok.com/en/2017/03/03/iranian-university-launches-pashtu-faculty.

Rafiq, Arif, 'Pakistan's Resurgent Sectarian War', United States Institute of Peace, November 2014, https://www.usip.org/sites/default/files/PB180-Pakistan-Resurgent-Sectarian-War.pdf.

Rafique, Aisha, Tahir Maqsood and Asima Naureen, 'Pak–Iran Cultural and Historical Ties', *IMPACT: International Journal of Research in Applied, Natural and Social Sciences* 2(11) (2014): 149.

Rafique, Najam, 'Prospects of Pakistan–Iran Relations: Post Nuclear Deal', *Strategic Studies* 36(3) (2016): 1–20.

Rahim, Nazim and Asghar Ali, 'The Sino-Indian Geo-Strategic Rivalry: A Comparative Study of Gwadar and Chabahar Ports', *The Dialogue* 13(1) (2018): 85–104.

Rana, Amir and Waqar Gillani, 'Iran Not Funding ISO: Shirazi', *Daily Times*, 24 November 2003, http://archive.vn/ab3QO.

Ranta, Paras, 'Why Chabahar Agreement is Important for Iran?' *Observer Research Foundation*, 17 July 2017, https://www.orfonline.org/expert-speak/why-chabahar-agreement-important-for-iran.

Rasa News Agency, 'Pakistan's Majlis Wahdat-e-Muslimeen Condemns the Terrorist Attack in Ahvaz', 28 September 2018, https://en.rasanews.ir/en/news/440720/pakistan%e2%80%99s-majlis-wahdat-e-muslimeen-condemns-the-terrorist-attack-in-ahvaz.

Rashid, Ahmad, *Taliban* (London: Yale University Press, 2000).

Regencia, Ted, 'Iran Warns Pakistan to Crack Down on Jaish al-Adl', *Al-Jazeera*, 16 February 2019, https://www.aljazeera.com/news/2019/2/16/iran-warns-pakistan-to-crack-down-on-jaish-al-adl.

Reuters, 'Karzai Says His Office Gets "Bags of Money" from Iran', 25 October 2010, https://www.reuters.com/article/us-afghanistan-karzai-idUSTRE69O27Z20101025.

Rieck, Andreas, *The Shias of Pakistan: An Assertive and Beleaguered Minority* (New York: Oxford University Press, 2015).

Roshangar, Baresh, 'Mohseni: Prozha-e Bast Salta-e Iran dar Manteqa' ['Mohseni: The Project of Iran's Expansion of Hegemony in Region'], *Kabul Press*, 19 April 2009, https://www.kabulpress.org/article3319.html.

Rubin, Barnett R. and Abubakar Siddique, 'Resolving the Pakistan–Afghanistan Stalemate', United States Institute of Peace, October 2006, https://www.usip.org/sites/default/files/SRoct06.pdf.

Rubin, Michael, 'Strategies Underlying Iranian Soft Power', American Enterprise Institute, 7 March 2017, https://www.aei.org/research-products/journal-publication/strategies-underlying-iranian-soft-power.

Saghafi-Ameri, Nasser, 'The Afghan Drug Problems: A Challenge to Iran and International Security', *Iranian Review of Foreign Affairs* 1(2) (2010): 213–36.

Saikal, Amin, *Iran Rising: The Survival and Future of the Islamic Republic* (Princeton: Princeton University Press, 2019).
Samii, Bill, 'Iran/Afghanistan: Still No Resolution for Century-Old Water Dispute', *Radio Free Europe*, 7 September 2005, https://www.rferl.org/a/1061209.html.
Sarkar, Saurav, 'Understanding Iran's Moves in the Afghan Endgame', *South Asian Voices*, 26 March 2019, https://southasianvoices.org/understanding-irans-moves-in-the-afghan-endgame.
Sawahel, Wagdy, 'Overseas Campuses Expanded in Drive for "Soft Power"', *University World News*, 19 January 2013, https://www.universityworldnews.com/post.php?story=2013011813380699.
Sawahel, Wagdy, 'Iran, Saudi Arabia Vie for Influence over Afghan HE', *University World News*, 15 December 2017, https://www.universityworldnews.com/post.php?story=20171212141208319.
Sawhney, Asha, 'Chabahar Port: Unlocking Afghanistan's Potential', Center for Strategic and International Studies, 8 April 2019, https://www.csis.org/chabahar-port-unlocking-afghanistans-potential.
Schneider, Tobias, 'The Fatemiyoun Division: Afghan Fighters in the Syria Civil War', Middle East Institute, 15 October 2018, https://www.mei.edu/publications/fatemiyoun-division-afghan-fighters-syrian-civil-war.
Seerat, Rustam Ali, 'Iran and Saudi Arabia in Afghanistan', *The Diplomat*, 14 January 2016, https://thediplomat.com/2016/01/iran-and-saudi-arabia-in-afghanistan.
Shackle, Christopher, 'Punjabi', *Encyclopaedia Iranica*, 2005, http://www.iranicaonline.org/articles/punjabi-indo-aryan-language.
Shah, Ali Zaman, 'Geopolitical Significance of Balochistan', *Strategic Studies* 37(3) (2017): 126–44.
Shamil, Taimur, 'This Muharram, Gilgit Gives Peace a Chance', *Herald*, 12 October 2016, https://herald.dawn.com/news/1153556.
Sharafedin, Bozorgnehr and Julia Payne, 'Iran Resumes Fuel Exports to Neighbouring Afghanistan', *Reuters*, 24 August 2021, https://www.reuters.com/world/middle-east/iran-resumes-fuel-exports-afghanistan-after-taliban-request-union-says-2021-08-23.
Sheikholeslami, Ali, 'Iran–Afghanistan Trade is More than $1.5 Billion, President Karzai Says', *Bloomberg*, 5 August 2010, http://www.bloomberg.com/news/2010-08-05.
Shitte News, The, 'A Particular Mindset is Trying to Push Shia Muslims to Wall', 7 June 2012, http://shiitenews.org/shiitenews/pakistan-news/item/1338-a-particular-mindset-trying-to-push-shia-muslims-to-wall.
Shiite News, The, 'Shia Parties Will Observe Chehlum of Qassem Soleimani in Pakistan', 21 January 2020, https://shiitenews.org/shiitenews/pakistan-news/item/108498-shia-parties-will-observe-chehlum-of-qassem-soleimani-in-pakistan.
Shuster, Simon, 'Is NATO to Blame for Russia's Afghan Heroin Problem?' *Time*, 12 June 2010, http://content.time.com/time/world/article/0,8599,1996120,00.html.

Sial, Safdar, *An Analysis of Emerging Pakistani–Iranian Ties* (Oslo: Norwegian Peacebuilding Resource Centre, 2015).

Skjærvø, Prods Oktor, 'Kartir', *Encyclopaedia Iranica*, 2011, http://www.iranicaonline.org/articles/kartir.

Slavin, Barbara, 'NIC Predicts Water Shortage, Oil Glut for Iran in 2030', *Al-Monitor*, 11 December 2012, https://www.al-monitor.com/pulse/originals/2012/al-monitor/nic-iran-water-oil.html#ixzz2H2WpjnGn.

Smyth, Philip, 'Hizballah Cavalcade: The Lion of Damascus, and Afghans, and Africans', *Jihadology*, 30 July 2013, https://jihadology.net/2013/07/30/hizballah-cavalcade-the-lion-of-damascus-and-afghans-and-africans-oh-my-fighters-from-exotic-locales-in-syrias-shia-militias/#_ftn2.

Smyth, Philip, 'Iran's Afghan Shiite Fighters in Syria', *Washington Institute*, 3 June 2014, https://www.washingtoninstitute.org/policy-analysis/view/irans-afghan-shiite-fighters-in-syria.

Solhdoost, Mohsen and Mahmoud Pargoo, 'Iran's Nontraditional Security Challenges Under the Taliban Rule', *Global Policy* 13(1) (2022): 146–51.

Solomon, Ty, 'The Affective Underpinnings of Soft Power', *European Journal of International Relations* 20(3) (2014): 720–41.

Spooner, Brian, 'Baluchistan i. Geography, History and Ethnography', *Encyclopaedia Iranica*, 1988, http://www.iranicaonline.org/articles/baluchistan-i.

Spry, Damien, 'What is Soft Power? Hint? It's Not Footing Sam Dastyari's Bills', *The Conversation*, 7 September 2016, https://theconversation.com/what-is-soft-power-hint-its-not-footing-sam-dastyaris-bills-65026.

Stobdan, P., 'To Make Chabahar a "Game Changer" Central Asian States Need to be Roped In', *IDSA Comment: Institute of Defence Studies and Analyses*, 12 December 2017, https://idsa.in/idsacomments/to-make-chabahar-a-game-changer-central-asian-states_pstobdan_121217.

Strickland, Patrick, 'Why are Afghan Refugees Leaving Iran?' *Al-Jazeera*, 17 May 2016, https://www.aljazeera.com/indepth/features/2016/05/afghan-refugees-leaving-iran-160511103759873.html.

Subtelny, Maria Eva, 'Arts and Politics in Early 16th Century Central Asia', *Central Asiatic Journal* 27(1/2) (1983): 121–48.

Syed, Baqir Sajjad, 'Iran Wanted Expanded Relations with Pakistan', *Dawn*, 14 August 2015, https://www.dawn.com/news/1200373.

Szostek, Joanna, 'The Power and Limits of Russia's Strategic Narrative in Ukraine: The Role of Linkage', *Perspectives on Politics* 15(2) (2017): 379–95.

Szuppe Maria, 'Herat iii. History: Medieval Period', *Encyclopaedia Iranica*, 2003, http://www.iranicaonline.org/articles/herat-iii.

Taye, Safiullah and Zahid Shahab Ahmed, 'Dynamics of Trust and Mistrust in the Afghanistan–Pakistan Relationship', *Asian Studies Review* 45(4) (2021): 557–75.

Tehran Times, 'Iran Capable of Boosting Electricity Exports to Afghanistan', 19 October 2019, https://www.tehrantimes.com/news/441270/Iran-capable-of-boosting-electricity-exports-to-Afghanistan.

Terrill, W. Andrew, 'Iran's Strategy for Saving Asad', *Middle East Journal* 69(2) (2015): 222–36.
The Nation, 'Wahdat-e-Muslimeen protest against US', 14 May 2018, https://nation.com.pk/14-May-2018/wahdat-e-muslimeen-protest-against-us.
The News, 'US Sanctions: Pakistan Refuses to Work on Gas Pipeline Project with Iran', 12 May 2019, https://www.thenews.com.pk/print/470290-us-sanctions-pakistan-refuses-to-work-on-gas-pipeline-project-with-iran.
The News, 'Islamic Countries Urged to Stay Away from Imperialist Forces', 10 February 2020, https://www.thenews.com.pk/print/611570-islamic-countries-urged-to-stay-away-from-imperialistic-forces.
The News, 'MWM Protests in Karachi Against Killing of Soleimani', 4 January 2020, https://www.thenews.com.pk/print/593358-mwm-protests-in-karachi-against-killing-of-soleimani.
Tober, Diane, 'My Body is Broken Like My Country: Identity, Nation and Repatriation among Afghan Refugees in Iran', *Iranian Studies* 40(2) (2007): 263–85.
Tolo News, 'Afghanistan, Iran Trade at $2.8 Billion', 27 February 2017, https://tolonews.com/afghanistan/afghanistan-iran-trade-28-billion.
Tolo News, 'Ismail Qaani was Appointed as the Quds Forces Commander after Soleimani was Killed in US Airstrike', 3 January 2020, https://tolonews.com/afghanistan/who-soleimani%E2%80%99s-successor-ismail-qaani.
Townsend, Mark, 'Special Forces Find Proof of Iran Supplying Taliban with Equipment to Fight British', *The Guardian*, 22 June 2008, https://www.theguardian.co.uk/uk/2008/jun/22/military.afghanistan.
Tran, Mark and Saeed Kamali Dehghan, 'Iran Mosque Bombing Kills Dozens', *The Guardian*, 15 December 2010, https://www.theguardian.com/world/2010/dec/15/iran-chahbahar-suicide-bombing-mosque.
United Nations, *World Drug Report 2014* (Vienna: United Nations Office on Drugs and Crime, 2014), https://www.unodc.org/wdr2014.
United Nations, *World Drug Report 2016* (Vienna: United Nations Office on Drugs and Crime, 2016), https://www.unodc.org/doc/wdr2016/WORLD_DRUG_REPORT_2016_web.pdf.
United Nations, *World Drug Report 2017* (Vienna: United Nations Office on Drugs and Crime, 2017), https://www.unodc.org/wdr2017/field/Booklet_2_HEALTH.pdf.
Uthman, Muhammad, 'Indian Outreach in Iran and Afghanistan: Regional Implications with Focus on Pakistan', *The Dialogue* 13(1) (2018): 53–70.
Vatanka, Alex, 'The Guardian of Pakistan's Shia', *Hudson Institute*, 1 June 2012, https://www.hudson.org/research/9863-the-guardian-of-pakistan-s-shia.
Vatanka, Alex, *Iran and Pakistan: Security, Diplomacy and American Influence* (London: I. B. Tauris, 2015).
Vogelsang, W. J., 'Herat ii: History, Pre-Islamic Period', *Encyclopaedia Iranica*, 2003, http://www.iranicaonline.org/articles/herat-ii.

Voll, John O., 'Trans-state Muslim Movement s and Militant Extremists in an Era of Soft Power', in T. Banchoff (ed.), *Religious Pluralism, Globalization, and World Politics* (New York: Oxford University Press, 2008).

Wallis, Emma and Reza Shirmohammadi, 'Iran: Tensions Intensify for Afghan Migrants, as Red Cross Chief Visits', *Info Migrants*, 10 May 2022, https://www.infomigrants.net/en/post/40414/iran-tensions-intensify-for-afghan-migrants-as-red-cross-chief-visits.

Wang, Hongying and Yeh-Chung Lu, 'The Conception of Soft Power and Its Policy Implications: A Comparative Study of China and Taiwan', *Journal of Contemporary China* 17(56) (2008): 425–47.

Wastnidge, Edward, 'The Modalities of Iranian Soft Power: From Cultural Diplomacy to Soft War', *Politics* 35(3/4) (2015): 346–77.

Weinstein, Adam, 'South Asia's Shiites are Eschewing Sectarianism', *Foreign Policy*, 7 January 2020, https://foreignpolicy.com/2020/01/07/iran-pakistan-shiism.

Weitz, Richard, 'Iran and Afghanistan: More of the Same', *Central Asia-Caucasus Analyst*, 7 February 2014, https://www.cacianalyst.org/publications/analytical-articles/item/13002-iran-and-afghanistan-more-of-the-same.html.

Wilson, Ernest J., 'Hard Power, Soft Power, Smart Power', *Annals of American Academy of Political and Social Science* 616 (2008): 110–24.

Winter, Tim, 'Geocultural Power: China's Belt and Road Initiative', *Geopolitics* 26(5) (2021): 1376–99.

Yarshater, Ehsan, 'The Persian Phase of Islamic Civilization', in Peter J. Chelkowski (ed.), *The Gift of Persian Culture: Its Continuity and Influence in History* (Salt Lake City, UT: University of Utah Press, 2011).

Yousefi, Golam Hossein, 'Calligraphy', *Encyclopaedia Iranica*, 1990, http://www.iranicaonline.org/articles/calligraphy.

Yudina, Natalia and Oksana Seliverstova, 'External Language Policy and Planning as Part of Soft Power Policy', 4th International Scientific and Practical Conference, 1–4 October, Volgograd, Russia, 2019.

Zahab, Mariam Abou, 'The Politicization of the Shia Community in Pakistan in the 1970s and 1980s', in Alessandro Monsutti, Silvia Naef and Farian Sabahi (eds), *The Other Shiites: From the Mediterranean to Central Asia* (Bern: Peter Lang, 2007).

Zahid, Farhan, 'The Zainabiyoun Brigade: A Pakistani Shiite Militia Amid the Syrian Conflict', *Terrorism Monitor*, 27 May 2016, https://www.refworld.org/docid/57567e114.html.

Zambelis, Chris, 'Is Iran Supporting the Insurgency in Afghanistan', *Terrorism Monitor*, 7(33), 6 November 2009, https://jamestown.org/program/is-iran-supporting-the-insurgency-in-afghanistan.

Index

Abbas, Allama Raja Nasir, 89–90, 91, 93, 111
Abd al-Rahman Jami, 24
Abd al-Rahman Khan, 25
Abdullah, Abdullah, 114, 143
Abdullah II bin Al-Hussein, King of Jordan, 10
Afghan–Soviet War, 8, 10, 54–5, 61–2
Afghanistan
  overview of relationship with Iran, 2–3, 10–11
  geostrategic location, 55
  historical connections with Iran, 21–6
  Iran's cultural influence, 72–80, 156–7: broadcast media, 9–10, 73–4, 78; cultural centres, 75–6, 81–4, 86; educational engagement, 9, 74–5, 76–8, 95; humanitarian aid, 78–9; promotion of Shi'a ideology, 77–8, 79–80
  Iran's economic relations and influence, 116–24, 155: business activities, 116–17, 118; infrastructure projects, 66, 67, 117–18, 121–2; Iran's 'look east' policy, 119, 120; post-Taliban reconstruction project, 116, 117–18; trade with Afghanistan, 6–7, 117, 119–21, 123–4; use for political purposes, 122–3
  Iran's national security interests, 54–61: during Afghan–Soviet War, 54–5; Shi'a and Sunni factions, 55–6; during Taliban first administration, 56; US invasion and aftermath, 56–61, 153; western provinces as buffer zone, 116
  Iran's political influence, 96–105: activities of IRGC/Quds Force, 113–14; connections with Pashtun groups, 98–9; financial assistance to Karzai government, 97–8, 101–2, 118–19, 122–3; prior to first Taliban regime, 96; relations with Taliban see under Taliban; use of economic relations, 122–3
  points of contention with Iran, 33–47: Afghan refugees, 37–43, 45; drug trade, 34–7; water-sharing of Helmand River, 43–7
  refugees in Iran, 10, 37–43, 45, 137–8, 155–6
  relations with Pakistan, 120
  Shi'a fighters in Syria see under Syrian conflict
  Shi'a population, 1
  trading links via Chabahar Port, 7, 54, 63–8, 69–71, 118, 120, 123–4
Afkhami, Amir Arsalan, 35
Ahmad, Shamshad, 125
Ahmadi-Moqaddam, Brigadier General Esma'il, 59–60
Ahmadinejad, Mahmoud, 4, 89, 98
Ahmed, Zahid Shahab, 63
Akbarzadeh, Shahram, 101
Alfoneh, Ali, 113–14
Allameh Tabataba'i University, 9, 76–7
Alvi, Arif, 86
Aman, Fatemeh, 44, 133
Amini, Hussein, 83, 126
Amirabdollahian, Hossein, 104
Amr ibn al-Layth, 23
Ardakanian, Reza, 121
Azimi, Basir, 45
Aziz, Sartaj, 69
Aziz, Shaukat, 127

Babaei, Hamid, 139
Balochistan, 68, 83, 84, 126, 128–9, 133; see also Gwadar Port
Baluch militant groups, 48–51
Bandar Abbas Port, 63, 65–6
Bandi Salma Dam, 44
Barzegar, Kayhan, 59, 120
Basit, Abdul, 50
Basit, Saira, 48

Behsoodi, Ayatollah Wahid, 142
Behzad, Kamal al-Din, 24
Belt and Road Initiative (BRI), 16, 123–4, 134
Bhatnagar, Stuti, 63
Bhutto, Benazir, 30, 85, 110
Bhutto, Zulfiqar Ali, 110
al-Biruni, 22
Bodde, Peter, 131–2
Bodman, Samuel, 131
bonyads, 5
Borujerdi, Alaedin, 44
Bosworth, Clifford Edmund, 23, 27, 28
broadcast media, 4, 9–10, 73–4, 78, 117
Bukhari, S. Muhammad Raju Shah, 29
Bush, George W., 9, 57

calligraphy, 28–9
Carter, Stephen, 54, 116
Chabahar Port, 7, 54, 63–8, 69–71, 118, 120, 123–4
Chehlum ceremonies, 93
China, 54, 68–71, 123–4, 130, 134, 155
Chong, Alan, 15
Clinton, Hillary, 111
Cole, Juan, 30–1

Daudzai, Mohammad Omar, 77, 98
Dehghanpisheh, Babak, 146–7
drug trade, 34–7, 113
Durrani, Ahmad Shah, 21
Durrani dynasty, 25

energy projects, 7, 45–6, 121, 128–31, 131–3
energy supply, 61, 70, 121, 122, 123, 127

Farabi Cinema Foundation, 5
Fatemiyoun Brigade, 11–12, 136–7, 138, 139, 141, 142
Feizi, Hiva, 6
Ferdowsi University of Mashhad (FUM), 76
Filkins, Dexter, 122–3
Frye, Richard, 27

Gardiz, Seyyed Ali-Shah Mousavi, 114
Ghalib, Mirza Asadullah, 83
Ghani, Ashraf, 45, 46, 64, 100, 114
Ghani, Owais, 83, 126
Ghaznavid dynasty, 23–4, 28
Gopal, Anand, 121

Greater Khorasan, 22–5
Gwadar Port, 54, 68–71

Haidar, Nazir Ahmad, 122
Hamadani, General Hussein, 135–6
Hamid, Shadi, 16
Hanaf, Abdul Salam, 104
hard power, concept of, 15–16, 17
Hashemi, Nader, 136–7
Hazara communities, 25, 38, 56, 72, 84, 87, 98, 104–5
Hekmatyar, Gulbuddin, 10, 56, 98
Helmand River dispute, 43–7
Herat, 22, 24, 25, 75–6, 117, 121–2
Hezb-e Islami, 10
Hezbollah, 4, 135, 136
Hirmand River *see* Helmand River dispute
Honerdoost, Mehdi, 69
Hoveida, Amir Abbas, 43
humanitarian aid, 78–9
Hussain, Agha, 124
Hussain, Syed Ghayoor, 82–3
Hussaini, Arif Hussain, 9, 88–9, 105, 106, 107, 108
Hussein, Allamah Jaffer, 87–8

Ibrahimi, Niamatullah, 101
Ibrahimi, Rauf, 143
iFilm TV, 4
Imam Khomeini Relief Committee (IKRC), 77, 78–9
Imam Reza shrine, 85
Imamia Students Organisation (ISO), 8, 11, 91–2, 92, 107, 109–10
India, 7, 54, 63–8, 120, 124, 129–30
international sanctions, impact of, 39, 63–4, 67
Iqbal, Muhammad, 31, 82, 83
ISIS, 101
Islamic Culture and Relations Organisation (ICRO), 3–4, 73
Islamic Republic of Iran Broadcasting (IRIB), 4, 9–10
Islamic Revolutionary Guard Corps (IRGC)
  activities of Ismail Qaani in Afghanistan, 113–14
  recruitment of fighters for Syrian conflict, 12, 135–6, 138, 139, 140, 146, 148
Islamic State of Khorasan Province (ISKP), 101, 104, 114

Ismail, Reza, 139
Israel, 4, 111, 135

Jadhav, Kulbhushan, 68
Jafari, Mohammad Ali, 50–1
Jafri, Abbas, 151
Jaish ul-Adl, 10
Jalandhari, Hafeez, 30
Japan, soft power, 14
Jaysh al-Adl (Army of Justice), 48, 49–50, 51
Jenkins, William Bullock, 5
Jiwna, Shah, 29
Jödicke, Ansgar, 16
Jundallah (Soldiers of God), 48–51

Kaboli, Ayatollah Mohaghagh, 140
Kabul University, 74–5, 118
Kamal, Abdol Moghset Bani, 78–9
Kamal Khan Dam, 44–5, 46, 47
Karzai, Hamid, 9, 44, 57, 97, 117, 118–19, 122, 123
Kasuri, Khurshid, 126
Al-Kawthar (TV channel), 4
Kerry, John, 132
Khamenei, Ayatollah Seyyed Ali, 40, 46, 103, 107–8, 110, 111, 125, 132, 146
Khan, Abdul Waheed, 76
Khan, Field Marshal Ayub, 81
Khan, Habibullah, 25
Khan, Imran, 31, 85, 91, 129
Khan, Raja Muhammad, 48
Khana-e-Farhangs, 75–6, 81–4, 86, 107, 156, 157
Kharazi, Kamal, 44, 125
Khatam al-Nabyeen Islamic University, 77–8, 118
Khatami, Mohammad, 6, 57, 125–6
Khatibzadeh, Saeed, 42
Khomeini, Ayatollah Ruhollah, 76, 106, 107, 110
 commemoration of, 88
Koepke, Bruce, 59

Lahore, 28
language, importance to soft power, 14
languages *see* Pashto; Persian language; Urdu
literature *see* poetry and literature
Liwa Fatemiyoun *see* Fatemiyoun Brigade
Liwa Zainebiyoun *see* Zainabiyoun Brigade

London Conference on Afghanistan Reconstruction (2006), 57, 117
'look east' policy, 119, 120; *see also* Chabahar Port

Mahmud of Ghazni, Sultan, 24, 28
Majidyar, Ahmad, 106, 109
Majlis Wahdat-e-Muslimeen (MWM), 8, 89–91, 92–3, 109, 111–12
Mandaville, Peter, 16
Mansour, Mullah Akhtar, 99
Al-Maqdisi, 27
Massoud, Ahmad Shah, 113
McChrystal, General Stanley A., 58
media *see* broadcast media; print media
Mehdi, Mawlawi, 104–5
Meidani, Rahim, 43
Milani, Mohsen, 120
Mitra, Ryan, 65
Moaseseh Hemayat Sabz e Parsiyan, 79
Modi, Narendra, 64
Mohammad Reza Shah Pahlavi, 1, 61, 63, 80–1, 124
Mohammadi, Ahmad, 90
Mohaqiq, Mohammad, 142, 143
Mohseni, Grand Ayatollah Muhammad Asif, 77–8, 118
Moosa, Hujjat al-Islam Maulana Aqeel, 107
Moosavi, Syed Hamid Ali Shah, 88, 92
Mottaki, Manouchehr, 117
Mousavi, Seyed Abbas, 146
Muhammad, Prince, viceroy of Multan, 28
Mujahid, Zabihullah, 36–7, 42, 103
Musharraf, Pervez, 89
al-Mustafa International University (MIU), 5
Muttaqi, Amir Khan, 42, 114

Nader, Alireza, 38, 72, 73, 98–9, 100
Nader Shah, 30
Al Nahyan, Sheikh Abdullah bin Zayed, 111
Naqvi, Allamah Hasan Zafar, 92–3
Naqvi, Allamah Sajid Ali, 11, 89
Naqvi, Maulana Haider, 107
Naqvi, Syed Jawad, 107
Nasr, Vali, 110
Nasser, Jamal Abdel, 124
National University of Modern Languages (NUML), 87
Nazari, Abdul Latif, 104

Nazeri, Hooshang, 46
Noor, Atta Muhammad, 101–2
Noor, Nasir Ahmad, 121
Northern Alliance, 56, 57, 97, 113
Nowruz celebrations, 4, 85–6
Nye, Joseph, 13–14, 15, 16, 33

Ohnesorge, Hendrik W., 17
Omid-Mehr, Ali Akbar, 107
opium trade, 34–7, 113
Ostovar, Afson, 139

Pakistan
  overview of relationship with Iran, 1–2, 11
  border with Iran, 51
  concerns over Chabahar Port, 63, 67–8, 69–71
  cooperation with United States, 61–3
  economic relations with Iran, 124–34, 155: agreements for economic cooperation, 124–9; energy and infrastructure projects, 7, 121, 127, 128–31, 131–3; impact of United States, 131–4; trade between the countries, 7, 126–8, 129, 131–4
  historical connections with Iran, 26–32
  impact of Gwadar Port, 68–71
  Iran's cultural influence, 80–94: cultural centres, 107; educational engagement, 83, 86–7, 107; language and literature, 81–4; on Pakistani media, 83; pre-Islamic Republic, 80–1; religious soft power, 84–6, 93–4
  Iran's national security interests, 61–3
  Iran's political influence, 105–13: activities of IRGC/Quds Force, 59, 113; connections with political parties, 87–92, 110–13, 154; influence on Shi'a groups, 105–10, 112–13
  points of contention with Iran, 48–51: Baluch militant groups, 48–51; links with Saudi Arabia, 51–3, 61–2, 111
  relations with Afghanistan, 120, 123
  relations with United States, 8, 61–3, 130, 131–4
  sectarian violence, 9, 86, 108–9, 125
  Shi'a fighters in Syria *see under* Syrian conflict
  Shi'a population, 1, 29–30
  zakat religious tax, 8–9, 106

Pakistan Peoples Party (PPP), 110–11
Pakpour, General Mohammad, 50
Pant, Harsh V., 62
Pashto, 25
Persian Empire
  foundation of, 21
  legacy in Afghanistan, 21–6
  legacy in Pakistan, 26–32
Persian language, 8, 25–6, 30–1, 73–4, 79, 81–4
Peshawar Alliance, 55–6
Peykan, Shokriye, 139
pilgrimages, 2, 85
poetry and literature, 23, 28, 31, 81–3
port projects *see* Chabahar Port; Gwadar Port
print media, 83

Qaani, General Ismail, 113–14
Qadi Abul-Hasan, 28
Qatar, 100, 130
Qizilbash troops, 30
Qomi, Hassan Kazemi, 47, 103, 105
Quds Day celebrations, 76, 78, 88, 106
Quds Force, 59, 113–14
Quetta, 84
Qureshi, Shah Mehmood, 50

Rabbani, Burhanuddin, 10
Ra'ees, Wahabuddin, 78–9
Rafsanjani, Akbar Hashemi, 60, 121
Rahmani, Reza, 129
rail links, 66, 67, 117, 122, 127
Raisi, Ebrahim, 85, 102–3, 129
Razavi, Allamah Sayyed Ahmad Iqbal, 90
refugees, Afghan, 10, 37–43, 45, 137–8, 155–6
religion, importance to soft power, 16–17
Reza Shah Pahlavi *see* Mohammad Reza Shah Pahlavi
Rice, Condoleezza, 131
Rieck, Andreas, 29, 30, 88, 111, 112
Rigi, Abdolmalik, 50
Rigi, Hamid, 50
Rizvi, Allama Agha Ali, 93
road projects, 66, 67, 117, 120, 122
Rouhani, Hassan, 5, 45, 60, 64, 66–7, 68, 69
Rubin, Michael, 21
Russia, drug addiction, 34

Safavid dynasty, 24–5
Saffarid dynasty, 23
Sahar TV, 4
Saikal, Amin, 36, 41, 50
Salahuddin, Dr, 81
Salehi, Ali Akbar, 39, 60
Salem, Hilmi, 77
Salman bin Abdulaziz Al Saud, King of Saudi Arabia, 130–1
Sasanian Empire, 22–3, 26–7
Saudi Arabia
  consequences of stance on Qatar, 100
  non-recognition of Taliban, 123
  relations with Pakistan, 51–3, 61–2, 111, 130–1, 133, 134, 150–1
Saulat, Mobin, 132–3
Shafi, Mohammad Musa, 43
Shahi, Agha, 106
Shahriari, Hossein Ali, 46
Shapur I, King, 26–7
Shapur II, King, 27
Sharif, General Raheel, 68
Sharif, Nawaz, 110, 128, 132
Sheikholeslam, Hossein, 60
Shi'a populations in South Asia, 1, 29–30
Shinwari, Muzammil, 39
Shirazi, Nasir Abbas, 111–12
Shirazi, Syed Nasir, 91, 92
Sial, Safdar, 132, 133
Singh, Manmohan, 64
Sipah-e-Muhammad Pakistan (SMP), 109
Sistan and Baluchestan Province, 48, 49, 51, 83, 126; *see also* Chabahar Port
Smyth, Philip, 137
soft power, concept of, 13–18, 33
Soleimani, General Qasem, 8, 92–3, 113
Soviet Union, 54–5; *see also* Afghan–Soviet War; Russia
Stobdan, P., 66
student exchange programmes, 14, 76–7, 83
Sufism, 24, 29
Sunnis, Iranian influence and support, 94, 98
Syrian conflict, recruitment by Iran, 135–52
  fighters from Afghanistan, 11–12, 135–45, 151–2, 156–7: operational presence, 138–9; recruitment methods, 136–8, 139–40; response of Afghan government, 139, 143–5; role of Afghan religious leaders, 142–3
  fighters from Pakistan, 12–13, 145–52, 156–7: operational presence, 146–7; political and governmental response in Pakistan, 149–50; reaction of religious leaders in Pakistan, 148–9; recruitment methods, 145–6; response of Pakistani army, 150–1
  reasons for Iranian involvement, 135

Tajikistan, 4, 113
Taliban
  first regime 1996–2001: Iran's security concerns over, 56; Iran's support of Northern Alliance, 56, 113; support in Pakistan for, 62; water-sharing of Helmand River, 43–4
  during US-led presence in Afghanistan: benefits from opium production, 34; Iran's links with, 9, 10–11, 58–61, 99–101, 114
  following return to power in 2021: Iran's relations with, 42–3, 47, 102–5, 114, 123, 153, 154–5; stance on opium production, 36–7
Tehrik-e-Jafaria Pakistan (TJP), 11, 89
Tehrik-i-Nifaz-i-Fiqah-i-Jafaria (TNFJ), 87–9, 106
television channels, 4, 9–10, 73–4, 78, 117
Tenet, George, 58
Turkey, 124–5, 127
Twenty-year Vision Document, 5, 134

Umayyad dynasty, 23
United Arab Emirates (UAE), 65, 123
United States
  Iran's position against, 4, 10, 55, 56–61, 88–91, 92–3
  nuclear agreement with India, 130
  Qasem Soleimani assassination, 92–3
  relations with Pakistan, 8, 61–3, 130, 131–4
  tsunami relief to Indonesia, 16
Urdu, 31, 82
US–Afghanistan Strategic Partnership Agreement (SPA), 59
al-Utbi, Muhammad ibn Abd al-Jabbar, 22

Vajpayee, Atal Bihari, 63
Vatanka, Alex, 30, 84, 108, 131
Vogelsang, W. J., 22

Wastnidge, Edward, 6
water-sharing disputes, 43–7
World Hazara Council (WHC), 105

Xuanzang, 22–3

Yakta, Rahim Muhammad, 122
Yaqub, 23
Yarshater, Ehsan, 28
Yazdi, Danesh, 118

Zahab, Mariam Abou, 86
Zainabiyoun Brigade, 12–13, 145–7, 151
Zardari, Asif Ali, 30, 50, 110, 111, 130
Zarif, Mohammad Javad, 5, 45, 46, 47, 70, 99, 100, 128
Zia-ul-Haq, General Muhammad, 8, 11, 61, 106, 107, 125
Zoroastrianism, 22, 23, 27
Zuhair, Tahir, 114

EU representative:
Easy Access System Europe
Mustamäe tee 50, 10621 Tallinn, Estonia
Gpsr.requests@easproject.com

www.ingramcontent.com/pod-product-compliance
Lightning Source LLC
Chambersburg PA
CBHW051128160426
43195CB00014B/2381